First World War
and Army of Occupation
War Diary
France, Belgium and Germany

33 DIVISION
100 Infantry Brigade
King's Royal Rifle Corps
16th Battalion
16 November 1915 - 30 November 1919

WO95/2430/3

The Naval & Military Press Ltd
www.nmarchive.com
Published in association with The National Archives

Published by

The Naval & Military Press Ltd

Unit 10 Ridgewood Industrial Park,

Uckfield, East Sussex,

TN22 5QE England

Tel: +44 (0) 1825 749494

www.naval-military-press.com

www.nmarchive.com

This diary has been reprinted in facsimile from the original. Any imperfections are inevitably reproduced and the quality may fall short of modern type and cartographic standards.

© **Crown Copyright**
Images reproduced by permission of The National Archives, London, England, 2015.

Contents

Document type	Place/Title	Date From	Date To
Heading	WO95/2430/3 16 Battalion King's Royal Rifle Brigade		
Heading	33rd Division 100th Infy Bde 16th Bn K. R. R. C. Nov 1915-Nov 1919		
Heading	33rd Div 16th K.R.R.C. Vol I Nov 15-Nov 19		
War Diary	Perham Down Camp	16/11/1915	16/11/1915
War Diary	Southampton	16/11/1915	16/11/1915
War Diary	Havre	17/11/1915	18/11/1915
War Diary	Buichy	18/11/1915	18/11/1915
War Diary	Abbeville	19/11/1915	19/11/1915
War Diary	Thienne	19/11/1915	19/11/1915
War Diary	Boeseghem	22/11/1915	22/11/1915
War Diary	Isbergues	23/11/1915	23/11/1915
War Diary	Ecleme	25/11/1915	25/11/1915
War Diary	Annezin	25/11/1915	25/11/1915
Heading	33rd Div 16th K.R.R.C. Vol 2		
War Diary	Perham Down Camp	16/11/1915	16/11/1915
War Diary	Southampton	16/11/1915	16/11/1915
War Diary	Havre	17/11/1915	18/11/1915
War Diary	Buichy	18/11/1915	19/11/1915
War Diary	Abbeville	19/11/1915	19/11/1915
War Diary	Thienne	19/11/1915	19/11/1915
War Diary	Boeseghem	20/11/1915	22/11/1915
War Diary	Isbergues	23/11/1915	23/11/1915
War Diary	Ecleme	25/11/1915	25/11/1915
War Diary	Annezin	30/11/1915	09/12/1915
War Diary	St Hilaire	10/12/1915	28/12/1915
War Diary	Gonnehem	29/12/1915	29/12/1915
War Diary	Bethune	30/12/1915	31/12/1915
Heading	16th K.R.R.C. Vol. 3 XXXIII (100)		
War Diary	Bethune	01/01/1916	02/01/1916
War Diary	Harley Street	03/01/1916	05/01/1916
War Diary	Bn.Hd.Qs Harley St	05/01/1916	07/01/1916
War Diary	Harley St	07/01/1916	07/01/1916
War Diary	B Hd. Qrs. Harley St	09/01/1916	10/01/1916
War Diary	Annequin North	11/01/1916	13/01/1916
War Diary	Fouquereuil	14/01/1916	22/01/1916
War Diary	Annequin Fosse	23/01/1916	06/02/1916
War Diary	Montmorency B Ks Bethune	07/02/1916	12/02/1916
War Diary	Annequin North	13/02/1916	13/02/1916
War Diary	B. 1	14/02/1916	22/02/1916
War Diary	Le Quesnoy	23/02/1916	25/02/1916
War Diary	B. I.	26/02/1916	29/02/1916
War Diary	B.I. Beuvry	29/02/1916	29/02/1916
War Diary	Beuvry	01/03/1916	08/03/1916
War Diary	Z 2	08/03/1916	12/03/1916
War Diary	Beuvry	13/03/1916	16/03/1916
War Diary	Auchy Sector	17/03/1916	20/03/1916
War Diary	Beuvry	21/03/1916	24/03/1916
War Diary	Oblingham	25/03/1916	02/04/1916
War Diary	Cuinchy Left Sector	02/04/1916	06/04/1916

War Diary	Le Quesnoy	07/04/1916	10/04/1916
War Diary	Cuinchy Left Sector	10/04/1916	14/04/1916
War Diary	Le Quesnoy	15/04/1916	18/04/1916
War Diary	Oblingham	19/04/1916	25/04/1916
War Diary	Beuvry	26/04/1916	30/04/1916
War Diary	Auchy Left	01/05/1916	04/05/1916
War Diary	Beuvry	05/05/1916	08/05/1916
War Diary	Auchy Left	09/05/1916	14/05/1916
War Diary	Beuvry	15/05/1916	15/05/1916
War Diary	Auchy Left	15/05/1916	15/05/1916
War Diary	Beuvry	16/05/1916	16/05/1916
War Diary	Oblingham	17/05/1916	07/06/1916
War Diary	Beuvry	08/06/1916	09/06/1916
War Diary	Auchy Left	09/06/1916	13/06/1916
War Diary	Beuvry	14/06/1916	16/06/1916
War Diary	Cuinchy Left	17/06/1916	21/06/1916
War Diary	Cuinchy Right	22/06/1916	24/06/1916
War Diary	Cuinchy Left	25/06/1916	30/06/1916
Heading	100th Inf. Bde. 33rd Div. War Diary 16th Battn. The King's Royal Rifle Corps. July 1916		
War Diary	Cuinchy Left	01/07/1916	02/07/1916
War Diary	Gorre	03/07/1916	06/07/1916
War Diary	Busnettes On Bas Rieux	07/07/1916	09/07/1916
War Diary	Vecquemont	10/07/1916	10/07/1916
War Diary	Morlancourt	11/07/1916	13/07/1916
War Diary	Becordel-Becourt	13/07/1916	15/07/1916
War Diary	High Wood Map Ref Martinpuich Trench Map 1/20000	15/07/1916	15/07/1916
War Diary	High Wood Attack	15/07/1916	18/07/1916
War Diary	Wood Trench	18/07/1916	20/07/1916
War Diary	Bazentin La Petit	20/07/1916	21/07/1916
War Diary	High Wood	21/07/1916	21/07/1916
War Diary	Mametet Wood	22/07/1916	22/07/1916
War Diary	Becordel Becourt	23/07/1916	26/07/1916
War Diary	Camp Near Dernancourt Albert	27/07/1916	31/07/1916
Heading	100th Brigade. 33rd Division 1/16th Battalion King's Royal Rifle Corps August 1916		
War Diary	Camp N	01/08/1916	01/08/1916
War Diary	Dernancourt	02/08/1916	07/08/1916
War Diary	Mametz Wood	07/08/1916	10/08/1916
War Diary	High Wood	11/08/1916	15/08/1916
War Diary	Camp Near Becordel	16/08/1916	18/08/1916
War Diary	Montauban Alley	19/08/1916	22/08/1916
War Diary	Carlton Trench	23/08/1916	25/08/1916
War Diary	Mametz Wood	26/08/1916	27/08/1916
War Diary	Nr Becordel	27/08/1916	31/08/1916
War Diary	Molliens Au Bois	31/08/1916	31/08/1916
War Diary	Talmas	01/09/1916	01/09/1916
War Diary	Beaumetz	02/09/1916	03/09/1916
War Diary	Fortel	04/09/1916	04/09/1916
War Diary	Hericourt	05/09/1916	05/09/1916
War Diary	Ternas	06/09/1916	07/09/1916
War Diary	Halloy	08/09/1916	09/09/1916
War Diary	Gaudiempre	10/09/1916	11/09/1916
War Diary	Humbercamps	11/09/1916	12/09/1916
War Diary	Souastre	12/09/1916	19/09/1916
War Diary	Line Fonquevillers	20/09/1916	20/09/1916

War Diary	Trenches Fonquevillers	21/09/1916	25/09/1916
War Diary	Souastre	26/09/1916	26/09/1916
War Diary	Coullemont	27/09/1916	28/09/1916
War Diary	Lucheux	29/09/1916	29/09/1916
War Diary	Bouquemaison	30/09/1916	18/10/1916
War Diary	Corbie	19/10/1916	21/10/1916
War Diary	Meaulte	21/10/1916	22/10/1916
War Diary	Mansel Camp	22/10/1916	25/10/1916
War Diary	Bricqueterie Camp	25/10/1916	30/10/1916
War Diary	Hogs Back Trench T9.d.2.8 Bn Hd Qrs	30/10/1916	31/10/1916
War Diary	Hogs Back Trench	01/11/1916	02/11/1916
War Diary	Lesboeuf	02/11/1916	06/11/1916
War Diary	Carnoy	07/11/1916	07/11/1916
War Diary	Citadel Camp	07/11/1916	09/11/1916
War Diary	Airaines	10/11/1916	10/11/1916
War Diary	Conde Folie	11/11/1916	03/12/1916
War Diary	Morlancourt	04/12/1916	05/12/1916
War Diary	Bray	06/12/1916	25/12/1916
War Diary	Bray Sur Somme	26/12/1916	27/12/1916
War Diary	Ailly Le Haut Clocher	28/12/1916	19/01/1917
War Diary	Bray	20/01/1917	20/01/1917
War Diary	Bray Camp 112	21/01/1917	23/01/1917
War Diary	Suzanne	24/01/1917	26/01/1917
War Diary	Clery Sur Somme	27/01/1917	31/01/1917
War Diary	Trenches	01/02/1917	07/02/1917
War Diary	Suzanne	08/02/1917	19/02/1917
War Diary	P.C. Merton	20/02/1917	23/02/1917
War Diary	Clery Sector	24/02/1917	26/02/1917
War Diary	Trenches (Clery Sector)	27/02/1917	27/02/1917
War Diary	Frise Bend	28/02/1917	03/03/1917
War Diary	Suzanne	04/03/1917	05/03/1917
War Diary	Corbie	06/03/1917	02/04/1917
War Diary	Bertangles	02/04/1917	03/04/1917
War Diary	Beauval	03/04/1917	04/04/1917
War Diary	Barly	04/04/1917	05/04/1917
War Diary	Mondicourt	06/04/1917	07/04/1917
War Diary	Souastre	08/04/1917	12/04/1917
War Diary	Mercatel	12/04/1917	15/04/1917
War Diary	Moyenneville	15/04/1917	21/04/1917
War Diary	Croissilles	22/04/1917	23/04/1917
War Diary	St Leger	24/04/1917	25/04/1917
War Diary	Berles Au Bois	26/04/1917	01/05/1917
War Diary	Blairville	02/05/1917	02/05/1917
War Diary	Moyenneville	03/05/1917	11/05/1917
War Diary	St Leger	11/05/1917	15/05/1917
War Diary	Moyenneville	16/05/1917	19/05/1917
War Diary	Croisilles	20/05/1917	24/05/1917
War Diary	Moyenneville	25/05/1917	27/05/1917
War Diary	Croissilles	28/05/1917	31/05/1917
Miscellaneous	100th Inf Bde Report on Operations of May 20-22, 1917	24/05/1917	24/05/1917
Miscellaneous	100th Inf Bde Herewith Report On Operations On 20-22 May 1917	24/05/1917	24/05/1917
Miscellaneous	A Form Messages And Signals.		
Operation(al) Order(s)	16th K.R.R. Battn. Operation Orders No 2		
Miscellaneous	A Form Messages And Signals.		

Miscellaneous	Messages And Signals.		
War Diary	Moyenneville	01/06/1917	01/06/1917
War Diary	Berles Au Bois	02/06/1917	20/06/1917
War Diary	Moyenneville	21/06/1917	24/06/1917
War Diary	Croissilles	24/06/1917	30/06/1917
War Diary	Moyenneville	01/07/1917	02/07/1917
War Diary	Forceville	03/07/1917	03/07/1917
War Diary	Mirvaux	04/07/1917	04/07/1917
War Diary	Breilly	05/07/1917	29/07/1917
War Diary	Breilly Sur Somme	30/07/1917	31/07/1917
War Diary	Longpre	01/08/1917	01/08/1917
War Diary	Tetegham	02/08/1917	05/08/1917
War Diary	Ghyvelde	06/08/1917	17/08/1917
War Diary	Coxyde	18/08/1917	26/08/1917
War Diary	Ghyvelde	27/08/1917	27/08/1917
War Diary	Teteghem	28/08/1917	31/08/1917
War Diary	La Commune	01/09/1917	13/09/1917
War Diary	Lederzeele	14/09/1917	15/09/1917
War Diary	Steenvoorde	16/09/1917	16/09/1917
War Diary	Fontaine Houck	17/09/1917	18/09/1917
War Diary	La Clytte	18/09/1917	22/09/1917
War Diary	Kreustathoek Area	23/09/1917	23/09/1917
War Diary	Zillebeke Area	24/09/1917	27/09/1917
War Diary		25/09/1917	27/09/1917
War Diary	Kreustathoek Area	28/09/1917	28/09/1917
War Diary	Sercus	29/09/1917	30/09/1917
War Diary	Sercus Area	01/10/1917	04/10/1917
War Diary	Tatinghem	05/10/1917	05/10/1917
War Diary	Neuve Eglise	06/10/1917	15/10/1917
War Diary	Messines Sector	16/10/1917	24/10/1917
War Diary	Ypres I.2.d.7.4	24/10/1917	31/10/1917
War Diary	Ypres	01/11/1917	05/11/1917
War Diary	Neuve Eglise	06/11/1917	10/11/1917
War Diary	Messines	11/11/1917	14/11/1917
War Diary	Neuve Eglise	15/11/1917	15/11/1917
War Diary	Locre	16/11/1917	18/11/1917
War Diary	Brandhoek	18/11/1917	24/11/1917
War Diary	Potijze	25/11/1917	29/11/1917
War Diary	Passchandaele Area	30/11/1917	03/12/1917
War Diary	Hamburg Farm	04/12/1917	06/12/1917
War Diary	Ypres Area	06/12/1917	06/12/1917
War Diary	Brandhoek	06/12/1917	09/12/1917
War Diary	Winnezeele Area	10/12/1917	13/12/1917
War Diary	Ypres Area	14/12/1917	20/12/1917
War Diary	Ypres	21/12/1917	21/12/1917
War Diary	Winnizeele	22/12/1917	03/01/1918
War Diary	Brandhoek	04/01/1918	04/01/1918
War Diary	Ypres	05/01/1918	09/01/1918
War Diary	Hamburg	10/01/1918	12/01/1918
War Diary	Potijze	12/01/1918	13/01/1918
War Diary	Brandhoek	14/01/1918	17/01/1918
War Diary	Seine	17/01/1918	19/01/1918
War Diary	Passchandaele	20/01/1918	21/01/1918
War Diary	Ypres	21/01/1918	25/01/1918
War Diary	Passchandaele	26/01/1918	27/01/1918
War Diary	Brandhoek	27/01/1918	28/01/1918

War Diary	Esquerdes	29/01/1918	20/02/1918
War Diary	Brandhoek	21/02/1918	22/02/1918
War Diary	Zonnebeke	22/02/1918	28/02/1918
War Diary	Ypres Zonnebeke Sector	01/03/1918	05/03/1918
War Diary	Ypres	06/03/1918	06/03/1918
War Diary	Zonnebeke Sector	06/03/1918	08/03/1918
War Diary	Zonnebeke	09/03/1918	14/03/1918
War Diary	Ypres	14/03/1918	18/03/1918
War Diary	Zonnebeke	19/03/1918	26/03/1918
War Diary	Ypres	27/03/1918	30/03/1918
War Diary	Zonnebeke	31/03/1918	31/03/1918
Heading	100th Brigade 33rd Division. 1/16th Battalion King's Royal Rifle Corps April 1918		
War Diary	Zonnebeke	01/04/1918	04/04/1918
War Diary	Vlamertinghe	05/04/1918	06/04/1918
War Diary	Penim	07/04/1918	10/04/1918
War Diary	Aubigny	11/04/1918	11/04/1918
War Diary	Caestre	11/04/1918	11/04/1918
War Diary	Revelsberg	11/04/1918	11/04/1918
War Diary	Neuve Eglise	11/04/1918	13/04/1918
War Diary	Minimum Reserve Revelsberg	12/04/1918	13/04/1918
War Diary	Hille Farm	13/04/1918	15/04/1918
War Diary	Hill 70	15/04/1918	17/04/1918
War Diary	Westoutre	18/04/1918	18/04/1918
War Diary	Mont De Cats	18/04/1918	20/04/1918
War Diary	Ochtezeele	20/04/1918	25/04/1918
War Diary	St. Marie Cappel	26/04/1918	30/04/1918
War Diary	Neuve Eglise Hill 70 (S 5 C T 2)	30/04/1918	30/04/1918
War Diary	St Marie Cappel	01/05/1918	01/05/1918
War Diary	La Sablon	02/05/1918	03/05/1918
War Diary	Steenvoorde	04/05/1918	05/05/1918
War Diary	Wattou Area	06/05/1918	08/05/1918
War Diary	Brandhoek Area	09/05/1918	15/05/1918
War Diary	Poperinghe East Area	16/05/1918	23/05/1918
War Diary	Watou Area	24/05/1918	29/05/1918
War Diary	Dirty Bucket Corner	30/05/1918	05/06/1918
War Diary	Ypres Canal	06/06/1918	10/06/1918
War Diary	Brandhoek	11/06/1918	15/06/1918
War Diary	Ypres Canal	15/06/1918	24/06/1918
War Diary	Brandhoek	25/06/1918	30/06/1918
Heading	To 100th Inf Bde Herewith War Diary For July		
War Diary	Ypres Canal	01/07/1918	10/07/1918
War Diary	Brandhoek	11/07/1918	15/07/1918
War Diary	Ypres Canal	16/07/1918	25/07/1918
War Diary	Brandhoek	25/07/1918	31/07/1918
Heading	To 100th Inf. Bde Herewith War Diary For Month of August		
War Diary		01/08/1918	09/08/1918
War Diary	Brandhoek	10/08/1918	14/08/1918
War Diary	Canal Sector	15/08/1918	17/08/1918
War Diary	Proven	18/08/1918	21/08/1918
War Diary	Zudrove	21/08/1918	28/08/1918
War Diary	Sus. St Leger	28/08/1918	15/09/1918
War Diary	Bazentin Le Petit	16/09/1918	17/09/1918
War Diary	Lechelle	18/09/1918	18/09/1918
War Diary	Equancourt	19/09/1918	30/09/1918

Miscellaneous	Operations An Account of the Part taken by 16th K.R.R.C. in Attack Upon Ossus on 29-9-18		02/10/1918	02/10/1918
War Diary			01/10/1918	03/10/1918
War Diary	Cavalry Support Area S. of Vaucellette Farm		04/10/1918	11/10/1918
War Diary	E of Troisville		12/10/1918	14/10/1918
War Diary	Clary		15/10/1918	21/10/1918
War Diary	Bertry		21/10/1918	22/10/1918
War Diary	K 16 Square		23/10/1918	30/10/1918
War Diary	Forest		01/11/1918	07/11/1918
War Diary	Petit Madberge		08/11/1918	23/11/1918
War Diary	Clary		24/11/1918	13/12/1918
War Diary	Breilly		14/12/1918	14/12/1918
War Diary	Camps En Amenois		15/12/1918	15/12/1918
War Diary	Andainville		16/12/1918	16/12/1918
War Diary	Andainville		17/12/1918	05/01/1919
War Diary	Martin Eglise		06/01/1919	28/02/1919
War Diary	Dieppe		01/03/1919	07/03/1919
War Diary	Sanvic.Le.Havre		08/03/1919	31/03/1919
War Diary	Sanvic		01/04/1919	30/04/1919
War Diary	Sanvic Le Havre		01/05/1919	15/05/1919
War Diary	Sanvic		16/05/1919	31/05/1919
War Diary	Sanvic. (Le Havre)		01/06/1919	24/06/1919
War Diary	Harfleur (Le Havre)		25/06/1919	28/06/1919
War Diary	Harfleur		29/06/1919	31/08/1919
Miscellaneous	D.A.G. G.H.Q. British Troops In France And Flanders.		03/10/1919	03/10/1919
War Diary	Harfleur		01/09/1919	31/10/1919
War Diary	Harfleur		01/10/1919	31/10/1919
War Diary	Havre		01/11/1919	14/11/1919
War Diary	Havre		01/11/1919	30/11/1919
War Diary	Havre		14/11/1919	30/11/1919

WO/95/2430/3

16 Battalion King's Royal
Rifle Brigade

33RD DIVISION
100TH INFY BDE

16TH BN K. R. R. C.
NOV 1915 – NOV 1919

16th K.R.R.C.
Vol I

7978/
IO/

November 1915. **WAR DIARY** 16th (S) K.R.R.C.
or
INTELLIGENCE SUMMARY.

Army Form C. 2118.

(Erase heading not required.)

Hour, Date, Place	Summary of Events and Information	Remarks and references to Appendices
16th Nov 1915. PERHAM DOWN CAMP	16th K.R.R. Strength {30 Offrs 994 other ranks proceeded to SOUTHAMPTON in (64 horses & mules, 19 vehicles, 9 bicycles) 3 trains.	Appendix I. List of Officers
7 p.m. 16th SOUTHAMPTON	Embarked.	
2 a.m. 17th HAVRE	Arrived at HAVRE. Disembarked 7 AM, marched to No 1 Camp Sst Ste.	
11.30 AM 18th HAVRE	Marched to Gare MARCHANDISE. Entrained (1 train). Started 3.30 PM	1 M.o. left in Hospital
12 MIDNIGHT BUICHY	Drew rations with hot coffee at various points. (Small fort.)	
3 AM 19th ABBEVILLE	Hot water for coffee. Supply indents.	
1 PM 19th THIENNES	Detrained, marched to billets in neighbourhood of BOESEGHEM	2nd Lt PARAVICINI. Rpt. to Hospital
20, 21, 22 nr BOESEGHEM	Route marches, looking at trenches & musketry training. Lt HORSFIELD	Rpt. NORLEDGE was/admitted Hosp
	appeared from BOULOGNE.	
9.30 AM 23rd IPSBERGUES.	Marched to IPSBERGUES. Stopped till 25th	
10 AM 25th ECLEME	Marched to ECLEME - Very slotted billets - Stopped till 30th (continued	
	training)	
9.30 AM ANNEZIN	Marched to ANNEZIN.	

16th K.R.R.C.
Vol: 2

19/1798

Army Form C. 2118.

WAR DIARY
or
INTELLIGENCE SUMMARY.

Army Form C. 2118.

December 1915   16th (S) K.R.R.C.

(Erase heading not required.)

Hour, Date, Place	Summary of Events and Information	Remarks and references to Appendices
16th Nov 1915 PERHAM DOWN CAMP	16th K.R.R. Strength (30 Offrs 994 Other Ranks) proceeded to SOUTHAMPTON in 3 Trains	Appdx I. List of Officers
7 pm 16.11.15 SOUTHAMPTON	Embarked (by two steamers 19 Offrs & 9 bicycles)	
2 AM 17.11.15 HAVRE	Arrival at HAVRE Disembarked 7 am & marched to No 1 Camp in Huts.	1 Offr left in Hospital
5.30 PM 17.11.15 HAVRE	Marched to GARE MARCHANDISES. Entrained (1 train) Started 3.00 pm 30 Offrs 972 Other Ranks	
12 midnight BULCHY	Train had to wait for Offrs Supply Return (French Govt)	
8 AM 18.11.15 ABBEVILLE		
1 pm 19.11.15 THIEMPE	Detrained & marched 5 billets in neighbourhood of BOESEGHEM	2 Lt PARAVICINI. Rpt to Hospital
20.21.22 Nov BOESEGHEM	Route marches, inspections etc. Open ground training.	
9.30 AM 23 Nov 15 ISBERGUES	Marched to ISBERGUES. Stopped till 10' (entrained training)	Lt MORLEDGE admitted to hospital
10 AM 24.11.14 ECLEME	Marched to ECLEME. Von Sectional billets. Stopped till 30' (entrained training)	Horsified by depart for BOULOGNE
9.30 AM 30.11.15 ANNEZIN	Marched to ANNEZIN. Entrained training.	
1.12.15 "	Rgt WEAR & 6 guns of Transport at ABBEVILLE Sgt CARR 6 guns M.G. at HALTE. 1 Sgt 32 men for course of Instruction	
4.12.15	at E.6.n. Rgt hsp. 36 Amb. 4 days later	Rgt hsp. 36 NW1 A8 Agar
4.12.15	A Coy. 30 Offrs 104 OR (2nd Platoon) attached to CAMERONIANS and 8th SCOTTISH RIFLES. 10.30 am for tour of Instr in Trenches M.Gs & Guides at WINDY CORNER Temp Lt Col ADRIAN B. COOBAN to be Temp A/Major. Detail 16 Sept 15 Order R.G.I. No 15.	
5.12.15	B Coy. 30 Offrs & Platoon attached from Coy with Sgt. PLATT. Corpl GODDARD	Rgt hsp. 36 NW1 A8 Agar
5.12.15	2 Lt FRANCIS returned from course	
5.12.15	A Coy. & Platoon to both WINDY CORNER 2 pm W.S.L.2 R.N.F.	
6.12.15	C+D by route to BETHUNE 2 pm. To furnish working parties daily - 3 Coys	3 men & 180th Tunnelling Co attached RE BEUVRY Permananent attached
6.12.15	missing parties daily - 3 Coys	
6.12.15	3 Nh attached to 183rd RE BEUVRY. Working party 1 Offr. 1/2 Platoon of CORRS	

Army Form C. 2118.

WAR DIARY
or
INTELLIGENCE SUMMARY.   16th (S) K.R.R.C.

December 1915

(Erase heading not required.)

Hour, Date, Place		Summary of Events and Information	Remarks and references to Appendices
7am 7.12.15	ANNEZIN	Rfn BANNISTER died of wounds to present 11 Corps. 4 Platoon started 14 Bde F Tunnl Det (1 Pl Down 13 2 (En) NW 3 RWF)	3 pm to 1805 Tunnel Co.
"	"	2 Platoon A & 4 to assist to relieve at 9.8.	RE BEUVRY
8.5am	"	One officer & 18 of DURA BETHUNE & employment to keep in between 11.30am & 7.30pm. Details came to 16 to report to find Wire on 9".	Permits attached
3pm	"		
		9 Platoon attached to Tunnel Det. 2. 19 Bde. Mining continued	Ref. Resp. 36 C NW A8 Ag ac
8.12.15	"		
9.12.15	"	Bn marched to St HILAIRE via trackpack down E to HAMEL thence S by bus. Mineports hoisted up by bus from CHAMBOYD Bks - BETHUNE	Lt LEWER MG Cass St BALL 9th to 4th WISQUES 2Lt WARNE 2Lt MANSELL
10.12.15	St HILAIRE	Bn. cleaning & general orders.	
11.12.15	"	Bomb & TM courses begun. Remainder in Reg. Bn. Beyond tres.	
12.12.15	"	Capt HARRISON out to GORRE to arrange billets for trench position.	
13.12.15	"	A & B Coy bus run on convoy to trenches GIVENCHY. Lewis left at 5 am from PONT LEVIS. Order to march from trenches to WINDY CORNER with detail between platoons & WESTMINSTER BRIDGE Trenches.	Ref. Resp. 36 C NW A9 ac A8 With 7th Queens.
		between sections received.	
13.12.15	"	Extract from LONDON GAZETTE dated 26 Nov 1915 -	
		"Kings Royal Rifle Corps.	
		Temporary LIEUT. JAMES R. SMITH to be Temporary Captain.	
		Dated 11th November 1915"	
14.12.15	"	Bn ready for trenches, MGs, TMs, grenade up ready in CCl.	
		Buses 10 yds to MG Holmes & BLR to BOURECQ.	
15.12.15	"	C.O. left in advance & Bn to collect A+B Coy & march	3.15 Ref. Coy to HC
14.12.15		from A 6.30 pm.	Ref Resp. 36 NW A9 ac A8 WK 5 ESSEX

Army Form C. 2118.

WAR DIARY
or
INTELLIGENCE SUMMARY. 16th (S) K.R.R.C.

December 1915.

(Erase heading not required.)

Hour, Date, Place	Summary of Events and Information	Remarks and references to Appendices
9.15 a.m. 16.12.15 St Hilaire	Sgt Can to be reported to B.M.G. Officer in Gen'l Instr.	By Rifle Grenades.
7.15 p.m. 17/12/15 "	C & D Coys returned from Trenches for two R & F Killed 1 Wounded 7	
10 a.m. "	Remainder of 13th Ed. Specialist course, Bde Route march.	
	Lieut S.S. Scott + 12 men to Maxim M.G. Course.	
9.44 30th, 10th up & 18th "	Courses and Coy training continued –	
11.30 A.M. 19th Bn "	No parade strong as possible, clean fatigue dinner, for letters	
	+ demonstration on gas attack. All ranks made to tea pass	
	into a room filled with gas.	
19th "	Lieut Parkin + Sgt Green to School of Instruction at Troop Rag.	
22 "	36A W.27 c 5.9 to report between 3pm + 4pm.	
20th "	Snipers Instr mr "Snipersopes" Bttn Courses + training	
	Continued – Work on improving billets continued –	
21st "	Bde Courses continued + other courses per as with	
	Battn.	
22nd " "	Bde + Bn Courses for Specialists continued – Improving billets	
	Staff Ride + Tactical Exercise on ground for Junior	
	Capt & 2nd in Command.	

Army Form C. 2118.

WAR DIARY
or
INTELLIGENCE SUMMARY.

1st / 15th K.R.R.C.

December 1915.

(Erase heading not required.)

Instructions regarding War Diaries and Intelligence Summaries are contained in F.S. Regs., Part II and the Staff Manual respectively. Title pages will be prepared in manuscript.

Hour, Date, Place	Summary of Events and Information	Remarks and references to Appendices
23rd Dec 15 St HILAIRE	Continued Training + improvements	
24th " "	Staff Ride for C.Os + 2 in Comds with Brigadier. Continued Training + improvements. Lieut LEWER, Sgt BALL, L/C WARNE, MANSELL reported on return from M.G. Course. Sgt WHITE to Div¹ School BETHUNE in charge of prisoners.	
25th Dec " "	CHRISTMAS DAY. Holiday – Batt'n not available being still...	
26th Dec " "	Continued training.	
27th Dec " "	Continued training.	
9.10 AM 28th Dec St HILAIRE	Marched to GONNEHEM.	
12.15 AM 29th Dec GONNEHEM	Marched to BETHUNE. In billets 2 Coln & Town – 2 Dn FRANCIS. 1 Section 1 Coy 12 Coy agn Coy to Bn H.Q.
30th " BETHUNE		for Trench Mortar Bolty.
9.30 AM 30th Dec BETHUNE	C O d Bn. Adj & 2 I C Cos reconnoitred 98th Bde H.Q. + own grand.	
" " "	by 14th R.F. own Section A1. CUINCHY SECTOR.	
6 pm "	Lecture to Officers at 2 Dn H.Q. on Aeroplanes + Trench Warfare.	
6 pm "	Conference of C.Os at 1st Bde H.Q. 100 + 1 B.	
" "	Lt PARAVICINI tried at a offices ad court Braft.	
" "	L/C PASKIN reported in action from Courses.	
9 AM "	1 Sgt & men to Divisional Salvage Coy	

16th K.R.R.C.
Vol: 3

Sept. XXXIII (3)

Army Form C. 2118.

WAR DIARY
or
INTELLIGENCE SUMMARY.

January 1916   16th K.R.R.C.

(Erase heading not required.)

Hour, Date, Place	Summary of Events and Information	Remarks and references to Appendices
1st Jan. BETHUNE	Whole Bn. got baths but supply chain did not work.	
	Lieut. Clarke and A.M.O. Gr & 2nd S.S.R.H. and R.F.M.O. moved	2 officers R.F.N.R. 4 wounded
	out to BEUVRY. No. 17 Ply Gatrigs tried to P.O.CH 23.12.15 succeeded 2 officers, R.F.N. Lyttmers 4 wounded Pioneers Idd 1.1.16.	
6.45 A.M. 2 Jan. BETHUNE	Bn moved to HARLEY STREET. Intervals between Coys. & BEUVRY	
	E. of BEUVRY & ANNAQUIN intervals between Platoons; &	
	ANNAQUIN into into between Sections. Took over Section	
	of from 17 ROYAL FUSILIERS of the CUINCHY SECTOR	
	At 11 AM Enemy sprung 2 large mines & heavy shelling on	
	followed immediately by intense bombardment of held trenches	
	and fire from ADCHY & large calibre 5.9 + 4.2 &	
	trenches of LA BASSEE M.G's to QUARRY TRENCH	
	Our front line badly damaged, & of LA BASSEE ROAD & chiefly	
	by our smell mount trench parapet	
	N. of LA BASSEE RD. both blown in below, B.m bays	R.F.A. 4 killed 27 wounded
	and damaged by bombardment. WATERLOO PLACE	
	SEYMOUR STREET and PARKLANE suffering most.	
	Enemy Crater put down & Sutton Alt. Bombardment ceased	
	at 2 P.M. Considerable shelling at night.	

WAR DIARY or INTELLIGENCE SUMMARY.

January 1916 18th K R R C

Army Form C. 2118.

Hour, Date, Place	Summary of Events and Information	Remarks and references to Appendices
3rd Jan 16 HARLEY STREET	Work of repairing, deepening & keeping clear of water, the interesting & heavy shelling from 3 P.M. to 4.30 P.M. Chiefly directed on CUINCHY SUPPORT POINT and Communication trenches EDGWARE RD & CONDUIT ST. Badly damaged. Sniping and M.G.'s very active the night. Retaliated with rifle grenades & late in night - Work of repairs continued.	3/ R+F Wounded
4th Jan 16	B. Coy relieved A. Coy in sub-station S.B. Nr BRAGGS Rd. C. Coy relieved B. Coy. D. Coy held line in reserve in billets in HARLEY ST. C. Coy in CUINCHY SUPPORT POINT. CAMBRIN SUPPORT POINT, and BRADDELL KEEP - General cleaning and repairing trenches - Some wiring done on right front.	2. R+F Wounded.
5th Jan 16 "	BRADDELL'S KEEP shelled from 9.45 A.M. to 10.30 A.M. no damage. Evacuating billets from SEYMOUR ST. cleaning communication trenches, & deepening sap trench to crater - Strengthening front line parapets. Some shells & CUINCHY SUPPORT POINT	4/
M.P.M	+ THE LANE. Slightly damaged - Bombin Smoke grenade posts disposed within our ettier into ? the LA BASSÉE Rd. two reconnaissance par????	

WAR DIARY
or
INTELLIGENCE SUMMARY

January 1916 1/5th K.R.R.C.

Army Form C. 2118.

Hour, Date, Place	Summary of Events and Information	Remarks and references to Appendices
5th Jan. B.H.Q. HARLEY ST	Our RIFLE GRENADE post near the TOWER got 3 shots home to enemy sniper loophole in old entries. Sniping from LA BASSEE RD silenced by Grenadiers	
6th Jan " " "	B. Co relieved C. Co in front line, during morning. A " D " " " " " BRADDELL'S KEEP shelled from 9.45AM to 10.30AM. Some shells near CUINCHY SUPPORT POINT & PARK LANE afternoon & evening. Gun of SHORTCUT temporarily withdrawn 2-3pm while track to Keel at Gun Emp being moved upright on old SHORT CUT SAP. Work on Keel — clearing & improving entrances — found misfires	2 R.F. Wounded
7th Jan " " "	Work on trenches entrances — Off and Ams traffic being arranged for by Rationing Trenches also Comn—— CUINCHY SUPPORT POINT. STAFFORD REDOUBT. BRADDELLS KEEP & HARLEY ST. loop trench. Enemy snipers very active against New RIFLE GRENADES.	
11.3-0 p.m.	HARLEY ST shelled with S.9 - Both 2nd in command & telephone	
12.30 AM	Reman wounded. "	91 2 killed 2 Grenadier 3 wounded

WAR DIARY or INTELLIGENCE SUMMARY

Army Form C. 2118.

January 1916 — 16th K.R.R.

Hour, Date, Place	Summary of Events and Information	Remarks and references to Appendices
night 27/8th Jan HARLEY ST.	HARLEY ST. shelled, inter mittently, garrison of SEYMOUR ST. withdrawn to CONDUIT ST. &	
Jan 8th "	all front line on alert prior to mine being sprung.	
4.30 am " "	Mine successfully sprung, the front of No 6 Sap. being occupied by WORCESTERS. Garrison SEYMOUR ST. formed up again & returned firing by on M.G. — Enemy opened rapid + M.G. fire — appears to form a few bombs & low M.G. fire from own trench return, 9.5" + 4" & heavy trench mortars fire by guns — continued till 6 A.M. Enemy began to shorten — Lost + M.G. to. In Rt. lu. A1. killed by little driven of bichum —	1 killed 5 wounded
8 am " "	16th K.R.R. CUINCHY SUPPORT POINT, BRADDELLS KEEP + CAMBRIN tunnel spiral dept detail — too well not much damage. front line + support in plain. Kit in before took place during morning (o) relief " " communication trenches Constant repairs + carrying up rations so on at day.	

Army Form C. 2118.

WAR DIARY
or
INTELLIGENCE SUMMARY.

January 1916.   16th K.R.R.C.

(Erase heading not required.)

Instructions regarding War Diaries and Intelligence Summaries are contained in F.S.Regs., Part II and the Staff Manual respectively. Title pages will be prepared in manuscript.

Hour, Date, Place	Summary of Events and Information	Remarks and references to Appendices
9th Jan 1916 HARLEY ST	Intermittent shelling. Working on repairing and improving all points damaged. Orders at LA BASSEE Rd but to be moved by day.	1 Rfn killed.
10th " "	Intermittent shelling. Bn relieved by the 1st Queen's at dusk. Relief complete and Bn in billets at ANNEQUIN NORTH by 10.30 p.m. arriving by TOURBIERES LOOP.	
11th " ANNEQUIN NORTH	Got baths & change of underlinen for men - 480 officers men on various working parties at night. PONT FIXE, HARLEY ST.	
12th " ANNEQUIN NORTH	Remainder of men got baths & change. Working parties on roads & splinter proofs - 380 men on various parties at night.	
13th " ANNEQUIN NORTH	2/Lt Howard reported to Dist H.Q. in BETHUNE for course of Instruction in Sniping. Various working parties.	
14th " FOUQUEREUIL	Bn marched to FOUQUEREUIL, 9 miles, via BETHUNE + ANNEZIN. A Coys turned off at BETHUNE + took up billets in FOUQUIÈRES. Billets rather scattered in both villages. Lieut HICHENS) rejoined from Course at BETHUNE Sergt HASTINGS)	Further Casualties reported. 1 Wounded 2.1.16 1 " 7.1.16 2 " 8.1.16 2 " 11.1.16

(73989) W4141—463. 400,000. 9/14. H.&J.Ltd. Forms/C. 2118/10.

WAR DIARY or INTELLIGENCE SUMMARY

Army Form C. 2118.

January 1916. 16th K.R.R.

Hour, Date, Place	Summary of Events and Information	Remarks and references to Appendices
15th Jan. FOUQUEREUIL	Resting and cleaning up – M.G. lectures under LIEUT. WATTS & SCOTT reported – men in trenches have not rested.	
16th Jan "	Revd. Duncan held voluntary service 10.A.M, 11 A.M & 6.30 P.M. 2nd Lieut PARAVICINI to Common at BETHUNE at Divl School Sergt Turner left. Company training.	
9.30 " 17th Jan "	2nd Lieut PEARSON & 16 joined Bn. Grenadier Course for instruction. Sergt BASHFORD attended as Sergt Instructor and Rfn STANNING on Asst Instructor at FOUQUEREUIL – Company training & Draft Sergt Martin, Corpl Ranz, Corpl Brown + 32 Rfn joined & taken on the strength. Companies, M.G's in training	
17th Jan "	Lieut ADRIFIELD + 3 men to LEWIS GUN course BETHUNE. 1 NCO + 4 men to T.M Course at FOUILLARD BKS. Sergt CARR on Instructors class M.G course BETHUNE.	
10 am 18th " "	Bn. pot ball in BETHUNE – Nothing of company training, M.G's, Inspection + fitting in panders to not – 2nd Lieut CHOWARD reported on completion of "Sniper" course. Capt WALLACE A/Adj to J.B. from Lectures. 5.30 pm Trench Weapons	

4 pm " " " P.J.

(73989) W4141—463. 400,000. 9/14. H.&J.Ltd. Forms/C. 2118/10.

WAR DIARY
or
INTELLIGENCE SUMMARY

Army Form C. 2118.

January 1916   16th K.R.R.

(Erase heading not required.)

Hour, Date, Place	Summary of Events and Information	Remarks and references to Appendices
19th Jan. FOUQUEREUIL	Coy training – Grenading, M.G., Bayonet – wiring by night. Gas helmets etc.	
20th Jan "	Same as above. The G.O.C. Division inspected various parties. Transport.	
21st Jan "	Same as above – Sergt Heald & Rfn Pratt instruction in repair of gun locks.	
22nd Jan "	Same as above. The C.O. & Capt from each Coy & 2nd Gunner from each Officer went to reconnoitre our trenches Z.D.	
23rd Jan. ANNEQUIN FOSSE	16th KRR moved from FOUQUEREUIL & FOUQUIERES & ANNEQUIN FOSSE taking over from 2nd Midx. Marched at 1:30 pm via BETHUNE & BEUVRY. Relieved BRAYS KEEP – CHURCH KEEP WEST. Coys under orders of O.C. 18th Bn.	
24th Jan	Bn relieved 20th & 19th R.F. Guides at R.E. Dump 4:00 pm – held from MUD TRENCH Exclusive to R1 inclusive with RAILWAY KEEP. { A Coy on Right of B in Centre (C on left Boundary this in support.) { Mud Tr & Mr Road & R1 to Q2 Q1 & R1. D Coy in Reserve holding Railway Keep. Got 100 I.B. in Gunwerk in centre of relief. * 1st Queens on our left. Leics Corps on our right. Relief complete 8:45 pm.	2 Rfn wounded.

Army Form C. 2118.

WAR DIARY
or
INTELLIGENCE SUMMARY.
(Erase heading not required.)

Instructions regarding War Diaries and Intelligence Summaries are contained in F.S. Regs., Part II and the Staff Manual respectively. Title pages will be prepared in manuscript.

Hour, Date, Place	Summary of Events and Information	Remarks and references to Appendices
25th Jan. Z.O.	Work on firing steps & bomb throw funnels. Warning to patrol at night. 2nd Lt Grant wounded while out.	2nd Lt GRANT wounded
26th Jan. Z.O.	Orders to move to Z.1. before generally cancelled – Patrols & covering parties sent in before.	{1 Rfn Killed 3 wounded} {1 Cpl Killed, 1 wounded}
27th Jan. Z.1.	Moved to Z.1. at 12 noon relieved the 1st Queens. D. Coy holding right – B. Coy left of front line. A – HAMILTON TRENCH & C – OLD BOOTS	
28th Jan. Z.1.	Enemy bombarded unanswered 10 A.M. and continued till 6 p.m. Very intense & knocked both front, support & communicating trenches about. Tho left of SIMS KEEP was also battered. B & C Coy front was t- our Art silent. Enemy reinforced 2 platoons B. Coy to assist A Coy. relieved B. Coy. who had not suffered much reversed on the right. 1/2 C. Coy. detailed to	Capt DONALDSON wounded R+F 21 Killed R+F 30 wounded
29th Jan. Z.1	BORDON TRENCH, whilst the other 2 platoons who had suffered most & B. Coy retired to AVNEQUIN 3. B. Coy. Work of improving trenches dead recovered continued. 2nd Lt O.G.B. Capt G. BOTHNELL killed out on patrol, recovered	

WAR DIARY or INTELLIGENCE SUMMARY

Army Form C. 2118.

January 1916 16th (S) K.R.R.

Hour, Date, Place	Summary of Events and Information	Remarks and references to Appendices
29 Jan	[illegible]	
29 Jan 2 P	[faded] ...our German trench... took observations – he was willing to [fetch?] a [bomb?]. A German party [attacked?] by them... then made his way back with valuable information. Has since been introduced to the G.O.C. 100th I.B. Repairing wire & patrols as before. A [fresh?] fog in the early morning, both our own working parties were busy, though a desultory [fire?] was kept up [illegible] Capt Wynne was shot through the back by the German shorts [?] [Captain?] 9 am Bitchen's [?] [illegible] affected by tear shells [?]	Capt WYAND killed R+F 3 killed 2 wounded that [Hollers?] wounded
30th Jan	Coy S.M. H.A. HAMILTON D Coy had gone to [?] from a patrol that was out in front. In spite of heavy M.G. fire he went over the parapet & worked his way towards the [wire?]. He found 2 men lying within 5 yards of the enemy's wire, riddled with bullets. On [finding?] one of them still alive, he tried to drag him away, the other being wounded in the [shoulder?]. He endeavoured by every effort to help him forward, the man was dead when he [illegible] [illegible] is [illegible] [condition?] [illegible] been [?] attd to G. O. C. 100 I.B.	2 Lt Horsfield to Dr 2/Lt [Fallon?] [Blessed?] Major D. Oates [Coward?] [?] [Coldring?] Verdin Le Bethune.

Army Form C. 2118.

WAR DIARY
or
INTELLIGENCE SUMMARY.

January 1916 16th K.R.R.

(Erase heading not required.)

Instructions regarding War Diaries and Intelligence Summaries are contained in F. S. Regs., Part II and the Staff Manual respectively. Title pages will be prepared in manuscript.

Hour, Date, Place	Summary of Events and Information	Remarks and references to Appendices
31 Jan. Z.1	2 N.C.O's + 20 men to 2.5.1st (or R.E. (Tunnels Co.)) for fatigue duties. Ripping + wiring trenches continued. Known + patrols as previously approximates. Reinforcement was received from G.O.C. 33 Div to be published — "The General Officer Commanding 33 Div Division wishes to convey to the 16th K.R.R his keen appreciation of the soldierlike spirit shown by the Battn in the recent bombardment." Capt Kelk reported to duty from Course of Instructions	1 Appx Nominal list

[signatures]

WAR DIARY
or
INTELLIGENCE SUMMARY

Army Form C. 2118.

16th K.R.R.

February 1916.

(Erase heading not required.)

Hour, Date, Place	Summary of Events and Information	Remarks and references to Appendices
1st Feb. Z1	Continued work on shoring & revetting trenches. Saps, Snipers posts, M.G. emplacements etc. Patrols unmolested.	1 Rfn wounded
2nd Feb. Z1	B + C Coys relieved A + D, in front line. 2 Platoons A Coy to BORDON IV. Dr. Ho & to ANNEQUIN South. Went patrols by night. Captured work in trenches.	
2nd Feb. Z1	Work as usual. 2 Lt C.H. Park reported for medical attention to R.A.P. Noah Sapr 5. Back up.	Rustle head caught up between dug-outs 4 & 5 1 am 5
4th Feb. Z1	A + D Coys relieved B + C. 2 platoons B to BORDON IV. Work on Brit + ANNEQUIN SOUTH HIGH St. A little rain on back.	
5th Feb Z1	Relieved by 1 CAMERONIANS. Guides to CAMBRIN CHURCH. 4.30 p.m. orders cancelled at 11 p.m. Continuous work repairing + clearing trenches. Especially Back St + High St. Orders taken by 2 R.W.F. opposite Noah Ca on our left - 9.30 PM.	
6 Feb Z1	1 Cameronians relieved us in front line. 12" R.F. relieved A + B Coy at ANNEQUIN. Relief completed by 7.15 pm. Bn. marched to MONTMORENCY By. BETHUNE. ARTHUR H.Q. + No 9 Pn. billetted during relief.	1 Rfn killed 1 Rfn wounded. R.S.M. Mita reported on arrival from England

Army Form C. 2118.

February 1916 16th K.R.R.

WAR DIARY
or
INTELLIGENCE SUMMARY.
(Erase heading not required.)

Hour, Date, Place	Summary of Events and Information	Remarks and references to Appendices
7th Qrs. MONTMORENCY BKS. BETHUNE	Rest & Clean up	
8th Feb. " "	C.O. Inspection in Barracks – Coy. work. Too soon on fatigues R.E. Yard. Replacing lorries & deficiencies from Q.M. Stores. C.O. attended meeting at Bde. Hd. Qrs. held by Army Boyd.	
9th Feb. " "	No battn. Clean up – Training to replace what was knocked in. Training to leaders. Coy. arrangements.	
10th Feb. " "	Bombing Course commenced at FOUQUEREUIL. Instructors – 2nd Lt. GONNER + Sergt BASHFORD. 32 R + F attended also 2nd Lt HICHENS. 2nd Lt. AVERDICK. GRANT + CORK. (2nd Lt. Lewin M.G. Course at Montmorency Bks. 2nd Lt. Paravicini Short Mortar Course Col. Ode L. Williams acts. Brig. 100 I.B. inspected Bks.	
11th Feb. " "	Courses + training under Coy. arrangements.	
12th Feb. " "	Bn. Route March to Arques + Coy. training – Courses to Lieut Hitchens hut to Arques to have been talks. Orders received to march to BEUVRY. in 13th + to B 2 buts on 14th.	

WAR DIARY or INTELLIGENCE SUMMARY

February 16th K.R.R.

Army Form C. 2118.

3.

Hour, Date, Place	Summary of Events and Information	Remarks and references to Appendices
13th Feb. ANNEQUIN NORTH	Major Sitwell + Captain Capt. Thomas, Murray + Smith + Lt. Gamer went to Sector B.I. Shown round by 21st R.F. Battalion marched at 4 pm from MONTMORENCY BKs. BETHUNE to ANNEQUIN N. Took over billets from 1st Middx. 2/Lieut. Giddens + Davies reported their arrival from ENGLAND.	
14th Feb. B.I.	2/Lt. Davis, Orley + Young + draft of 1 Sgt. 82/cpls. 62 R.F. arrived from Base. Capt. DONALDSON rejoined from Hospital. Met guides in Harley St. 4.30 p.m. D. Coy took over R. from firing + SpoilBank Keep left front line, with N. Yorks firing, A.C. left front line in PONT FIXE + ORCHARD REDOUBT. B. + C. Coy in PONT FIXE NORTH. Relief reported complete 7.15 pm. Very wet night — Ride + ORCHARD RD, FINCHLEY RD, CHEYNE WALK, — left being of communication trenches available on left bank. PIONEER trying to reclaim flooded Comm. Trenches + clearing WILLOW RD. drains.	1 Rfn wounded.
15th Feb. B.I.	Work on Rifleman Ryan, + Rfn Bloomfield funerals.	Lt. Hicklers attached Eye reported not to expose flames.

WAR DIARY
or
INTELLIGENCE SUMMARY.
(Erase heading not required.)

Army Form C. 2118.

Thines 16th K.R.R.

4.

Hour, Date, Place	Summary of Events and Information	Remarks and references to Appendices
15th Feb. B.1.	Very wet night & day. Water gaining at trenches very bad. Draining, cleaning, repairing trenches. Working parties from Bn. C. Coy - Worcesters under R.E. & Pioneers. ENEMY Sniped a few rifle grenades into front lines. The left front, N. of FINCHLEY RD. left unoccupied. Enemy M.Gs enfilade Working parties began to gain on water. Willow	Put no rifle man on left.
16th Feb. B.1.	RD. Drain running freely, but helps B. 2 men from own front line. Work to his & french's. Brilliant moon light made patrolling & working both sides impossible. Duel between M.G's present. Clearing PONT FIXE defences begun.	2 men wounded.
17th 2b. B.1.	B. Coy relieved A. firing line much improved, & C. " D. great deal of work done, ground on repairing stronghold extn - Work on Clearing PONT FIXE Defences, continued. Pioneers began in Strathcona Walk.	1 Officer wounded. 2d Lt Mansfield – 2/gt Fielder returned from Comn. Gd. School.

Army Form C. 2118.

January 16th K R R

WAR DIARY
or
INTELLIGENCE SUMMARY.
(Erase heading not required.)

Instructions regarding War Diaries and Intelligence Summaries are contained in F.S. Regs., Part II and the Staff Manual respectively. Title pages will be prepared in manuscript.

Hour, Date, Place	Summary of Events and Information	Remarks and references to Appendices
18 Feb B.1	Work on repairs & improvements continues. Very bright moonlight - M.G. duels - Usual & fit wiring parties - Weather very bad. Water scarce on purpose. Co[y]s to 8th R.Munster Fus. reported & relieved. Village Line shelled during day. Trenches - B.2 on N. appeared to be getting Minenwerfers. 4 were put established - Claim 3 kits. Finchley Rd very bad indeed. (Clearing & draining throughout.) Lata Motortraversea in CHEYNE WALK & PARADOS of LEFT FRONT Trench.	2/Lt AVERDICK Sgt Mowbray 5 Gunner shots. 1 Rfn wounded.
19th Feb B.1	1 Co[y] T. R. Munster Fus. attached for Instruction also 16 snipers. One of our planes fit to ground down into our lines S. of Canal A. Sutor. Aeroplane hand fight & returning - One or more passed over B.1 apparently very low & loved on [bombs?]. Sniper driven fit to left front. Germans heard calling to our own, & shouted "K.R.R." Some things hung from our own lines rather more active over Orchard Redoubt. M.G. fire rather more active over Orchard Redoubt. Some rifle grenades fell in R front line near Canal. No damage.	
10.30 a.m.		
10.30 - 11.30 p.m.		

WAR DIARY 1/5 K.R.R.
INTELLIGENCE SUMMARY
February

Army Form C. 2118.
6

Hour, Date, Place	Summary of Events and Information	Remarks and references to Appendices
20 Feb B.1.	A relieved B & D Coys in front line after dark. Considerable Arty. duel to North. At barrier trains & Cr Lane & fire to South. Had a mine, but could not locate it to S.	Capt Thomas proceeded on leave.
11 p.m.	Warned that an attack might be expected presently. Bn. H.Q. Coy. Scouts wounded & had his attack	Weiss changed to E. Lieut. Watkins Thomas RAMC relieved by Lieut. W. Bower on evening of —
1.30 p.m.	A few shells lunge fell near ORCHARD REDOUBT O.C. 9th Dublin Fus. came to make arrangements as relief on 22 Feb.	Rev. J. Duncan also proceeded on leave Sh.f. 17 Feb.
6 p.m.	Draft of 18 men arrived — 2 left at BEUVRY 1st Reserve from 20 Riflemen (Oxf. Bucks. L.I.) Draining & cleaning out Trenches. Signed Reserve Transport & —	
21st	Aeroplane head replaces, dropped bomb on BETHUNE.	
B.1.	2 men of draft left at BEUVRY report their arrival. Usual work again & improvements, drawing in.	2nd Lt. Cooper proceeded on leave.
	Brig. Gen. Baird came round. Another plane can to fire behind our lines. O.C. 9th Dublin & O.C. Coys came to look at Trenches.	Capt Donaldson sent to Hosp?
6.40 p.m.	Arranged to relieve tomorrow. Division front at GIVENCHY Sector.	

WAR DIARY
or
INTELLIGENCE SUMMARY.

(Erase heading not required.)

February 16th K.R.R.

Army Form C. 2118.

7

Hour, Date, Place	Summary of Events and Information	Remarks and references to Appendices
21st B.1.	The following message received B.M. 131. 21st "The Brigadier has much pleasure in forwarding the following — begin — Commander in Chief award of the D.C.M. to the following Cpl. C.S.M. H.A. HAMILTON 16th K.R.R.C. C.93. Corporal G. BOTHWELL 16th K.R.R.C. — Please inform the N.C.Os concerned and forward thro the competent Liaison " 9th B.G.C. — From 33 Division — Heavy snow.	
22. B.1.	Relieved by (9) 2nd DUBLIN FUS. On relief Bath Coy marched by Canal Bank to LE QUESNOY into billets Hard frost last night. Relief completed 10 p.m. 1 Officer + 4 N.C.Os per Coy left with DUBLIN FUS to acquaint them — hard frost with N. wind.	
23. LE QUESNOY	Rest & clean up — Hard frost at night — Orders received 10.30 am to move back to B.1. in Evening Cancelled at 1.00 pm	
24. LE QUESNOY	Hard frost & snow — Work under Coy arrangements. Test GAS ALARM — All ran stopped.	Capt. John Noone proceeded on leave.

(73989) W4141—463. 400,000. 9/14. H.&J.Ltd. Forms/C. 2118/10.

Army Form C. 2118.

WAR DIARY
or
INTELLIGENCE SUMMARY.

(Erase heading not required.)

February 16th K.R.R.

Instructions regarding War Diaries and Intelligence Summaries are contained in F.S. Regs., Part II and the Staff Manual respectively. Title pages will be prepared in manuscript.

Hour, Date, Place	Summary of Events and Information	Remarks and references to Appendices
23rd 24th / LE QUESNOY	Marched at 4.15 p.m. Relieved 9th DUBLIN FUS in B.1. Relief completed 8.30 p.m.	
26th B.1.	C. Coy in RIGHT Front. B. Coy LEFT FRONT. A & D. at PONT F x E. Snowing hard. Quiet night. Evacuated man of Dublins who died of wounds after relief completed. Working – FINCHLEY ROAD free of water. Pumping, General repairs & improvements – Some wiring down in preparation for move – Recon. Coy's making fatalis [?] – Own patrol got out to enemy wire, found it in good order. Threw bits in. Brig. General round. Lt Col. C.E. Lyle + Capt Harrison returned from leave.	
27th B.1	Trenches getting back again with melting snow, + after front – Pumping + again throughout sector. Patrols to wiring at night. A few shells put into CHEYNE WALK. Rifle grenades over ↓ on right.	
28th B.1.	C.O. + Officers 20th R.F. up to look round. – Pumping + repairs – 4 by Dublin into PONT F x E – CHEYNE WALK + FINCHLEY RD lights shelled.	
29th B.1.	ORCHARD REDOUBT + PONT F x E shelled 8.15 am till 9 a.m. Spport BANK shelled. Phone wire cut. Bn relieved by 20th R.F. after dark. Relief complete 10.20 p.m.	5th R.F. wounded. Working Pty 15th Middx 7 casualties

Army Form C. 2118.

WAR DIARY
or
INTELLIGENCE SUMMARY.

February 16th K.R.

(Erase heading not required.)

Instructions regarding War Diaries and Intelligence Summaries are contained in F.S. Regs., Part II and the Staff Manual respectively. Title pages will be prepared in manuscript.

Hour, Date, Place	Summary of Events and Information	Remarks and references to Appendices
29th B.I. + BEUVRY.	Trenches constantly in bad condition after thaw. Pumping & repair all day. Proceeded by Coy to BEUVRY after an interval. Last Coy in billets 3.30 a.m.	[signature] Comdg 16th K.R.R. 1/3/16

WAR DIARY
INTELLIGENCE SUMMARY

Army Form C. 2118.

16th K.R.R.

March

Hour, Date, Place	Summary of Events and Information	Remarks and references to Appendices
1st March BEUVRY	Last by rated billets from B.1. 3.30 a.m. Rest & clean up. Sgt. Rix (M. Gun) returned from leave.	
2nd March "	Men got baths & change of linen. Men proceeded to Bn Instructor School 1 N.C.O. & 2 men. " LEWIS GUN " Sgt. Com in Inst. Attending 2'Lt Oxley & 5 men } In BÉTHUNE. " Grenades " Sgt. Bashford & Rpt Gosford in Instruction Attending 2'Lt Giddens 18 other ranks.	
3rd March "	2'Lt Pearson & 4 R&F to ANNEZIN course of telescopic sights. 2'Lt Cooper returned from leave. Pts Dr & detail billets. Bn carrying on. Sniping & Observation intoxication General. " " " Housfield Wiring " " Cooper Signalling " " Watts M.G Class for Officers under Lt Watts " " NCOs men " Scott " " " " M.O. Lectures & Stretcher bearing " Lis Gowans. The whole draft in Grenades & bombing. Through accidental explosion 2 Pts killed, 7 wounded 1 off " 3 Revd J. Dunstan returned from leave.	

Army Form C. 2118.

WAR DIARY
or
INTELLIGENCE SUMMARY

March 1916.   16th K.R.R.

(Erase heading not required.)

Hour, Date, Place	Summary of Events and Information	Remarks and references to Appendices
4 March. BEUVRY.	Courses continued. 1 Officer 100 men on working party in trenches. Heavy rain.	
5 March "	Parade Service 7.30 a.m. Evening service 7 p.m.	
6 " "	2 Officers 150 men on working parties in trenches. Courses continued. C.O. & Coy. Comdrs. conference at Bn. H.Q.	
7th " BETHUNE 3 p.m.	Courses continued. C.O. & Coy Commanders to Z.2. that has been dengh., to arrange relief with 4 SUFFOLK & 2 ARGYLL & SUTHERLAND. 15-6 pm. 2 other ranks to "Permanent tps." Div. Demonstration by "B" Co. Proceeded with the WORCESTERS. 1 good trench at ANNEZIN. 1 good trench at BEUVRY	Dist. Rifle Cpl.
8 " "	Bn. marched to Z.2. viâ CAMBRIN ALLEY. Cams. in for some shelling at CAMBRIN & CAMBRIN ALLEY — No damage	

WAR DIARY or INTELLIGENCE SUMMARY

Army Form C. 2118.

March 1916   16th K.R.R.

Hour, Date, Place	Summary of Events and Information	Remarks and references to Appendices
8th March Z.2	Trenches inspected after being handed over. Lgd & 9 hrs to front line. Relief completed by 10.45. B Coy front BOYAU ST GIL. A Coy in reserve C " " 11 to 16 WIMPOLE ST. D " " 16 to 20 10 cwt iron LEWIS KEEP B - # 2 - No 2 Sect MAISON ROUGE ALLEY. Patrols, repairing, cleaning. Heavy GRENADE fight from 2am to 7am to D.S. Arr heard on both sides 	
9th " Z.2	Patrols, repairs, cleaning. At 4.45pm enemy exploded MIDNIGHT CRATER. Consolidated by 5 to 7. 1 pm to 1.30 pm Coy relief Quiet night.	2 OR killed 1 Sgt, 2 Rf wounded

WAR DIARY 16th K.R.R.

March 1916

INTELLIGENCE SUMMARY

Army Form C. 2118.

4

Hour, Date, Place	Summary of Events and Information	Remarks and references to Appendices
10th March Z.2	Moved Bn HQ to A.26.d.3.5. A. Coy relieved D. on left front. Boyaux 16-20 intensive. Pumping, baling, cleaning and repairing. Capt MUNEY sent to BETHUNE sick. Bright fine around the trenches.	
11th March Z.2	2'Lieut AVERDIECK killed by Sniper in Boyau 16. Cleaning, relaying & repairs.	1 O.R. Killed.
12th " Z.2	Bn relieved by the 1st QUEEN'S after dark. Conference of OC's at Bn HQ 2pm. Relief completed by 9 pm - marched back to BEUVRY & took over the same billets as before - last Coy in by 11.30 pm. 2'Lt AVERDIECK buried at CAMBRIN.	
13th " BEUVRY	5 Officers 4/o R+F on Working parties. Other ranks baths & change socks.	
14th " BEUVRY	5 Officers 410 R+F on working parties. Other ranks baths & change. Battn slowly passed through Divl Baths 5-6 pm. Bn beat WORCESTERS in reply Cup Tie 2-1.	

WAR DIARY or INTELLIGENCE SUMMARY

Army Form C. 2118.

March 1916. 16th K.R.R.

(Erase heading not required.)

Hour, Date, Place	Summary of Events and Information	Remarks and references to Appendices
14th March. BEUVRY	3 Civilians killed & 1 woman & French Soldier wounded at corner of BETHUNE ROAD. Bomb dropped & placed at BETHUNE during the ceremony of presentation of French Colours by Inhabitants. B. Coy. The Regt. Band Post was sounded & afterwards a salute from our armed sentries.	
15th March. BEUVRY	C.O. + Bombing Officer visited AUCHY SECTOR. 5 Officers with parties, to HARLEY ST. for work with R.E. DIvide for baths.	
16 March. BEUVRY	Battalion relieved 1st QUEENS in AUCHY SECTOR. D. Coy on right. BOYAUX 8 to 10 — A. " centre " 11 to 15 — B. " left " 16 to 20 — C. in reserve in WIMPOLE ST, Bn Hd Qr ho 2 siding MAISON ROUGE ALLEY. Relief completed 9.30 pm. BEUVRY slightly shelled 11.30 am.	
17 March. AUCHY SECTOR	2nd Lieut. R.S. LYONS killed by sniper. R/C. LIVESEY wounded.	2/L HOCKENHULL Killed

Army Form C. 2118.

WAR DIARY or INTELLIGENCE SUMMARY.

16th K.R.R.

March 1916.

(Erase heading not required.)

Hour, Date, Place	Summary of Events and Information	Remarks and references to Appendices
17th March AUCHY SECTOR.	Rfn FISH Wounded. Repairs, working parties cleaning & deepening trenches.	1 Rfn Wounded
18" "	Rfn HERRITY, KIBLE & Rfn MEAD, HUGHES, CAMPBELL & AINSWORTH wounded by rifle grenade in TWIN SAP. 2/Col NEWELL 15th CHESHIRE REGT. visiting for instruction. Lot B work on repairs & improving -	2/Lt HOWARD to hospital hurt. 1 Rfn Killed 4 " wounded.
19" "	MAJOR GEN HUNTER & Officers 35th Div visited trenches. 5.15 pm to 7.45 pm ENEMY violently bombarded trench on right (HOHENZOLLERN). We reported heavy trench mortar and WORCESTERS on our right reported a 2" mine. Everyone stood to arms wearing gas helmets. Enemy sent a lot of lachrymatory shells along whole front & up & down LA BASSÉE RD. & supports. Our fire retaliated. At 2 AM bombardment recommenced for about 40 minutes - he carried train -	

Army Form C. 2118.

WAR DIARY
or
INTELLIGENCE SUMMARY

March 1916 16th K.R.R.

(Erase heading not required.)

Hour, Date, Place	Summary of Events and Information	Remarks and references to Appendices
19th March. AUCHY SECTOR.	Learn opened - Major Sitwell 17 men wounded on tram 11 p.m. C Coy relieved B in front line.	
20th " "	Bn relieved by the QUEEN'S. Relief complete 9 pm No 7 Platoon B Coy left behind LEWIS KEER not returned.	1 Rfn killed C1165 Phipps wounded.
" "	Bn marched to BEUVRY. Old billets.	
21st BEUVRY	4 Officers + 300 men on working parties - remainder rest + clean up. 2/Lt GONNER, Sgt BASHFORD + 24 Gunners carried out a raid by the QUEEN'S. Covering Rifle Gde into enemy front line.	NEWTON RIFLE GRENADES. Raid in enemy front.
22 " "	4 Officers 336 men working parties.	
23 " "	2 Officers 210 men working parties. Remainder baths.	
24th " "	Bn marched to OBLINGHAM. 1.15 p.m. arrived 3.40 p.m. Very scattered billets. Many trans.	MAJ. COORAN went on leave.
25th OBLINGHAM	Coy training in the (?) arrangements. A piano platoon & lecture formed. 2/Lt HOWELL 2 NCO'S	

Army Form C. 2118.

WAR DIARY
or
INTELLIGENCE SUMMARY.

March 1916. 16th K.R.R.

(Erase heading not required.)

Hour, Date, Place	Summary of Events and Information	Remarks and references to Appendices
26th March OBLINGHAM	Voluntary Church Parade at 11 am. 30 men inoculated. 2/Lt. K.G. DENNISS joined from O.T.C. H.Q.	
27th "	2 Officers & 200 men on working parties, heads of 5 hrs. Training under Coy arrangements. Mr Cluson commenced Gyrations. Wiring LEWIS M.G. Stretcher Bearers Signals, Transport The Corps Commander 11 Corps, held a reception at BOULEVARD VICTOR HUGO, BETHUNE 3 p.m. to meet all officers. 2/Lt PEARSON - 16 men to Bde. M.G. Course BETHUNE. S/t GREEN to ditto. 2/Lt YOUNG, 16 men to Bde Grenadier Course BETHUNE. S/t BASHFORD + RFN CRAWFORD to ditto. 2/Lt CORK, 4 men Bde Gymnastic Course BETHUNE. No.7 Platoon returned from LEWIS KEEP.	

Army Form C. 2118.

WAR DIARY
or
INTELLIGENCE SUMMARY.

(Erase heading not required.)

Brunel 1916. 16th K.R.R.

9.

Hour, Date, Place	Summary of Events and Information	Remarks and references to Appendices
27th March DRLINGHAM	Draft of 36 R+F joined from 19th S.Bn K.R.R. 2/C BIRCH. Tried by F.G.C.M. at BETHUNE.	
28th "	Coveren as usual. Shapers fired course on range at ANNEZIN. Bn. Battn. at BETHUNE. Inspected by Corps. Bde Dist Anal. (Lt. Cuptn 4-1. 4th round.	
29 "	Adjt. Ptn at 9.30 a.m. + 2.30 p.m. Maj SITWELL returned off leave, + Capt. Hon L. LINDSAY proceeded on leave. Sentence of F.G.C.M. on 2/C BIRCH promulgated on Pte. Broad of A.A. Sec 9.(?) 3 years P.S. Commutted suspended.	
30 "	Bn paraded at 10.30 a.m. for inspection by Brig Gen A.W.F. BAIRD. C.M.G. D.S.O. Comdg 100th I.B.	
31st "	Course as usual. Training taken by companies.	

Cupman
16th Bn.

16 KRRC Vol 6
XXX IV

WAR DIARY
or
INTELLIGENCE SUMMARY

April 1916 16th K.R.R.

Army Form C. 2118.

Hour, Date, Place	Summary of Events and Information	Remarks and references to Appendices
1st April OBLINGHAM	Battalion marched to LE QUESNOY and took over billets from 6th Bn The King's (Liverpool) Regt. 4 p.m. The C.O. & Coy Comds (Cos) went to CUINCHY Batt Sector. Left Battalion to look round.	
2nd "	Billets taken over by 1/5 Scottish Rifles 6 p.m. Bn marched via (Canal Bank) to left sector CUINCHY. Bn marched into relief of 2nd Argyll & Sutherland Highrs. Sector (Brickstacks) to relief of 8.60 p.m. Relief completed 8.60 p.m. A Coy on right front. B centre. D. Left front. Bayonet 32-37 m. Bayonet 37 & 40. Bayonet House & 54. C in reserve at ESPERANTO TERRACE. Hd Qrs KINGSCLERE.	
CUINCHY LEFT SECTOR	16 Rifle Bde. on our right. Big minnies put over 4-3 p.m. on our right. At WOYONITZA. 1-3 Khings bomb put on to our own Bn Snr. Academy. Enemy Trench Mortars 4—940 p.m. front & supports. Improving communication trenches between supports & front line. Cleaning trenches. Putting up parados from 6 to T.A. Central trench. Enemy Arty. making 3 places in trench pretext aint. Big fire round ST LAWRENCE.	1 Officer wounded

WAR DIARY or INTELLIGENCE SUMMARY

Army Form C. 2118.

16th K.R.R.

April 1916

(Erase heading not required.)

Hour, Date, Place	Summary of Events and Information	Remarks and references to Appendices
4th CUINCHY LEFT SECTOR.	Enemy shelled The Bulge, Canal Bank, & whole of Left shelled 6.a.m. 11/7/12 Intermittent small minnies, + rifle grenades during the day. Works on dugs legs at Banbury x Berkshire LANE. The Bulge, Opening Lower Old Kent Rd + Coldstream Lane- Carryn Stores, Wiring + patrols. Patrols out from our Enemy Patrols. Pionier Platoon finished wiring towards COLDSTREAM LANE + LOWER OLD KENT ROAD	2 Rfn Howell wounded 6 a.m. died on way down C.S.M. Laurence Rfn Fletcher Killed (Rfn Scott) (Rfn Kiln) wounded
5" " "	Began helping with NEW OXFORD ST. Work repairing + reburying through out extra - Wiring + patrolling Big MINNIE landed behind No 10 Breastwork, in donnays + 3 more T.M.s detonated 4 to 1 - others judged to be 4000 yds, + T.M.n. HARLEY ST. Shells were normal. Enemy parachute lights came down in DEAD MAN LANE, N.8 (and + on our right at night. Lot of shelling + heb M.G's Several strains were sent up. Wiring parties returned. Col. + Capt. The I/Queens taken up to take round.	
6" " "	Two OSE (m) of Queens + 2 J 175 K.R.R. up at 10.30 AM. to look round. Considerably shelling at various times during day in various parts of the front- no damage to trenches or inmates. Pionier Platoon working in DAWSON ST. Bn relieved by the I/QUEENS. Relief completed 8.45 p.m handed back to L.E. QUEENS on Canal Bank.	Rfn Boast wounded.

WAR DIARY / INTELLIGENCE SUMMARY

Army Form C. 2118.

April 1916. — **16th K.R.R.**

3.

Hour, Date, Place	Summary of Events and Information	Remarks and references to Appendices
7th Ap. LE QUESNOY.	Clean up + rest. Intelligence Officer + Patrol Leaders had Conference.	Bn played draw 3-3 with 2nd S.W.B. & Semifinal Divl Cup.
8th " "	Training under Coy arrangements. Lecture by B.I.O. 3 p.m.	
9th " "	Major Stewart goes to Aire on a Senior Officers Artillery Course. Capt Snell returned from leave.	
10th " "	Conversion of Lyd. Dirck evacuated to three years penal Servitude, granted in accordance with Army Corps orders. Relieved 1st Queens in Cuinchy Left Sector. Relief complete 9.45 p.m. 2nd Worcesters on our right.	
Cuinchy Left Sector.	A Coy left front Coy — B Coy Reserve in Esperanto Terrace. C Coy right Coy — D Coy Centre Coy. Patrols sent out from each Coy in front line. Report all normal.	
11th	Lieut Parkin goes on leave. Yesterday was quiet on the whole line; two Minnies only being sent over. Tunnel between Coy H.Q. and Signallers dug out (right Coy) completed. Work on dug outs and claiming of Borjan 33 proceeded with. Bridstock keep notched with stores.	

WAR DIARY or INTELLIGENCE SUMMARY

Army Form C. 2118.

16th K.R.R.C.

April 1916

Hour, Date, Place	Summary of Events and Information	Remarks and references to Appendices
Crunchy Left Sector. 11th (cont). 12th " "	New front trench started from S.W. corner Brickstack No 2 to join Oxford Street near Brickstack No 1. This work done at night by the sapping platoon. Bad weather hampered work considerably. Brigadier visited the Boise with General Anderson. Lieut Hitchens proceeds on leave. — All leave cancelled till further orders. Work carried on in new front line trench, which is now almost complete. Six cadets are attached, two to each company in the front line, for training as platoon commanders. A small raid was carried out on our left at midnight. At 9.10 pm a patrol under head keeper and M.S. of Queens with Sgt Shafton and 7 men , went out from the left front with the object of finding a gap in the enemy's wire. They saw a Hun patrol previously, then proceeding along a light railway, which runs from our line to the German's. They came to a mound close to the enemy's wire. Here the Sgt sighted some Huns, and unfortunately fired with his revolver. At once the Germans began bombing. The Sgt was seen to fall and groan. The rest thinking he was killed and owing to the intensity of the fire, returned.	

WAR DIARY
or
INTELLIGENCE SUMMARY

April 1916   16ᵗʰ K.R.R.C.

Army Form C. 2118.

5.

Hour, Date, Place	Summary of Events and Information	Remarks and references to Appendices
12ᵗʰ (cont) Quinchy A1+1.	Half an hour later the Tofft returned, slightly wounded. He said the protruder [?] is be dead and when the bomber came at to look for him he shot twice with his revolver, and returned.	3.45pm Cooks "A" Killed. 13.07 Cpl Shapton "A" wounded (slight) 1.55pm Throw "C" wounded
13ᵗʰ	At 11am a loud explosion was heard, and débris was seen to be flung into the air from the SPOTTED DOG HOUSE. It is thought that a Minnie had a premature, and no exploded. This is probably true, as a Minnie has been seen to fire from this house for the past few days. The enemy shelled Hurley Street in the morning with light shells. Working parties to the trenches were carried out. Minnie fired Aerial cards but did no harm. A meeting of Coy Commanders was held at Batᵗⁿ H.q. to discuss a "getting B" work when at rest. At 6 P.M. we exploded three mines by the HOHENZOLLERN, which started an artillery bombardment lasting an hour. The Germans was active, but returned no shrapnel. Our patrols were active but encountered no Germans.	c12.16 Rfmn T. Roach "C" Killed c12.30 " 6 Hall "A" wounded c13.04 " B.H. West "B" wounded

Army Form C. 2118.

16th K.R.R.C.
6.

WAR DIARY
or
INTELLIGENCE SUMMARY.

April 1916

(Erase heading not required.)

Hour, Date, Place	Summary of Events and Information	Remarks and references to Appendices
14th CUINCHY LEFT.	Quiet day. Work completed on dug-outs; and trenches repaired. 1st Queens relieved 16 K.R.R. Relief complete 9 P.M. Battalion proceeded to billets in LE QUESNOY. Capt Deedes returned from leave.	
15th LE QUESNOY	Major SITWELL reported return from Command at AIRE. Lieut FRANCIS returned to duty into D. Co. HICHENS reported return without leave on reaching BOULOGNE.	
16th " "	Rest & clean up. Church Parade 7.30 A.M. 9.15 A.M. 6.30 P.M. Lecture from Col. Hopkin headed in after Board of Inquiry. 2 Officers 240 men on working parties.	
17th " "	Training under Co. arrangements. 2 Officers 200 men on working parties. Interpreters and Billeting party went to OBLINGHAM and took over billets from 5th Scottish Rifles ready to take over billets on arrival. Bn. beaten by 2's A & S. Highrs 2-1 in Semi-final for Divl Cup. 2d Lt Francis, 2d Lt Horsnail + 16 O.R. to Sniping Course BETHUNE.	

WAR DIARY or INTELLIGENCE SUMMARY.

Army Form C. 2118.

April 1916 — 16th K.R.R.C.

7.

(Erase heading not required.)

Hour, Date, Place	Summary of Events and Information	Remarks and references to Appendices
18th LE QUESNOY	Bn. moved to OBLINGHAM, marching via BETHUNE on relief by 20th R.F. Each Bn. marched independently - relief completed by 3.30 p.m.	Weather wet + cold winds.
19th OBLINGHAM	Clean up, work on billets improvement - last draft inspected by Med. Officer. Lecture in BETHUNE to 10th + 4 N.C.Os. per Co. truck in by transport wagon - Bayonet fighting - Lecture to Officers + all N.C.Os. & from "Discipline" + Courage opened. 2 Lt Young 7 NCOs + 16 men 13th Bombing Instruction. 2 Lt Hayes " " " 1 NCO + 8 men ". C/S. Hodgson " " " 1 NCO + 8 men in m.Tr. Vickers M.G. St. from m.Tr. 1 NCO + 4 N.C.Os. Working party with Bayonet Fighting 2 Lt Dunn + 12 men R.E. Scott 2 Lt Pearson + approved by Brigadier. Programme	Heavy rain.
20th OBLINGHAM	Work carried to programme. Riding School for young Officers - under Transport Officer - 1 Lt Scott. 2 " Ortley. 2 " Gardner. n.i. Cocker. " " Davies. " " Fielden. Working party with R.E.	Ground very wet.

Army Form C. 2118.

WAR DIARY
of 16th K.R.R.C.
April 1916.
INTELLIGENCE SUMMARY.
(Erase heading not required.)

Hour, Date, Place		Summary of Events and Information	Remarks and references to Appendices
21st	OBLINGHAM.	Training as per Programme. Lecture by Med. Off. "Sanitation." 1 Sgt. 20 men working party.	
22"	"	Training as per Programme. Baths & change of underclothes in BETHUNE. 1 Sgt 20 men working party.	
23"	"	Early service 7.30 am. Bn paraded 9.15 am marched to BETHUNE & paraded review at 10.30 am. Ensuing 6.30 p.m. Lt Francis, 2/Lt Howard + 16 men reported return from Sniping Course. Men on Battn. Roster this on parade — ten men on Bn Route march. Bn paraded. Route OBLINGHAM.	Rfn Watson killed 2/Lt Young + 6 O.R. wounded Accident at Rifle Bombing School.
24th	"	Course at 9.45 am, passing W36c3.8. at 10 am. Route OBLINGHAM — Mt BERENCHON — Road junction at P.36.b.1.3. — GONNEHEM — CHOQUES — VENDIN-LES-BETHUNE. Bn got in 1.30 p.m. Major SITWELL. Capts HARRISON + SMITH Lieuts FRANCIS + WATTS 2/ Lt. GRANT, DAVIES + GIDDENS + 4 N.C.O.s proceeded by Bus to BEUVRY + reconnoitred the 2' LINE DEFENCE SYSTEM—	

WAR DIARY
or
INTELLIGENCE SUMMARY.

(Erase heading not required.)

April 1916. 16th K.R.R.C.

Army Form C. 2118.

9.

Hour, Date, Place	Summary of Events and Information	Remarks and references to Appendices
25th OBLINGHAM	Training as per programme. (Cleaning up - probationers etc. Coys attached to 100 I.B. B.S.B.O.G. - Probationers	
26th BEUVRY	B. relieved 2nd A. & S. High[landers]. at BEUVRY, marching in via BETHUNE at 3 pm. Handed over billets at OBLINGHAM to Train Accn. Party. Bn Sick Parade J.C.M. at LIGHTOURENAY BKS	
27th "	BETHUNE 6 am. 1 Officer + Cpl + 9 men working parties at CAMBRIN. Gas warning from 16- 9 am. 9-12 muskets. Improving billets. Running + Phys. Ex. 7.30 am. Bayonet fighting to by Coys. M.G. + Bombing Classes - high patrols. 150 men on working parties. 2 Officers + 30 men attached R.E. 212th (s). ANNEQUIN SOUTH for special work. Gas noticed (slight) in our billets from redemption shells 2 Officers + 100 men carrying party. (wire) 8-9 am.	
28th "	Musketry - bayonet, phys. ex. under (?) arrangements. M.G. + Bombing. high patrols. 3 Officers + 330 men on working parties.	

WAR DIARY or INTELLIGENCE SUMMARY

Army Form C. 2118.

April 1916   16th K.R.R.C.   10

Hour, Date, Place	Summary of Events and Information	Remarks and references to Appendices
28th BEUVRY	Some heavy shells put over - one known hit, artillery in billeting area. Warning of gas attack from Bn M.G. Canal. C.O. + O.C. Coys to AUCHY LEFT to arrange relief. Training under Coy arrangements	
29th "	on 30th.	
30th "	Bn relieved 1st QUEENS in AUCHY LEFT. Also 1 Coy took over front of 2' WORCESTER front to assist 1/6 SCOTTISH RIFLES who are under. C. Coy on Rght. Railway inclusive to Boyau G. D.Co in Centre Boyaux 9-6. B. Coy on left 16-20. A.Coy Garrisoning Lewis Keep, Sussex Keep, Arthurs Keep + 1 platoon in reserve in Wimpole St. 1 Officer, 2 returns 98t M.G.Coy attached for instruction 4 " " 3-N.C.O. 100t M.G.Coy attached in trenches. 2LT GIDDENS, 1 N.C.O to Lewis M.C. (course) at CAMIERES 4 N.C.O. to Vickers M.G. Course	Cpl DCol (cont 16th K.R.R.)

16 KRRC
Army Form C. 2118.
XXIII Vol 7

WAR DIARY
or
INTELLIGENCE SUMMARY

16th K.R.R.C.
May 1916

(Erase heading not required.)

Hour, Date, Place	Summary of Events and Information	Remarks and references to Appendices
1st AUCHY LEFT	Work – Principally at SAP HEADS & Craters, improving cover & building communication ways – Continuing on a big dug out in SIDING I. (connects ARTHURS KEEP – BHQ by phone. Enemy threw lot of T.M's over on Bn on our left 2 R.W.F. Certain amount of light T.M's mostly + M.G. on front & right. 4.20 & 5.30 mm trench Mortars in rear – a lot of duds. a little evening & usual patrol. Went out to S.E. M.Gs kept up bursts & sprays on enemy wire. Retaliation & Rifle grenades, with our own the on got the upper hand. a lot of aerial activity – Work on Sap Heads & Craters continued – Improvements general.	2 Rfn wounded rifle grenades accident
2	Continuation on deep dug out SIDING I. Intensive bombardment & trench mortar report that Enemy held S. Lip of MIDNIGHT CRATER. Examined the same T. Enemy put some 3.9 near BOYAU III & a lot of whizz bangs in retaliation for our 6 pm work on this front line on trenching actions. 9 of our Fighting Vickers bombarded by + apparently h.c. M & and BH heavy planes.	2 Rfn wounded rifle grenades accident

WAR DIARY
or
INTELLIGENCE SUMMARY

Army Form C. 2118.

16th K.R.R.
May 1916.

2.

(Erase heading not required.)

Hour, Date, Place	Summary of Events and Information	Remarks and references to Appendices
3rd May. AUCHY LEFT.	Very quiet night. Dull morning - one 18pdr shell return came. Minnies fell on R.W.F. birds on our left. Our T.M's reply tended to settling mins. Enemy retaliated with M.G. rifles. Work on Twin Crater bank completed. Shot wt made from craters & left sup of R.W.F. craters, to keep enemy Pioneer wire, and patrols out over ground, N of MIDNIGHT. Not many airplanes up this evening. Lot of firing at daylight. Work continued. Repairs, & improvements to B de G trench.	1 Pte wounded 2 Pte grants & 1 Pte wounded R.G. accident. Stab.Alsts. found Effect— for own Effective—
4th May " "	Reconnoitred Willow Support LINE S. according. Patrols out in patrol Japs & German wire. Relieved by 1st QUEENS. Relief completed 9.50 p.m. Moved to old billets in BEUVRY.	
5th May BEUVRY.	Rest & clean up. Majoris & Bn got baths & change. 2 Platoons D. Co commenced special instruction for a raid. 4 2/Lt FRANCIS + CORK. Wiring parties. 5 Officers 130 men on wiring parties. Course. Lt. Hagen Inst. Bn Bomb. Course.	

WAR DIARY or INTELLIGENCE SUMMARY

Army Form C. 2118.

May 1916.   16th K.R.R.C.   3.

(Erase heading not required.)

Instructions regarding War Diaries and Intelligence Summaries are contained in F.S. Regs., Part II and the Staff Manual respectively. Title pages will be prepared in manuscript.

Hour, Date, Place	Summary of Events and Information	Remarks and references to Appendices
6th May BEUVRY.	5 Officers 130 men on working parties - Physical &c., Bayonet fighting under Coy arrangements. Nos. 13 + 15 Platoons under Special instruction for raid -	
7th " "	Church Service 7.30. 9.30. 10.15. 11 a.m. + 6.30 p.m. 4 Offrs 230 men Working parties + training. Special training for 13.15. Platoon. Scheme submitted & passed by Bde. Bn. relieved 1st QUEENS in AUCHY LEFT + 1 (Right) Coy	1 Offr Wounded on working party.
8th " "	of 2 WORCESTERS - Left Front Coy + Russell's Keep. "A" Coy. Centre Coy "B" Coy. Right 2nd Coy (--) "C" Coy. Reserve Coy "D" Coy - 1 Platoon - SIMS KEEP 1 " - Arthur's Keep 1 " - Windsor St. tie expired. 1 Platoon left in BEUVRY. QUEEN'S Lewis Keep for Thomas Relief complt 9.55 p.m. 4 Officers 166 men working parties.	Lt Hitchens on leave 8-5-16 to 15-5-16.

WAR DIARY or INTELLIGENCE SUMMARY

16th K.R.R.C.

May 1916.

Army Form C. 2118.

4.

Hour, Date, Place	Summary of Events and Information	Remarks and references to Appendices
May 9th AUCHY LEFT.	Continued work on BABY & QUEENS Craters — (Queen's blown by Enemy on night of 5th and carried by the Queen's). Party went out & Western Twin to Queen's defended — New trench connecting W. lip of Queen's & Baby commenced. Covn sap in R.W.F. connecting centre & left saps — digging out shelters commenced. Cleaning & repair in trenches. Patrols out reconnoitring. E. & MIDNIGHT places — Crater & Enemy saps back to his front lines — Some wiring — Enemy put in a heavy bombardment 8.15 to 8.45 p.m. on Back St., BURBURE & Alley MAISON ROUGE Alley. Raid ordered for 1 am 10/5/11th Cancelled by Division in view, heavy barrage put on evening from R.W.F. Crater to Boyau 22 back by Art. T.M. & Rifle Grenades + M.G's — 9.37 p.m. to 9.55 p.m. + again from 11.30 — 11.35 p.m. The first draw heavy retaliation, no casualties but second did damage to parapets between Boyau 10 - 16 - in places.	Rgt Holroyd, died on 10th - R. Birks - R. Sparrow } Wounded Capt. S. Moore - J. Davey
May 10th " "		

WAR DIARY
INTELLIGENCE SUMMARY

May 1916 — 16th K.R.R.C.

Army Form C. 2118.

5-

Hour, Date, Place	Summary of Events and Information	Remarks and references to Appendices
May 10th AUCHY LEFT	At 10 a.m. 2nd in command, Platoon left at BEURY. relieved QUEEN's Platoon in LEWIS KEEP 3.30 p.m. Work continued in Craters + repairing damage. Aeroplanes Hy'd A Coy on left front. D. Coy relieved A Coy on left front.	
May 11th AUCHY LEFT	Work in TWIN + QUEEN'S Craters continued. Repair of damage. Lot of 9 hour Art. work on both sides in morning. 4 p.m. a mine went up in Hollenzollern Sector, followed by intense Art. Bombardt. Our guns retaliated + heavy, but died till 7 p.m. A big explosion. We turn at THE DUMP. Some damage down to HIGH + BACK STREETS. Corner of ARTHUR'S KEEP + BOYAUX 15 & 9 C. Coy men knocked in.	Lt. Lever in comm. 11.5.16 to 18.5.16. 3 Rfn wounded 1 shell shock M.G.C. in Arthur's Keep 1 killed 1 wounded.

Army Form C. 2118.

6.

WAR DIARY
or
INTELLIGENCE SUMMARY.

(Erase heading not required.)

May 1916 16th K.R.R.C.

Instructions regarding War Diaries and Intelligence Summaries are contained in F.S. Regs., Part II. and the Staff Manual respectively. Title pages will be prepared in manuscript.

Hour, Date, Place	Summary of Events and Information	Remarks and references to Appendices
May 12th AUCHY LEFT	Work done. Repairing damage by two days bombardment. Continuing sapping to QUEENS & BABY CRATERS - Mining shelters. Very quiet on this sector - A gun 77 H.E. + 4.2 Shrapnel. Good deal of Art. fire to N. + S. Another scheme for raid on night 15-16 cancelled.	21. 2 Rgs wounded.
May 13th "	Very quiet on this sector - Trench correct - Extra Twin, Baby + Queens posts cased in by est. chasses + repaired. Bad road had come in Northern TWIN repaired by stony trebs. Repair + improvements generally.	§ 1 Off 1 Rg wounded.
" "	No 13 Platoon K.R.R. Br raid night 15th/16th cancelled - during day. Wd. Left B zone height @ 10-15 + during day. Br. relieved by 1st QUEENS, + returned to BEUVRY. 2 Offs. 30 men opened wire parts - 8.30 p.m. Work carried on - 2 Offs + Wk.Cos + 40 men 7.30 carrying for R.E. p.m. 4 W.Cos + 40 men 7.30 carrying for R.E.	
May 14 "		
May 15th BEUVRY ~~BILLINGHAM~~ Bn	Rest + clean up - The platoon for Raiding party paraded 5.30 p.m. Capt. Guitt, 2 Lt Francis. 2 Lt Cork 42 O.R. marched to VILLAGE LINE + rested. Moved up to HIGH ST. to wait for Mine Kh exploded on signal for assault. Art. + T.M. + R.G. barage arranged for. 10 p.m. Art. barage commenced 2 minutes before Twin mine exploded unfortunately, +	2' W.Howard 5th Dir. School 1 Sgt 1 Rg wounded.

Army Form C. 2118.

WAR DIARY
or
INTELLIGENCE SUMMARY

May 1916.   16th K.R.R.C.

(Erase heading not required.)

Instructions regarding War Diaries and Intelligence Summaries are contained in F.S. Regs., Part II and the Staff Manual respectively. Title pages will be prepared in manuscript.

Hour, Date, Place	Summary of Events and Information	Remarks and references to Appendices
May 15th AUCHY LEFT	Enemy at once retaliated + by the time the MINE went up the firing up following men. The MINE was second larger than expected + dangerous. Reached Jerries but then allowed for — much part had great difficulty getting forward to MIDNIGHT SAP. Men filled in — 75 feet out but appear to have lost direction + worked diagonally to S.E. instead of due E + owing to the change in the ground counsel of the crater, failed to reach the Enemy trenches. "Bee in" was reported 10.30 p.m. Major Scott acted as Liaison Officer at B.H.Q. The Queens Party put bid & VILLAGE LINE + marched back to BEUVRY 11.30 p.m. arriving 1 a.m.	2/Lt Britten A. Casualties in raid past. 2/Lt Bramwell " Giles Harbour " Smith " Clive } wounded
May 16th BEUVRY	Battalion changed billets BEUVRY - DBLINGHAM with 5 Scottish — handed out of BEUVRY 3 p.m. Rifles — Bayonet fight + Phys. (cont.) Capt Smith Sgt Hamilton Ball BETHUNE Div Bayonet fight + Phys. (cont.) 2 Lt R.B. Downer "	

Picture: T.M. Command   2 Lt R.B. Downer

Army Form C. 2118.

WAR DIARY
or
INTELLIGENCE SUMMARY.
(Erase heading not required.)

May 1916   16th K.R.R.C.

8 –

Hour, Date, Place	Summary of Events and Information	Remarks and references to Appendices
May 19th DBLINGHAM	Clean up. Kit inspection of Arms &. MAJOR SITWELL, 2 Lt Cork + 20 men attended funeral in BETHUNE of men of QUEEN'S accidentally killed. Training under the Coy arrangements - Capt. Hon. W. L. Lindsay + 4 N.C.Os sent for course. Bombing Course - Sgt Bankford } on Instructors Rfn Crawford } Scouts Course - 2 Lt Pearson + 9 men - Brigade Courses 2 Lewis Gun + 4 men per Coy. Vickers M.G. Course - 2 Lt Kt Dawe 2 N.C.Os 3 men	2 Lt Watts on leave 17.5.16 to 27.5.16
May 18th "	Per Coura - Bayonet + Phys. Training under Coy arrangement 2 Lt C. W. Young + 4 Sgts. Per Boxing Competition Winners competed in Brigade Competition - Bantam under 9 st Light 9 — 10 st Middle 10 — 11 st Heavy over 11 st. 2 Lt P. Cole 60 men on working parties -	1 OR on leave

WAR DIARY
~~INTELLIGENCE SUMMARY~~

Army Form C. 2118.

May 1916. 16th K.R.R.C. G.

(Erase heading not required.)

Hour, Date, Place	Summary of Events and Information	Remarks and references to Appendices
May 19th OBLINGHAM	Baths at ECOLE DES JEUNES FILLES, BETHUNE used to A.M. — D Coy 9 am A Coy 11 am Headquarters 2 pm A " 10 " C " 12 noon Drill A.D. 3 pm — B.Y. 4 pm Work as per Programme — Young Officers under Adj. Stell 6.45 pm "potato" 1 Sgt 1 Cpl 20 men working party.	2 O.R. on leave.
May 20th "	Work as per Programme — Draft of 1 Sgt 1 Cpl 18 men arrived from 14th The K.R.R. of which part Hd.Qrs. Capt Loughton 2 Lieuts — O.R returned from leave A Coy 4 Cpls 100 men working pt. 9 am to 1 pm. " " " " " 2 pm to 6 pm. Pr Scotts night patrol with Major Stell. Battalion in Billets, training. H.	4 O.R. on leave
May 21st	8 Sgts 8 Cpls + 200 men on working parties Early Service 7.15 am Church Parade 9 am. Vol Service + H.C. 10.15 am Evensong 6.30 pm	2 O.R. on leave

WAR DIARY
INTELLIGENCE SUMMARY

May 1916 — 16th K.R.R.C.

Army Form C. 2118.

10.

Hour, Date, Place	Summary of Events and Information	Remarks and references to Appendices
May 22nd OBLINGHAM	Work as per programme. Bn. Scheme. Staff ride for Senior Officers. Coy. Schemes for Platoon commanders during N.C.O. & Sec Comdrs 16 N.C.Os + 200 men on working parties. Capt. Smith & 2/Lt Davies, 2/Lt Young & 1 O.R. returned from various courses. 1 N.C.O. & 8 Pvts to be transferred from A.K.P.D. Coy. to act as C.S.M.	4 O.R. on leave
May 23rd	Bde Route March. Head of Bn formed station & point 6.45 am. Route being 1/40000 Contoured Sheet N.21c 74 to proceed E. to Mt. BERNENCHON, thru road P.36 central GONNEHEM, CHOQUES and VENDIN-lez-BETHUNE. H. at 10.35 am. 16 N.C.Os & 205 men on working parties. Go an hour drill contd 6 pm. Sgt. Bradford slightly wounded by Rifle grenade accident.	4 O.R. on leave

WAR DIARY
or
INTELLIGENCE SUMMARY

June 1916 16th KRRC

Army Form C. 2118.

Hour, Date, Place	Summary of Events and Information	Remarks and references to Appendices
May 24th OBLINGHAM	Work as per programme. Bn. Staff Ride - C.O. 2 i/c Coyd & Capt Linton attended. Rendezvous 10am E.M.2.74. Capt Beale to Cavan at BOULOGNE. Lt Francis Took over Coy Adjt. Lt Capt Apps Ross - Brunker & Buckby joined & G.C. hn hn 6/7254 to Lieut Sharp on parade	2nd Lt Hogan. 7 O.R. on leave
May 25th "	Work as per programme & Historical parties P. Bn. Boxing Competition in the Theatre, BETHUNE 4 pm. Winners of Bn. competition and 2/Lt. Cliff & superintendent. from Band to play during the intervals. Rif. Belle & Hucker got into the finals of Bantam & Light Weight respectively. Sergt Cliff was knocked out 2nd round in the middle wt. R6. Newnes 1/6 Rattler Rifles.	4.O.R on leave

Army Form C. 2118.

May 1916   16th K.R.R.C.

WAR DIARY
or
INTELLIGENCE SUMMARY
(Erase heading not required.)

Instructions regarding War Diaries and Intelligence Summaries are contained in F.S. Regs., Part II and the Staff Manual respectively. Title pages will be prepared in manuscript.

Hour, Date, Place	Summary of Events and Information	Remarks and references to Appendices
26th OBLINGHAM.	Work on programme. Working parties 200. Men commencing for lectures on Discipline. To Officers - Capt Lindley a lecture on Gas and one by B unit Hunt. Progress shown E.N. ANNEQUIN on 28th.	
27th	Work on programme. C.O, 2 i/c & Adjt attended Bayonet fighting display at VENDIN SCHOOL. 2nd Lt Young, Sgt Stout, Corpl. Sutcliffe, Beaumont returned from Bayonet Course - also put (on "Very good") a report - Sgt Beaumont on a "Very good" one. 2nd Lt H.C. Davis returned from Bde M.G. Course. Move to N. ANNEQUIN cancelled.	3 O.R. on leave.
28th	2 Coy Comdrs sent to 15th Div Area to reconnoitre THE VILLAGE LINE. C.O's leave cancelled - Brigadier ill.	

Army Form C. 2118.

13

WAR DIARY
or
INTELLIGENCE SUMMARY.

May 1916   16th K.R.R.C.

(Erase heading not required.)

Hour, Date, Place	Summary of Events and Information	Remarks and references to Appendices
28th May OBLINGHAM.	2nd Lt Oxley & 16 Rfn returned from R & R Bombing Course. Church Parade 7.30 am	· 2 Lt Lipscomb on leave
" "	C.O. & notice 2 Coy Cmdrs joined him ANNEQUIN CHURCH 9. am 10.15 am	
29th	E.p. with G.O.C. and other Gen Staff to view (HOHENZOLLERN) VILLAGE LINE in 15th Brit area. Sector 300 men with Officers working in reliefs all day. Bayonet fighting for the Bn (Comns and recruits). Bn under orders to move at 2 hours notice in fighting order. All superfluous kit to be left under a guard, + stored in BETHUNE by the A.S.C.	2. O.R. on leave 3 Officers 120 men (approximately) during stay in OBLINGHAM.
30th		

Army Form C. 2118.

/4.

WAR DIARY
or
INTELLIGENCE SUMMARY

May 1916 16th K.R.R.C.

(Erase heading not required.)

Hour, Date, Place	Summary of Events and Information	Remarks and references to Appendices
May 30th OBLINGHAM	2 Coys Contd to mtd 16th & 1st Brigade areas, VILLAGE LINE under Bde arrangements. 160 men & Officers on working parties. Programme of work continued as per common. Battalion trained to the Coal Seam in 1 hour.	2 O.R. on leave.
31st "	C.O. & 2 Coys contd worked 16th & 1st Brigade areas, VILLAGE LINE under Bde arrangements. Programme of work & No common continued. 4 Officers 160 men working parties.	L/Scott & 1 O.R. on leave.

Ayshel D/Col
Comd 16th K.R.R.C.

Vol 3

Army Form C. 2118.

16. KRRC

XXXVI 15th K.R.R.C.

June 1916

WAR DIARY
or
INTELLIGENCE SUMMARY.
(Erase heading not required.)

Place	Date	Hour	Summary of Events and Information	Remarks and references to Appendices
ODLINGHAM	1st	6.30am	Work as per programme. Per course continued	
		8-12	Lts. Potts started firing M.G. Class	
		8.30am	Service Voluntary	
BILLINGHAM	2		Work as per programme. Bn course continued.	
		on above	2nd Lt Thorpe Thomas proceeded on relief by 2nd Lt Jenkyns	
			Rt to C.42 Off Rew. Chopped with "s"	2/O R in leave
			2nd Lt Pritty Cocker 6 month I.H.L. & found £1	
			A.Co morning rear Cofound by Brig Gen C/no 1.B. Congested 3 months J.D.	
			Prt. Hart + Priv £1. So R Malcolm Efnd (and X) Cpl.	
	3	2pm	Travel order for arrangements	
			Per course continued	2.O.R a.b. leave
			C + D. Coys morning roam + sports	
"	4	10.45	Church communion Voluntary. Staff ride for Capts	2 O R in leave

WAR DIARY

June 1916 - 16th K.R.R.C.

INTELLIGENCE SUMMARY

Place: OBLINGHAM **Date:** 4th

Extract from "London Gazette". Awarded the D.C.M. C267 Rfn Rock J.
Awarded the M.M. C6 L/Cpl. Raggett A.
   "   "   "   C1401 Rfn Harris A.

Rfn Rock "During the bombardment on Jan 28th, was in charge of the machine gun at the junction of Boyau 11 & the Rock Trench. The gun emplacement was blown in and all the team wounded. When the stretcher bearer came, Rfn Rock refused to be moved & remained with his gun till he had handed it over on arrival of the machine gun Officer of the 1/Queens. Rfn Rock was removed by his orders."

L/Cpl Raggett "For conspicuous good work in charge of the stretcher bearers & devotion to attending to the wounded during the heavy bombardments on 2 January, and again on the 28th January."

Rfn Harris "On night of 3/4th Jan volunteered to go out with Lance Corporal and attack a sniper who was causing great trouble. He crawled out and threw three bombs, and located a machine gun. He came back for more bombs, but 1st person had found..."

Army Form C. 2118.

WAR DIARY
or
INTELLIGENCE SUMMARY.
(Erase heading not required.)

June 1916. 16th K.R.R.C.

Place	Date	Hour	Summary of Events and Information	Remarks and references to Appendices
OBLINGHAM	5th		Work as per programme. Pg. courses continued.	2 O.R. on leave.
"	6th		Programme travelled owing to wet weather. Training under Coy arrangements.	
"	7th		Boy scouts & other parties proceeded to AUCHY LEFT to arrange things on transfer fm. 1st Cameronians. Training under Coy arrangements.	2 It. front conducting Officer & 2 O.R. leave. C.O. on leave. 2 O.R.
BEUVRY	8th	4 pm	Bn. relieved 20th R.E. in BEUVRY, marching via BETHUNE. Relief complete 4 pm.	
BEUVRY & AUCHY LEFT	9th	7.45p	Bn. relieved the 1st Cameronians in Left Subsector AUCHY LEFT. Guides at CAMBRIN CHURCH 9.30 pm. A Coy. Right & took over 1 Coy. 2/5 Warwicks in fire trenches — transferred into VILLAGE LINE & LEWIS Keep. Bayaux 8-10 A.M. D. Coy. Centre. C. Coy. Left. B. Coy. in Reserve in WIMPOLE St. & in LEWIS Keep. Bayaux 10A. & 16 ex. Bayaux 16 in & 20 in. Relief complete 10. p.m.	

Army Form C. 2118.

4.-

WAR DIARY
INTELLIGENCE SUMMARY.
(Erase heading not required.)

June 1916. 16th K.R.R.C.

Place	Date	Hour	Summary of Events and Information	Remarks and references to Appendices
AUCHY LEFT.	night 9th/10th	2.0am	At 2.Am a mine was fired to try and make E. Twin, Baby & Queen's Craters into one large one. All saps & front lines to HIGH ST. cleared between BOYAUX 13 & 18. As soon as mine went up, front line reoccupied, also sap. A party detailed length near lip of new crater & began digging in posts & sapping to consolidate. On explosion in front covered by T.Ms, Lytle Grenades & M.Gs. German retaliation did not commence for about 10 minutes, and was not very heavy. It is thought own mine exploded a German one and buried their galleries.	
"	10th		Sapped out from N. Twin tunnel way which was not damaged to old Queen's Post on edge of Crater. Found the Queen's Crater not joined to New Crater only separated by a narrow lip from E.Twin & Baby which had been blown into one, but will not towards the German line. Other work, wiring & lifting from Sapping from Sally Port to right front. Repairing HIGH & BACK STREETS. Continuing with dug out, own back cover and improvements generally in front line, HIGH ST. Rebuilding BACK ST. new ARTHUR'S KEEP.	

Army Form C. 2118.

WAR DIARY or INTELLIGENCE SUMMARY

June 1916. 16th K.R.R.C.

(Erase heading not required.)

Place	Date	Hour	Summary of Events and Information	Remarks and references to Appendices
AUCHY	10th	9.30pm	Coy. 2/Lt Harwicks attacked left to regain their Battalion at BETHUNE. Parties of Officers + N.C.O's of Diffrt Warwicks visited the lines during the day.	@ 2.30am 1pl. Thomas died wounded previous [?] night. [?] (086 Rfn
			Lieut. Scott 2/Lieut. Harwicks d'Etaples + 1 OR to leave.	Harvis died
LEFT		1 am	STOKES MORTARS put over 70 rounds. Enemy retaliated with obsy bomp.	
			2/Lt Pierson patrolled round our Craters. Winning + from with on night - winnings Left Flag. 9 wounded	
	11th		Had continued trouble on Right bombing post on line (N.2A) (Eastern Twins) also observation post. supplied at to add sandbags. Wiring and pressuring. Patrols on.	Rfn Stimson wounded
		11½pm	a front deal of Rifle-grenade fire on front line and HIGH ST.	
		10.30pm	a lively M.G. duel, our grenade got the upper hand. Some STOKES MORTARS	Rfn Cocks Killed - 1 OR wounded
		12.30am	drew retaliation from M's.	

WAR DIARY

Army Form C. 2118.

June 1916. 16th K.R.R.C.

INTELLIGENCE SUMMARY.
(Erase heading not required.)

Place	Date	Hour	Summary of Events and Information	Remarks and references to Appendices
AUCHY LEFT.	12th		Work through sectors continued. Firing line on left is gradually being rebuilt & pulled down & deep dugouts in HIGH ST. & deep dugout for bombs at Pt. H1 20, near junction of No 1 Siding & MAISON ROUGE ALLEY commenced. Wiring in barrier places & spirals 108 hours. Reversal of latrine crater. Continuation of steps toward – OVER HEAD COVER &c. C.O. & Coy Officers & Telegram & Bombing Officers in 1/QUEENS, came up to look round.	108 hours
"	13th		Bombardment of MAD POINT 6.20 p.m. to 7. p.m. by mortars re. Enemy retaliated SIMS KEEP firing list, & BOVAUX Pt & 9 slightly damaged. Work throughout sector continued – Work in craters especially, hampered by wet – Rd relieved by 1/Queens – Sape., O.P's & Snipers Posts Taken over at 6.30 p.m. Snipers at CAMBRIN CHURCH 9.30 p.m. Relief complete 11.20 p.m. 20 Rm. Water collecting in all trenches, rain all day, every knew at after – Marched back to old billets in BEUVRY.	20 Rm. leave

Army Form C. 2118.

WAR DIARY
or
INTELLIGENCE SUMMARY.

(Erase heading not required.)

Instructions regarding War Diaries and Intelligence Summaries are contained in F. S. Regs., Part II. and the Staff Manual respectively. Title pages will be prepared in manuscript.

16th K.R.R.C.

June 1916

7.

Place	Date	Hour	Summary of Events and Information	Remarks and references to Appendices
BEUVRY.	14th		Seven Officers and 290 other ranks on working parties to front line. Baths arranged for the remainder at the Divisional Baths. At 11 p.m. all watches were put forward one hour in accordance with Army Order.	2Lieut Young on leave. 2 Lt Granville Howell returned
"	15th		Same number of Officers and men on working parties — Baths arranged for the remainder. Battalion Commanders conference at Brigade HQ at 4 p.m, at which a new scheme of holding the line was explained. The Division will now take up post from boyau 1 to about the Ducks Bill. The new Brigade frontage from boyau 1 to boyau 36 exclusive.	1 O.R. on leave. 2Lt Grant returned from leave
"	16th		The 2nd Corps & and Company Commanders visited the new front. The usual working parties were supplied. The late Capt Dyand mentioned in despatches	2nd Lt Lethal returned from leave. 1 O.R. on leave.

Army Form C. 2118.

WAR DIARY
or
INTELLIGENCE SUMMARY.

June 1916.   16th K.R.R.C.

(Erase heading not required.)

Place	Date	Hour	Summary of Events and Information	Remarks and references to Appendices
CUINCHY LEFT	17th		Battalion relieved 1st Middlesex and one company A & S.H. in the trenches. D Coy left & left sector. B right centre. A right Coy. All four companies in the front line. One platoon (D) in BRICKSTACK KEEP, one platoon (C) in PARK LANE redoubt. One platoon (B) in HARLEY STREET. Trenches in a bad state. Relief complete 11.30 p.m. Battn. H.Q. HARLEY STREET. Trenches in a bad state. Went to a bombardment the night before. Night fairly quiet, with the exception of a large number of rifle grenades, which caused some damage.	1 O.R. on leave.
"	18th		A quiet day with the exception of T.M's and rifle grenades. Work carried on clearing OXFORD STREET. Dugouts started in C Coy front. Saps begun in front line. By Engineers & rifle R.E.	Major Sissell goes on leave. ✗
"	19th		Quiet morning. Work carried on as before. Brigadier visited line. Lively. About four half minos were exploded by the DUCKSBILL to our left. Incessant little T.M. and rifle grenade fire. Two organised strafes by our artillery and T.M's was ————— replied to by the enemy with more vigour.	16 O.R.s on leave. 4pm Hoct — wounded 4pt Hodgson " Briggs — " Johnson — wounded " Sgt Sill ? 4pt Eardell ? Sgt Bell — killed

✗ Group "A" following casualties. Rfm Cobb | Miles Ogden " Tyler } wounded " Crawford — killed

WAR DIARY
INTELLIGENCE SUMMARY

June 1916. 16th K.R.R.C.

Army Form C. 2118.

Place	Date	Hour	Summary of Events and Information	Remarks and references to Appendices
CUINCHY LEFT	20th		A small Mirques mine was blown by the enemy at 8.45 AM just north of krogan R3. We filled in 10 yds of trench. No casualties reported. The RE think the Germans drove a pipe from his advanced sap, and then blew. There was slight shelling at the time, but no harm done. Work continued on saps in front line and reclaiming trench damaged by mine. During the night the enemy heavily shelled the right centre Coy front causing casualties. A patrol under 2 Lieut Grant was unable to locate left lug observation confirmed its report of the RE referred to.	109 m line 2 Lieut Curtis returned. 2 Lieut Hoops struck off strength J Battn dig claiming Medical Board Spr. Johnson slightly wounded [list of names: Burrows, Leggatt, Lloyd, Bawtree, L/Cpl Harrison] Cpn. D & G ? killed whyatt 1 OR killed
"	2nd		At 7 PM the 1st Queens relieved us. The Battalion took up its position in the keeps and VILLAGE LINE and WIMPOLE STREET. See pages 13.14.	1 OR on leave

WAR DIARY
or
INTELLIGENCE SUMMARY

June 1916. 16th K.R.R.C.

Army Form C. 2118.
10.

Place	Date	Hour	Summary of Events and Information	Remarks and references to Appendices
CUINCHY RIGHT	22nd		A quiet day. Work begun on dugouts in VIRTUE STREET and 1 in RUSSELLS KEEP. At 9.30 PM a mine was exploded by us in the F.O. R.W.F. Crater. There was little retaliation. At the Divisional Horse Show held yesterday and today the Battn. won first prize for the pair of mules and limber competition. The light draft horse and man cast was fourth in its competition.	2 hrs only on leave.
"	23rd		At 2 AM the enemy exploded a series of large mines by the DUCKS BILL causing heavy casualties to the Brigade immediately North of us. Slight shelling of RUSSELLS KEEP and BACK STREET. The M.O. to the battalion Lieut Wathen Thomas goes to HAVRE to take up a hospital appointment. Lieut. DERRY succeeds him as M.O. to the battalion. Heavy rain.	1 O.R. on leave.
"	24th		Wire cutting operation started on our front by our guns. Enemy aeroplanes very active, flying low over our trenches. Yesterdays rain damaged the trenches, large parties of men employed draining and cleaning up. Battn. for the Baths.	1 O.R. on leave.

Army Form C. 2118.

WAR DIARY or INTELLIGENCE SUMMARY.

June 1916.   16th K.R.R.C.

(Erase heading not required.)

11.

Place	Date	Hour	Summary of Events and Information	Remarks and references to Appendices
CUINCHY LEFT	25"		Baths for the Battn in the morning. Relieve 1st Queens in trenches in CUINCHY LEFT. 6 Coy left. D right A & B left centre Coy. Relief complete 7.30. Throughout the day our batteries fired on German trenches.	10 ORs Leave. Pte HARKNESS died wounds in England.
"	26"	6 AM	At 6 AM a fight took place between four Fokker machines and four Vickers. One of our aeroplanes was brought down by CAMBRIN CHATEAU. The observer being killed by German rifle fire during the fight. Pioneers at work on building furniture for a new battalion H.Q. in VILLAGE LINE. Sapping Platoon at work on a new trench which runs from CLIVE ROAD towards the BRICKSTACKS. The new trench will avoid the fire of the Minnie. At 6.35 p.m. the Germans placed a mine on D Coys front between SIBSONS CRATER & IPSWICH doing damage to our saps causing casualties. Throughout the night our artillery fired in organised bursts of fire lasting 10 to 15 minutes. The Germans retaliation was smcell. Suffering from shock 16.	1 OR on leave. L/Cpl FOSTER dis. in hospital. c.9.20 p.m. Riflm Ruffel killed c.9.26 Riflm Edmunds died c.9.02 Cpl Brown killed. c.10.39 Riflm Hutchison killed. Wounded 4

WAR DIARY
INTELLIGENCE SUMMARY

Army Form C. 2118.

16th K.R.R.C.

June 1916.

12.

Place	Date	Hour	Summary of Events and Information	Remarks and references to Appendices
CUINCHY LEFT	27th		During the morning and afternoon three organised artillery bombardments took place. Little retaliation. At 11.30 pm the Glasgow Highlanders on our right raided the German trenches by MAD POINT. A company went over reconnoitring in the trenches for an hour; two machine guns and thirty eight prisoners were brought back. Two hostile were slightly blown in; our casualties two wounded. The Battalion "stood to" all the time and gave overhead rapid fire and front "bombs". The 13th Division well to our right discharged some gas, with some success.	1 O.R. on leave 1 conducting Offr. to Brewers Pte Fink (wds) " Putty " Ratcliff " Kirby " Pengfort " Buckle woud. " Putnam Shell " Patty to " " Panciville " " Wilson " " Jones "
"	28th		Rfm R Davis sentenced by F.G.C.M. to 3 mths F.P.No1 for absenting himself without leave Sentence commuted to 14 days F.P.N.1 by XI Corps Commander. At 4.15 pm the enemy exploded a mine just N of MIDNIGHT CRATERS at A.21.d.65.05 — no damage — after the explosion the enemy put over a barrage of shells, T.M. bombs & rifle grenades. Our artillery replied. At 4.50 p.m. We exploded a mine at A.22.a.2.6. among the JERUSALEM HILL CRATERS — Our Artillery put over a barrage — At 11.30 pm the enemy	Admitted to Hosp. Kidd

Army Form C. 2118.

WAR DIARY
or
INTELLIGENCE SUMMARY.
(Erase heading not required.)

June 1916. 1/65th K.R.R.C.

13 -

Place	Date	Hour	Summary of Events and Information	Remarks and references to Appendices
CUINCHY LEFT.	26"	11.30pm	The Enemy exploded a mine S.W. of RAILWAY CRATER. Little damage. At 5 pm. a heavy minnie was heard to turn N.of the CANAL. 2" Lt PEARSON + 2 men patrolled right round the enemy's new crater between MIDNIGHT and IPSWICH CRATERS - no signs of enemy supping or working towards it. The new crater is 30 yds in diameter, about 35 ft deep + very steep. There is a gap from 15 to 20 yds between it and IPSWICH + about 20 to 30 yds between it + MIDNIGHT - The E. lip is between 30 & 40 yds from enemy front line. Major SITWELL returned off leave. Capt. Dales came back from course at CONDETTE. Battalion relieved by the 1st QUEEN'S in front line + took over Keeps + VILLAGE LINE from them - A Coy / Platoon ARTHURS KEEP (32 men). 1 - Lewis - (32 men). 1 in CHURCH " WEST. Remainder to FACTORY TRENCH and LEWIS ALLEY.	Wounded 2/Lt Mr ... Killed 3 Rfn ...
"	29		B.Cy. 1 Platoon L RUSSELLS KEEP (32 men). Remainder to VILLAGE LINE. BURBURE ALLEY. 1 " - STAFFORD " (32 men). MAISON ROUGE ALLEY. H.Q. WIMPOLE STREET.	

WAR DIARY or INTELLIGENCE SUMMARY

Army Form C. 2118.

16th K.R.R.C.

June 1916.

14.

Place	Date	Hour	Summary of Events and Information	Remarks and references to Appendices
CUINCHY LEFT.	29th		C. Coy. 2 Platoons CUINCHY KEEP. 1 Sec. MOUNTAIN KEEP. 2 Secs. CAMBRIN SUPPORT POINT. 1 - TOURBIERES REDOUBT. 2 " BRADDELL POINT. 1 N.C.O. + 3 men CARTER'S " D. Coy. 1 Platoon RAILWAY KEEP. (3 men) Remainder To FACTORY TRENCH Sect. SIMS " " (32 "). Bn. H.Q. WIMPOLE STREET. M.Gunners WIMPOLE ST. Bombers BORDEN TRENCH. Casualties. Rfn. Matthews, Finch, Peters wounded. Shoesmith. L/C Dunlop, Rustin Jones killed Britain " " " Rfn Garretson hospital. 2/Lt TAYLOR Wounded. Rfn Bodkin "	
"	30.		6 Officers 220 on working parties. 2/Lt ATKINSON + 12 men reported for the Nanu. + returned to duty 3 recruits.	

100th Inf.Bde.
33rd Div.

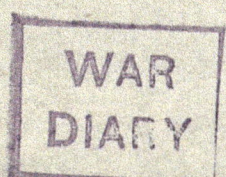

16th BATTN. THE KING'S ROYAL RIFLE CORPS.

J U L Y

1 9 1 6

33 July
Army Form C. 2118
16 K R R C
Vol 9

WAR DIARY
or
INTELLIGENCE SUMMARY.

100. 1/3 July 1916. 16th K.R.R.C.

Place	Date	Hour	Summary of Events and Information	Remarks and references to Appendices
CUINCHY LEFT	1st		The 100th I.B. carried out the following programme on night of 1/2 July.	
		12.15 am to 12.18 am	Art. bombardment RAILWAY POINT.	
		12.18 am	Mine exploded at MINE POINT. (No 5 mine) A small mine exploded at RAILWAY POINT.	
		12.45 to 1 am	4 Gas cylinders discharged from HUMPHRES SAP. (No 4 mine)	
		12.45 to 1.15 am	Smoke bombs fired from 3.7 T.M's between Boyaus 30 + 34.	
		12.18 am onwards	Artillery Barrage for 2' WORCESTERS.	
		12.19 am	2 Companies 2' Worcestres enter German Trenches RAILWAY POINT.	
		12.45 am	Mine exploded E of TWIN CRATERS (No 6 mine).	
		12.45 am	Party of 16 K.R.R.C. enter German Trenches N of MIDNIGHT CRATER.	
		12.48 am	Artillery Barrage for 16 K.R.R.C. starts.	
			With reference to above, the Bn took over front line & sps from S. Sgt of IPSWICH CRATER inclusive to BOYAU 20 from 7 pm to stand down.	A
			Raid: party left WIMPOLE ST. 11.1 pm via BRAINES WAY - THE DELL - BOYAU 21 - Beside the Art. Barrage at 12.48 am a rifle grenade barrage was put on under orders of 2/Lt Cooch at THE QUEENS LEWIS GUNS cooperated. 2/Lt Gaunt directed the Bn bombers cooperation of MILLS CUP & Rifle grenades from	

Army Form C. 2118.

WAR DIARY
or
~~INTELLIGENCE~~ SUMMARY.

July 16th K.R.R.C.

2.

(Erase heading not required.)

Instructions regarding War Diaries and Intelligence Summaries are contained in F. S. Regs., Part II. and the Staff Manual respectively. Title pages will be prepared in manuscript.

Place	Date	Hour	Summary of Events and Information	Remarks and references to Appendices
CUINCHY LEFS	night of 1st & 2nd		The Raiding Party under 2 2Lt PEARSON & DAVIS went over the top from Saps in the NEW CRATER & blown by the Enemy on 28th ult. passed through the N. gap by IRSWICH & S gap by MIDNIGHT. formed up on E side and attacked the German front line – Unfortunately just as they reached the German Wire they were caught by a M.G. on sitting flanks & bombers suffering heavily. They got in, worked outwards & blocked as per orders. They found no dugout, but one minor shaft. As it was lighted & could be seen the bombs were exhausted, so they bombed them down. When their supply of bombs were exhausted, Both Officers were wounded before reaching the trench. 2Lt PEARSON was hit by a in the arm, & 2Lt DAVIS was hit twice using his revolver. the last man left in the trench. Out of a party of 2 Officers & 40 men there were 11 wounded & brought in. Killed 3 – missing 11... Capt SMITH remained at the NEW CRATER in 16. Amongst their number 11..	/Numbers would in say.
			JAP Handford, 2Lt CORK & the 9 reserve men did fine work in collecting & carrying in the wounded.	
			The following averages were received:-	

T/134. Wt. W708-776. 50C000. 4/15. Sir J. C. & S.

Army Form C. 2118.

3.

WAR DIARY
or
INTELLIGENCE SUMMARY.

16th K.R.R.C.

July 1916.

(Erase heading not required.)

Place	Date	Hour	Summary of Events and Information	Remarks and references to Appendices
CUINCHY LEFT	2		"Brigadier congratulates all ranks on their gallant conduct last night whilst materially contributed to the general success of our operations." Following received from 33' Div. Brigr. "hopes found wishes you to convey his congratulations to E.B on their gallant efforts in connection with raid of A.B. last night. Following from General HAKING to 33' Div. begins - Please convey my congratulations to 10 for again distinguishing themselves. The raid of A.B. was most skilfully carried out and the effort of the E.B. to cooperate on the flank showed determination and gallantry in the face of considerable difficulties near. The Artillery also are to be congratulated on their accurate shooting and cooperation. Also the following letter to the C.O. from the Brigadier- "My dear Hyde I write to ask you to tell Smith & his company how very gallantly I know that they carried out last night's the work that was not there. Their loss were unfortunately heavy, but though we must all deplore them, they show that	

Army Form C. 2118.

4

WAR DIARY
or
INTELLIGENCE SUMMARY.

July 1916   16th K.R.R.C.

(Erase heading not required.)

Place	Date	Hour	Summary of Events and Information	Remarks and references to Appendices
CUINCHY LEFT	2		"Officers and men behaved with a determination that was beyond all praise. No Officer or man could have done more than they did, and I would be glad if you would take the earliest opportunity of telling your Officers and all ranks that the whole Brigade will be proud. Their Commander under your command - no one can express his own feelings a keener, but your fellows did last night all that it was humanly possible to do to drive us - I am proud. Their Officers & men will never be seen better in the day. Yours truly (sgd) Walter Nicol." The Army also wired congratulating all ranks of A.B. & E.B. – The WORCESTERS & tr... – The body of Pte ARNOLD was brought in from the new crater after dark – The Battalion was visited by the Brigadier and the G.O.C. Division – The Battalion was relieved by the 1/4th SUFFOLKS at night – Relief complete	
GORRE	3	1.5 am	marched to GORRE & took over billets of 1/4 SUFFOLKS. Rest and clean up. Hd Qrs, A & B. Coys & Transport in CHATEAU. F3b central. C. Coy. F3d central. D. Coy. F4a 2.10. F4d 5.10	

Army Form C. 2118.
5.

WAR DIARY or INTELLIGENCE SUMMARY

July 1916. 16th K.R.R.C.

(Erase heading not required.)

Place	Date	Hour	Summary of Events and Information	Remarks and references to Appendices
GORRE	3rd		2° Lieut (Temporary Captain) E. WENHAM from 2° Batt. reported and took over duties of Adjt. 7975 C.S.M. C.R. Trousdale from 2° Batt. reported and took over the duties of Regt Sgt Major - Both above are brought on the strength of the Bn. from this date.	
	4th		Working parties 5 Officers 400 men. Parades under Coy arrangements. Bde and Batt. specialist courses. Capt Thomas + 1 Sgt. to 1 Army Courses - CORDETTE Lieut Scott to Divl School Sgt Goddard on Instr to Bde Bombing BEUVRY 1 Sgt VENDIN 2° Lt Gilder + 7. O.R. Vickers M.G. Course BEUVRY. " Howell + 5. O.R. Stokes Mortar " " " Atkinson + 5. O.R. Bayonet fighting " " " Oxley + 20.O.R. Musketry Course CAMIERS. 7 to 18th inclusive.- Parades under Coy arrangements. - Batta from 9.30 A.M. to 6 P.M.	
"	5th		A. Coy Tactical Exercise under Major Futvoll.	

Army Form C. 2118.

WAR DIARY
or
INTELLIGENCE SUMMARY.
(Erase heading not required.)

July 1916   16th KRRC

Place	Date	Hour	Summary of Events and Information	Remarks and references to Appendices
GORRE	6th		Parades under Coy arrangements. Batn received orders for this notice to move until further notice. Bde Orders received that 100th Inf Bde would be relieved by 116th Bde & proceed to new billetty area BUSNETTES. Relief to be completed by 6.0 am on 7th July. Batn moved off 11:30 pm and marched all night arriving at new billets at 5:30 am.	
BUSNETTES or BAS RIEUX	7th		Batn rested. Parades under Coy Arrangements in morning. 1st EMGoways rejoined the Batn for duty from the 100th Bde.	
	8th		Received orders from Bde for train movement. To entrain at LILLERS at 1.50 am on the 9th. Batn paraded at 12.0 midnight and entrained. Strength 27 officers 877 other ranks. Total 904.	
	9th		Batn detrained at SALEUX at 9.15 am. We moved close to the station and had breakfast on the road side. Billeting parties went on to St SAUVEUR on the road Batn received orders from Bde to march to VECQUEMONT. Batn halted for lunch just W of AMIENS. Resumed march and arrived at VECQUEMONT at 6.0 pm very tired after this 17 mile march and were billetted in an old Silk Mill by the canal.	

T2134. Wt. W708-776. 500000. 4/15. Sir J.C. & S.

Army Form C. 2118.

WAR DIARY 16th KRRC
July
or
INTELLIGENCE SUMMARY.
(Erase heading not required.)

Instructions regarding War Diaries and Intelligence Summaries are contained in F.S. Regs., Part II. and the Staff Manual respectively. Title pages will be prepared in manuscript.

Place	Date	Hour	Summary of Events and Information	Remarks and references to Appendices
VECQUEMONT	10th		Batn rested during the day.	Map Ref AMIENS 1/100000
MORLANCOURT	11th		Batn: moved off to MORLANCOURT and bivouaced. All packs were stored in the village. Bn remained on short notice to move.	
	12th		Batn. rested all day. Marched off from camp 9.15 pm to BECORDEL-BECOURT and bivouaced in front of a battery of 9.2" hows.	
	13th		Batn. rested all day. Batn. received orders to STAND TO from 3.25 am and were under orders to move. Following men awarded the Military Medal. C10518 Rfm Hartley. C862 Rfm Ansell. R1064 Rfm Rhodes. Captn.& Hon Lindsay received orders from Bde to act as Liason officer and to report at Bde HQrs at 3.25 a.m. in the lt. Major Sitwell detailed to remain behind with 1st line transport.	
BECORDEL-BECOURT	14th		Batn STOOD TO at 3.25 a.m. After breakfast men drew picks + shovels (60% shovels 40% picks) Extra SAA was issued thus giving each man 220 rounds. Also 2 sandbags were allotted to each man. Extra Coy Orderlies were detailed for Action. Batn: marched off prepared for action at 10.30 am to FRICOURT where tea was obtained and the men rested. Orders were received from Bde to move forward into position of assembly in valley West of SABOT and FLATIRON Copse. Transport Echelons were left in rear under command of Bde. Batn arrived at position of assembly 9.15 pm and proceeded to dig themselves in and carry up ammunition, bombs, water to A&T and 1st Queens. All our picks + shovels were handed over to 1st Queens and 9th H.L.I.	Trench Map MARTINPUICH 1/20000

Army Form C. 2118.

WAR DIARY
or
INTELLIGENCE SUMMARY.

July   16th KRRC

(Erase heading not required.)

Instructions regarding War Diaries and Intelligence Summaries are contained in F. S. Regs., Part II. and the Staff Manual respectively. Title pages will be prepared in manuscript.

Place	Date	Hour	Summary of Events and Information	Remarks and references to Appendices
	14th	10.30pm	A Coy under Command of Major Cothrue was sent up in support of 9th HLI who were digging in W of Highwood. Both had little rest after fatigue parties had returned. Enemy teas shells caused some trouble during night.	
	15th		Bde received Bde Orders for Divisional Attack. The 33rd Division is to attack the enemy's SWITCH line in front of MARTINPUICH at 9.a.m. today. Frontage of attack is allotted as follows — 100th Inf.Bde on a frontage of 1000 yds. from a line drawn N+S through S.B.6.8.2 with its right resting on this line, 98th Inf Bde on left of 100th Inf Bde with right in touch with 100th Bde, and left resting on the MARTINPUICH — BAZENTIN LE PETIT Railway. The Artillery bombardment of German line will commence at 2.30 a.m. and will lift at 9.0 a.m. at which time the infantry will assault. They will advance as near the hostile trench as possible during the bombardment. 19th Inf Bde will be in position of assembly at 7.0 a.m. where it will be prepared to advance through 98th + 100th Bdes on MARTINPUICH after German SWITCH is captured. Assault of 100th Inf Bde will be carried out by 9th H.L.I. on right 200 yds E. of where it now rests and 1st Queens on left on frontage of 500 yds each. The left of 1st Queens 200 yds E. of where it now rests. 16th KRR will support the advance of 1st Queens and 9th HLI. 2nd Worcesters will be in Reserve. Units will be in position as follows by 8.A.M. 16th KRR in SDQ. In the event of SWITCH trench being taken with little loss orders will probably be received later to push on to MARTINPUICH but objective in first instance is only SWITCH Trench.	Map Ref. MARTINPUICH Trench Map 1/10,000 Map Ref. MARTINPUICH TRENCH Map 1/20000
	15th	7.am.	Early morning misty. Commanding Officer and Coy Commanders received orders to go up and reconnoitre Around of Attack. The CO proceeded to Hdqrs of 1st Queens at the CEMETRY at BAZENTIN LE PETIT Village. Coy Commanders reconnoitred road running SW & NE in SDQ. The three remaining Coys followed later	

WAR DIARY
16th KRRC
INTELLIGENCE SUMMARY
July

Army Form 2118.

Place	Date	Hour	Summary of Events and Information	Remarks and references to Appendices
High Wood Map Ref. MARTINPUICH Trench map 1/20000	15th		and took up their position in place of Assembly along road running SW & NE in S.D.9 and were ready for Attack at 8.0 a.m. Message was received from 1st Queens stating that they would not require us to support them owing to danger of crowding in Enemy's trench. Following a message from 1st Queens stating that they were not in touch with the 9th HLI, Bde orders were received, to act as circumstances required, but Attack must be closely supported and any Gap between 1st Queens & 9th HLI must be filled when Assault starts. While Batn was lined up for the attack 2nd Lt GRANT was hit in the thigh. At 9.10 a.m. our Artillery barrage lifted and "B and C" Coys were ordered to advance in half Coys in line. "C" Coy under Captain Donaldson on the left and "B" Coy under Captain Deedes on the right. "C" Coy came under hostile M.G. fire directly they began to advance and post heavily. Captain Donaldson was hit but remained with his Coy urging them on till he was hit a second time and forced to return to the dressing station. The Coy advanced to the old line vacated by the 1st Queens along sunken road running from N.E. corner of BAZENTIN le Petit village to N.W. corner of High Wood. After reaching this position they remained there, awaiting further orders. However upon	

Army Form C. 2118.

10

WAR DIARY 16th KRRC
or
INTELLIGENCE SUMMARY.

(Erase heading not required.)

Place	Date	Hour	Summary of Events and Information	Remarks and references to Appendices
High Wood Attack	July 15th		Seeing the 1st Queens retire owing to being held up by enemy's wire being uncut and hostile enfilade M.G. fire, and take up a position at cross roads S8b67, C Coy joined up with the 1st Queens right flank. Here they remained during the whole day under fire from enemy's M.G. and hostile sniping. 2Lt HICKSN'S was hit in the leg while leading his platoon and while bandaging his foot was again hit in the hand and died immediately. 2nd Lts Giddens and HOWARD brought the remains of their Coy out when their relieved. However 2nd Lt Howard soon went to the F.A. after discovering that his heel had been hit by M.G. bullet. 'B' Coy under the command of Captain DEEDES advanced in lines of half Coys on the right of 'C' Coy. The objective of the rt flank of this Coy was NW Corner of wood. Both lines of advance passed over a line where the enemy had previously dug themselves in and went up hill at the top of which they came in touch with the 9th HLI, most of whom were lying wounded or killed. Here they met the enemy's M.G. fire and only a small party of ten reached a position within 25 yds of the sunken roadway. Eventually only two of this party arrived back untouched. While holding this position they were enfiladed by M.G. fire from NW corner of wood and from isolated tree on the rise on the farther side of roadway about S.3.c.9.9.	Trench Map NATIN Perth 1/20000

Army Form C. 2118.

WAR DIARY 16th K.R.R.C.
or
INTELLIGENCE SUMMARY.
July
(Erase heading not required.)

Place	Date	Hour	Summary of Events and Information	Remarks and references to Appendices
HIGH WOOD ATTACK	15"		'B' Coy. under Lt Howell led the 1st line consisting of Nos 5 & 7 platoons. Capt. Deades and 2nd Lt Smulis brought over the 2nd line. A section of Lewis gunners also went over with this line. 2nd Lt Dennis is reported to have been hit three times before he was killed. Captain Deades was hit by M.G. bullet in the head and died immediately.	MARTINPUICH Trench Map 1/20000
		11:30 a.m.	'D' Coy under Captain Smith J.R. was sent up to reinforce the 9th H.L.I. The 2nd Worcesters who were also sent up to help the H.L.I. D Coy held a position along S edge of High Wood. Here they remained all day under intermittent shell fire & continual M.G. sniping. At 8.0 pm they withdrew to a line 50 yds back from edge of wood & dug in and made a support line in conjunction with 2nd Worcesters which ran from S. corner of Wood to H.L.I. trench. Lt Francis was hit in the arm.	
		3.0 am	At 3.0 am they were relieved by a Bn. from 19th Inf Bde and reached back to rest position without very many casualties.	
		12.30 pm	Report was received at Batn. Hdqrs. that Major Cooban had been killed and all his officers wounded. Lt Gonner was sent up to find the remainder of A Coy and take	

T/134. Wt. W708-776. 500000. 4/15. Sir J. C. & S.

Army Form C. 2118.

WAR DIARY 16th K.R.R.C.
or
INTELLIGENCE SUMMARY.

July.

Place	Date	Hour	Summary of Events and Information	Remarks and references to Appendices
High Wood	15"		Command. Upon reaching S.W. Corner of High Wood he was unable to find any of A Coy except a wounded Corporal who stated that a small remnant of A Coy had joined D Coy and were under his command. "A" Coy upon arriving at High Wood took up position along S.E. edge of wood. Here they received orders to advance through wood to further edge under cover of our Artillery barrage. At 9.0 am the barrage lifted they were found through wood and Capture [in?] trench at N. corner of wood. The Coy advanced in one line and after crossing first glade in wood were fired upon by M.G. Major Cochran is reported to have been killed a little to the right of German M.G. Blockhouse at 3.4.c.5.9. This Blockhouse was reported to contain two or three M.Gs which held up A Coy line of advance, causing many casualties. Capt Harrison was wounded in the arm. Lt Lewis had his leg broken and remained in a shell hole. He died of wounds. 2Lt Atkinson was reported wounded + missing at end of the day.	12
		2.30pm	Our M.O. and 2Lt Spero were both hit by pieces from the same shell. Enemy L Storming High Wood trenches with bombs. All wires cut.	
			Message received stating that ...."	

Army Form C 2118.

13

WAR DIARY 16th KRRC
or
July INTELLIGENCE SUMMARY.
(Erase heading not required.)

Place	Date	Hour	Summary of Events and Information	Remarks and references to Appendices
High Wood Attack.	15th	3.0 pm	Situation Report sent in. Remains of A + D Coys held S.W. edge of wood. These were reinforced by Bde on our Right. General line - joining W. of Bazentin le PETIT with N.W. corner of High Wood - being held by groups. No information from 1st Queens.	
		5.40 pm	Casualty Report. Number passed through Btn Dressing Station - 4 Officers 149 other Ranks. A report in that 2 Officers killed 6 wounded - not yet brought in.	
		7.45.	Colonel Kyffin Tart a the wrist by one of our own Shrapnel shells falling short. Captain Wenham the Adjutant took over Command of Batn. Lt Watts sent up with spare Lewis gun to try and put out of action M.G. in N. corner of High Wood. He was hit while going up into action. Shortly afterwards message received to send up 2 platoons to reinforce 2nd Worcesters. Our last 2 Lewis guns under charge of M.G. Sgt. and 30 men sent up to Capt. Smith.	
		10.20 pm	Message received stating that Colonel Darling of the 9th HLI had taken over the Command of our Advances.
			Situation. Remainder of B + C Coys were spread out in small groups between 1st Q. and 9th HLI. Rem: of A + D in trenches round High Wood under command of Capt. Smith.	

Army Form 2118.

14

WAR DIARY 16th K.R.R.C.
or
INTELLIGENCE SUMMARY.

July

Place	Date	Hour	Summary of Events and Information	Remarks and references to Appendices
High Wood Attack	15th	10.30 p	German prisoner brought down from High Wood and sent on to Bde Hdqrs.	
		10.45	Six Germans found on edge of road by Battn Hdqrs. 2 killed 4 wounded. From appearances it seemed as if they had broken through our line and had been hit by one of their own shells.	
	16th	2.10 am	Orders sent out from Bde that we should be relieved by the 19th Bde. The 20th Royal Fusiliers came up and took up the line of support previously held by us on previous morning. Battn marched back to (S.19.C.7.7.) Some small holes dug by previous Batta. Men very tired.	
	16th	2.20		
	16th		Rested all morning. Parties sent out in the afternoon and collected all their missing articles. Rain came on in the evening. Enemy sent gas-shells round the outskirts of our Camp. Men were obliged to put on Gas helmets - No Casualties.	
	17th		Rested all day. In the afternoon Batn had orders to move to Wood Trench which Mametz Wood. Batn. marched off at 9.15 pm and after a slow journey reached its destination. Battn Hdqrs in old German dug-out.	
	18th		Men improved trenches and rested as much as possible. Large party away all morning filling 80 petrol tins with water for a Bde. Dump.	

T2134. Wt. W708-776. 500000. 4/15. Sir J.C.&S.

WAR DIARY 16th KRRC

July

Army Form C. 2118.

15

Place	Date	Hour	Summary of Events and Information	Remarks and references to Appendices
Wood Trench	18th	6.15	2/Lt CORK went up to reconnoitre position held by 19th Inf Bde which we should support if necessary. A new draft of 79 other Ranks joined the Batn.	
	19th		Batn. rested during the day. Very hot weather. Draft of 3 new officers arrived at Bn Hdqrs. at 2.30pm. They were put in the following Coys. 2/Lt WHATELY A Coy. 2/Lt BRYAN B Coy. 2/Lt REED C Coy.	
		9.30pm	Very quiet all day. no shelling near our lines. Orders received from Bde Hdqrs to STAND TO at 4.0am in the morning since the 100th Inf Bde (less one Batn) had been detailed for Divisional Reserve during an attack on High Wood and German entrenchment 6½ North. The 7th Division on our right would also be carrying out an attack at the same time. Quiet night; no shelling.	
	20th	4.0am	STAND TO and ready to move at short notice.	
		11.0am	Had orders from Bde to push up and hold trench along road S9C.90 — S/6 A.39. and cover the withdrawal of the Bde from High Wood. Capt. Wenham received orders to report at 19th Inf Bde Hdqrs for instructions. Batn. was met by Capt. Wenham at 19th Bde Hdqrs and proceeded to position as ordered above. "A"+"C" Coys moved into position untouched but "B"+"D" were harassed by enemy's shells causing a few casualties.	

WAR DIARY 16th RRC

INTELLIGENCE SUMMARY

Army Form 2118.

16

Place	Date	Hour	Summary of Events and Information	Remarks and references to Appendices
	20th		2/Lt Cooper received shell-shock in a dug-out on the way up and also injuries which caused him to go to F.Amb. 2/Lt Paravicini and 2/Lt Oxley and a class of 5 other ranks joined the Bat. The former being attached to "A" Coy, the latter to "D" Coy. 19th Bde Orders were received here that 1 Coy would keep up supply of S.A.A, Trench Mortar Bombs & Water to dump at S. corner of High Wood. Each Coy was detailed in turn for this work accompanied with an officer. Few casualties occurred although the kept passing through heavily shelled area. Bat HdQrs was shelled heavily with 4.2 + 5.9 guns. After shelling had stopped one of our aeroplanes drove down a German machine so low that Bat HdQrs Coy opened rapid fire on it and at once caused it to drop rapidly into the village of BAZENTIN le PETIT.	Trench Maps MARTINPUICH 1/20000
Bazentin le Petit.	21st	10.30.	Orders received from 19th Inf Bde to move up at once and relieve force holding High Wood. Batn moved up by Coys and in spite of heavy barrage on Road, had very few casualties and by dawn we completed the relief of a vacated line. Almost immediately after taking up position in trench at S4632 Capt Smith and a party of "D" Coy were attacked by enemy with stick bombs	

Army Form C. 2118.

WAR DIARY 16th KRRC
or
INTELLIGENCE SUMMARY.
(Erase heading not required.)

July.

Place	Date	Hour	Summary of Events and Information	Remarks and references to Appendices
High Wood.	21st	5.40. a.m.	Capt Smith came back to BHQ to report. He was wounded by pieces of bomb. Sending him to retire to F.Amb. After this attack our position was as follows:— 3 Coys along E edge of Wood and C Coy along S. edge of Wood. Captain Wenham received verbal orders to take over the command of the forces defending High Wood thus adding the 1st Queens to his command. On our immediate right was a Batn of R. West Kents. All quiet during the day from enemy's shell fire but we suffered a great deal from enemy's sniping and M.G. fire at first until we sent out our snipers who succeeded in keeping down the enemy's fire. Hot sunshine all day. Our stretcher bearers did valuable work carrying down wounded. During the morning we lost three NCOs being crouched by snipers. The 212th R E Field Coy were up - making strong points round the wood at S4c35, S4c77, S4D20, S4c80. Communication poor at first until we had a line laid to Bde Hdqs. Orderlies had to run over the hill where a relay orderly was kept in readiness. During day our heliograph was able to send messages back. At night we had night lamps fixed up to an old german gun position.	Trench Map 1:20000

WAR DIARY 16th KRRC

Army Form C. 2118.

INTELLIGENCE SUMMARY

(Erase heading not required.)

Place	Date	Hour	Summary of Events and Information	Remarks and references to Appendices
High Wood	21st July	1.45 a.m.	Strength return sent to Bde Hdqs. 1st Queens. 5 Officers 225 other Ranks. 16th Hdqs. 1st Queens 22 Officers, 514 other Ranks. KRR. 6 Officers 214 other Ranks. Officers wounded – Lt Posavicini, 2nd Lt Oxley, 2nd Lt Reg. During the day we watched some exciting aerial combats.	
		4.30 p.m.	Casualty Report sent in to other Ranks 4 killed 49 wounded (approx) Situation Normal. Disturbances caused by our own shells dropping too close over our trenches.	
		6.25 p.m.	Orders sent out from 19th Bde to send out patrol on our left to get into touch with Bath on our left which orders was carried out by 1st Queens but was interfered with by German alarm on our relief. Orders handed over to relieving Bat. 1st Gordon Highlanders of the 154th Bde.	Trench Map Martinpuich 1/20000
		7.0 p.m.	Guides sent down for 4th Gordon relief.	
		7.30 p.m.	Orders received from 1008 B to proceed to BECORDEL-BECOURT when guides would show us bivouacing ground. Completion of relief to be reported at 19th Bde. Completion of move at PM to B. The Gordons were late owing to German barrage. We handed over and Bath marched back having lost several men owing to shells falling amongst them. Relief complete reported at 19th Bde at 12 midnight. Our Machine Gunners suffered during bombardment owing to our shells falling short.	

Army Form C. 2118.

WAR DIARY
or
INTELLIGENCE SUMMARY.
(Erase heading not required.)

16th RRC
July 19

Place	Date	Hour	Summary of Events and Information	Remarks and references to Appendices
MAMETZ Wood	22nd	12.15 am	Batn marched back through heavy barrage of Shells and Tear shells. Marched back	Martinpuich T.M. 2000.0
		4.34 am	to BECORDEL RESCORT where we were bivouaced in the field next to the 1st Queens. Batn	
Becordel Bescourt	23rd		rested all morning and after lunch moved to a next Camp. Draft of 18 other ranks arrived also another draft of 161 other ranks from trench hops about 1 mile away. Orders received orders morning to move. 62 D N3.	
			Marched passed VIVIERS Mill and arrived at camp at 12 noon. Major Sitwell ordered to join 33rd Div as Reinforcement Officer. Camp at E 90 Central. Captn Wadham assumed Command of Batn. Lt Sullivan is appointed Actg Adjutant. 2nd Lt Lipscombe is appointed Actg Quarter Master. 44 tents arrived and were distributed as per Coy at 4 tents. May 318 draft arrived other Ranks.	
	24th		Company Training. Settling down to Camp. Baths refitter. Lack of effective N.C.O.s. Reduced to one Sergeant & 7 Corporals for duty.	
	25th		Company Training. Congratulatory telegram from Lord Grenfell & members of Govening body. Specialist training.	
	26th		Company Training. Return of Dr Scott from course. 2/Lt Mason joined Batn for duty.	

Army Form C. 2118.

WAR DIARY 16th KRRC

July

INTELLIGENCE SUMMARY.

(Erase heading not required.)

20

Place	Date	Hour	Summary of Events and Information	Remarks and references to Appendices
Camp near DERNANCOURT ALBERT.	27th		Company Training. Bayonet Fighting Courses held by Bde. Weather hot. Men allowed to bathe in River ANCRE.	
	28th		Coy Training. Hot weather continues.	
	29th		" " " " Camp improvements carried out daily.	
	30th		Church Parade 10.0 a.m. taken by Capt Hon Lindsay. Brigade Parade for presentation of Military Medals by Gen: Landon 33rd Div. 11 awarded to 16th RR. 9 men presented.	
	31st		Coy Training. Specialist Classes. Hot weather – Bathing. NCOs receive Special training from R.S.M.	

100th Brigade.
33Rd Division

1/16th BATTALION

KING'S ROYAL RIFLE CORPS

AUGUST 1916

Army Form C. 2118.

August WAR DIARY 16th KRRC
or
INTELLIGENCE SUMMARY.
(Erase heading not required.)

Vol (1)

Place	Date	Hour	Summary of Events and Information	Remarks and references to Appendices
Camp N	1st		Training under Coy arrangements. Specialists parades carried on. Bayonet Fighting	Map ALBERT / Arras
DERNANCOURT	2nd		Very hot. Coy Training. Bay. Fighting sections kept up.	
	3rd		" " Coy Training. Bathing parades.	
	4th		" Coy Training. Lecture at Bde Hdqrs on Aircraft Communication by Capt Miles.	
		11:0 am	C.O. & A.C. Coys went up line to reconnoitre. Grant Competition in evening.	
	5th		Coy Training. P.M. Gas demonstration at Bde Hdqrs. D Coy party on fatigues.	
		1.15 pm	OC B & D went up line to reconnoitre. B Coy practised Night-Tunnel Relief near Camp.	
	6th	9.30 pm	Received orders from Bde to move on night of 6th/7th.	
			No Church parade. Voluntary Service. R.C. the parade Service at Bde Hdqrs at 10 am. Veryhot Sun Cool wind. Further details of move received. Packs sent away at 12.0 noon.	
	7th	2.15 am	Reveille. Tea 3.0 am. Marched off at 4.0 am 9 Officers 700 OR. Marched past Bde Hdqrs 4:15 am Route via Vivier Mill – N of Méault – Fricourt. Guides met us at cross-roads F9a 5.7. Went to Fricourt	
		6:40 am	Wood and took over from 16th Gordons. Breakfast 8.0 am. Rested & cleaned up Trenches.	
		9.0 am	Orders received from Bde to relieve 4th Kings in Mametz Wood. Relief to be complete by 3.0pm	
		1.0 pm	Batn marched off by platoons up to Mametz Wood. Relief complete 2.30pm	

Army Form C. 2118.

WAR DIARY of 16th KRRC
August
INTELLIGENCE SUMMARY.

(Erase heading not required.)

Place	Date	Hour	Summary of Events and Information	Remarks and references to Appendices
Mametz Wood	7th	5.30-6.30p	Our Artillery bombardment	Trench map Martinpuich 1/20000
		7.0p	Water parties sent to front line	
	8th		Major Howard joined Battn & took Command of Battn. Quiet night. Cleaning & improvement of trenches. Working parties all day. Gas shell barrage in valley in evening. Collecting of Salvage	
	9th	8.0a	Four Coy Commanders & M.G.O. reported at B.H.Q 2nd Worcesters to view the line. Draft of 16 sergeants & 3 Corporals reported for duty. Collection of Salvage & improvement of shelters.	
		9.30p	Orders received from Bde. to relieve 2nd Worcesters in front line between hours of 3pm & 8.30pm. Details of relief to be arranged by COs concerned. Quiet night.	
	10th	1.0p	Run Outs went up to line at 1.0p to take over trench stores. Coys started at 3.0p D.R.A.C. Very little shelling while relief was taking place.	
		2.15p	Draft of 2 Lieuts and 7 second Lieuts joined for duty just before leaving Mametz Wood. Lt Mason wounded slightly in hand while going up. Relief complete 8.15p. Names of Lts Bernard, Fardell, 2nd Lts Stearns, Tucker, Stone, Balshaw, Hope, Barrard, Inigo Jones. Lieut Fitzell went to Base Depot Etaples. Central Training School of reinforcements. Transferred to General List. Ration parties shelled.	

Major Fitzell went to Base Depot Étaples Central Training School of reinforcements

Army Form C. 2118.

WAR DIARY or **INTELLIGENCE SUMMARY**

16th KRRC   August

Place	Date	Hour	Summary of Events and Information	Remarks and references to Appendices
High Wood	11th	12.20 am	Enemy heavily shelled valley. Rifle & M.gun fire along whole line caused by a bombing attack in High Wood. Ceased at 1.0 a.m. Working parties greatly hampered. Patrol sent out from 'B' Coy. K.I. digging parties up to help men front trench.	
	12th		Quiet morning. 12 noon 1/4th Kings Liverpool Officers came up and took over strongpoints & Sniping.	
		4-6 p	Our heavy artillery bombardment of Wood Trench. Enemy retaliated with 8" shells. Blackwatch Trench shelled. 'C' Coy Hdqrs knocked in. ← casualties slight. Orders from Bde that 98th Bde would relieve us on morning of 13th. Enemy artillery ← active during the night. Showery during evening.	
	13	3.00	Lewis Gunners relieved. 4.0 am Hdqrs relieved. 5.0 am Coys started. Relief reported complete 7.15 am. All Coys went through valley Poloch to bivouac at Becordel Becourt. Rested during day. Rifle inspection.	
	14th		Cleaning up of Equipment & refitting.	
	15th		Working parties all day – 4.00 M.R.	

WAR DIARY
or
INTELLIGENCE SUMMARY

Army Form C. 2118.

AUGUST 1916.

Place	Date	Hour	Summary of Events and Information	Remarks and references to Appendices
Cnd nr Bde. J.C.	16th		Working parties of 2 officers 100 O.R. provided to S.14.6.2.5. Trench guides of 222nd Fd Coy R.E. Halfpick. Half drawn from R.E. dump. Work continued until 4:15 am. Parades 7-7:15am Trench - 9:30 am onwards Companies at disposal of 2nd Cpls - Specialist Officers under instruction. Brigade Sports held at camp at 6 p.m. Tug of war & Relay Races won by 7 Pioneers. Shock of strength having been included & declared.	
	17th		Parades as on 16th. Companies at disposal of 2nd Cpls	
	18th		Parades as on 17th	
MONTAUBAN ALLEY	19th		Batt'n moved to MONTAUBAN ALLEY at 4 p.m. Disposition of Companies. A Coy Montauban Alley, A1a.9.7. B2 Camp Trench, B2'C' Coy trench along Montauban Alley East of Bn HQ. D Coy Lot Trench. Bn HQ S.26.C.9.4. Montauban Alley. Officers solo in Montauban Alley. Chinning of obstacles - some sniping	
	20th		Carried on burning in "Shrapnel" "Magazine" trench	
	21st		Company Commanders reconnoitred position. Capt. Roberts, Capt. Sidey, & Lr. Working Party of 150 other ranks. 300 sandbags from No 6 dump & Green Dump. Another Partie under Lieut. Bernard & 2nd R Gaurard deepened LIVERPOOL TRENCH too length of 260ft. Avg 150ft deeper to a depth of 3'9" workers K 2'9". 13th August continued deepening to 3'9" & worked to b. aug at K 2'9"	

WAR DIARY
or
INTELLIGENCE SUMMARY.

(Erase heading not required.)

AUGUST 1916

Army Form C. 2118.

Place	Date	Hour	Summary of Events and Information	Remarks and references to Appendices
Montauban Alley	21st		Batt" relieved into 16th line. Reg.t Bryar. left of Dalvile Wood; 2 Coys in Subsektor "A". 2nd Hosalier & 2 Coys in Subsektor "H t". 1st Queens Reserve near Bde H.Q. Pioneer Regim.t moved into Montauban Alley. 1/6 KRR. Bernal.m Montauban Alley. 9th N.F. shelled & kept 2 Coys in support b 2thc, and rest of 2 Coys AVB in support of them relieving early on morning of 22nd b. Montauban Alley.	
	22nd		C. in D. Regt M./.A.H.I. evolved harassing on Coys of 3rd Hororian. Rat'n'd artillerist arrived. C. O.C. Cd. Ops direct with O.C. 2nd Hororian. Night of 22/23 B.n. relieved 3rd Honoreit. Reg.t. Bde Road Release 13. Dalvile Q. Coys A. Coy in Band line and in 2nd O. Trench; B. Coy in Shrap. Red. 1 Oaklew Trench with Capt Thomas. C. Coy, 1 Platoon Oaklew Trench & 1 Plat. Green Jacket Trench with Sec. B Lt. 2/Lt. Tacton. 2 Pleton. Callo. French under Capt Luken. 2/Lt. Cey and Chalk Trench. Carried parties for the Coys k mon lim 11-3.30pm of Sea & rest. Spaniste Left Montauban Alley at 5.30pm. B.n. H.Q. at Cavalu French	
Caft Trench	23rd		On morning of 23rd. Major Hormm) was known to be & wounded at Oakleaw French Whele 7.8 A.m. killed, there only one Stella burst Major opened. Capt Cantoust (M.O.) was accompanying	

T/134. Wt. W708-776. 500000. 4/15. Sir J.C. & B.

WAR DIARY or INTELLIGENCE SUMMARY

Army Form C. 2118.

AUGUST 1916

Place	Date	Hour	Summary of Events and Information	Remarks and references to Appendices
Cotton Trench	23rd		Capt. Thomas & Lieut. Tindall rejoined the Battn. Major Howard & Capt. Crabtree wounded & Lieut Farber having been shell shocked Lieut Farber assumed Command of "B" Coy. Capt E Durham assumed Command of Battn & Lieut R Scott took over duties of acting Adjutant. Lieut Richie RAMC joined for duty vice Capt. Crabtrorth. Enemy trench mortar & rifle shells caused some few casualties. Otherwise situation normal. On night of 23rd/24th Bolton line Cunis with its two 48 guns which included a rifle S/pr. Also positions and Kbg taken by A Coy. 'A' Coy moved up to Reg of Strong point line making way for Coy from 9/2nd Worcs on right. 'B' Coy moved up "C" Coy occupied Green Jacket Plum & Cherry Branches in rear of Orchard Branch. "D" Coy in Rear 12 in Cotton Trench.	
do	24"		3 Friend Cops engine-inferior apparent, tender - Rogers Coy Connaught 0630 for found Cope No litter reported and tried shelter in front trench. Enemy aircraft should not allow accounts of toshe	

T.J.134. Wt. W708-776. 500000. 4/15. Sir J.C. & S.

Army Form C. 2118.

WAR DIARY
or
INTELLIGENCE SUMMARY.

(Erase heading not required.)

AUGUST 1916

Place	Date	Hour	Summary of Events and Information	Remarks and references to Appendices
Carlton Tr	2ⁿᵈ		In accordance with 100.J.B. B.O. Order Batt. left line & proceeded into 110 Ave. & 2ⁿᵈ Ave. in which the Officers & Gunners Tea Trench & Communications Tr.	
			Supporting relief attack S.M.G. 53.80. The Royal 33ʳᵈ Brig'd Broadway and F2	
			LONGUEVAL - FLERS Rd inclusive to 33ʳᵈ Division	
			1ˢᵗ Divn on Left. 16 K.R.R.C. in Colony 2ᵈ Suffolks on Right - 9ᵗʰ H.L.I. in Brigade Reserve.	
			Continued position by Coy as 3.30 p.m. on 2ⁿᵈ. "A" Coy Ist line	
			B in Ictas Trench, "C" & one of "D" Coys Platoons Cluny Trench	
			to Longueval-Caterpillar Trench Road jnct. w/ East Bayham	
			also 2 Lewis Guns & "A, B, & C" & one of "D" Coy Laphonic Communication	
			from R.H.Q. & H.C.Coy. Mc Coy (Capt Lindsay) also had 2 Platoon in	
			Levred with all other Communications failed. "B" H.Q. arranged as before	
			The attack was preceded by a heavy bombardment of 2 hours & of the enemy	
			our intent. The order of advance was: "A" Coy first line, "B" second line	
			"C" How Lewis & D in Reserve. Zero hour was 5.45 p.m. The H.Q. Position		
		6.45 pm	attached thereof. Detailed Report on this Rpt at zero. One hour after zero "A" Coy moved on & close under barrage into "B" Coy Bay's &	
			no losses.	

Army Form C. 2118.

WAR DIARY
or
INTELLIGENCE SUMMARY.
(Erase heading not required.)

AUGUST 1916

Place	Date	Hour	Summary of Events and Information	Remarks and references to Appendices
Guillemont	21		'C' Coy & the same time moved on forward and reached line occupying this as soon as they could. 'A' Coy also moved forward into the trench as it lifted — the rate of lifting was 25 yds per minute — 'B' Coy 30's in rear conformed to 'A' Coys movements. The Third Obj. [crossed out] was got — the 3rd [crossed out] Somewhere became a factor in a foolish state, particularly recent to the first casualties on its first instance when A & B lines clear of the forward line. 'C' Coy conformed in 2 lines occupying the first line & Orchard Trench. The Attack was carried out as ordered and all objectives were taken by 'B' Coy during an about 100 yds beyond the final objective. 'A' Coy forming the covering party in front, lying 50 on 50 parallel to it. A Salient left between Left & 'Queens' Right but this have since been consolidated. We got one about 7.30 pm. Touch was held with Rgts on right.	
		7.30pm	2/Lts Cook and Ball (patrol) went + 2 Platoons of Reserve Coy & 30 reptd to front line + left to consolidate on trying & get touch + touch with 1st Queens to left + in dayls.	
		8.30pm	Comm. + send back to consolidate front line. Lt. Penner sent forward into reserve. 2 Platoons of 'D' Coy & sent to Cosk. Ending up in 503 front line.	

WAR DIARY
or
INTELLIGENCE SUMMARY

Army Form C. 2118.

AUGUST 1916

Place	Date	Hour	Summary of Events and Information	Remarks and references to Appendices
Guillemont	24th		The new front line was consolidated here & afresh & a surface held good thanks to faithful & the whole attack was carried out thoroughly fair our under the fairly any of the troops moving out immediately behind our own Barrage (which tho' (W) Germ-Counter from their own shells gave the troops no chance but tho' the Germans kindled (?) very quickly) made the work of the Reserve (?) very hard and the under in Callies trench although sent up by the B/C Coy when the barrage had initially stopped. Patrols were sent out from our sentry Watch points about one hour over front & to try to re-establish communication into 1st Queens on left the other Patrol succeeded in capturing a men point. The Enemy answered in small parties of 2 or 3 men thought & and carrying of 25% which were ope parties keep which we left on a Regt. ready to help. One feature of the Barrage of Scoville was the new system of fire of barrage adopted by the Artillery. We left some of 25 yds for minute from to two of the first lift this was the to keep the Infantry close up in each. By back then shrapnel without off or machine gun five except to the left. Here they were left up for a little bit afterwards but a small some of smoke close.	

T2134. Wt. W708-776. 500000. 4/15. Sir J. C. & S.

Army Form C. 2118.

WAR DIARY
or
INTELLIGENCE SUMMARY.

(Erase heading not required.)

AUGUST 1916.

Place	Date	Hour	Summary of Events and Information	Remarks and references to Appendices
Carlton Tr	2nd		Our casualties for the action are Killed - 1 Officer (2nd Lt Slee) 13 O. Ranks Wounded 2 Officers (2nd Lts Wheatley & Bevan) 72 O.R. Missing 29. O.R.	
			A large number of the casualties were only slight cases. Also many were due to the left of our Hawley line rather than advance & mostly with burst of M.G. & Rifle fire from the direction of WOOD TRENCH. Good work was done throughout the operation by the stretcher - bearers, being regular & accurate. Stokes Gunners also worked well & were in fire. The line of communication by wire to the front line was cut at 5.30 p.m. & many attempts to regain it were unsuccessful. Runners were kept from company HQ for this. The Battn & Coy Runners did splendid work, the R.M.O. Capt Doyle did good work between Battn R.Q. & the Dressing Stn at FRICOURT but was with the R.S.M. at the T.O.C. 1st I.B. MONTAUBAN ALLEY for the then 48 hrs without which was nearly 24 hrs at nearly the Battn HQ was shelled to hold it in readiness to the Transport lines. The R.S.M. was wounded by private cleaning his rifle when a communication to the front line with a hand bomb from the men in MONTAUBAN ALLEY.	NB

Army Form C. 2118.

WAR DIARY
or
INTELLIGENCE SUMMARY.

(Erase heading not required.)

AUGUST 1916

Place	Date	Hour	Summary of Events and Information	Remarks and references to Appendices
Carnoy Valley	25th		Early in the morning of the 25th 1/6 Batt was relieved by the 1st Midx, one Company of which had been on front line & one Company relieving 1st Objective & the French Skirmishers. 2 Coys of 1st Midx relieved the 2nd Hoc. on Right. The Batt on relief proceeded to Carnoy Trench. In afternoon 7 Sec 1st 25th Batt was relieved by a Company from Cork & proceeded to Mametz Road arriving at 8.45 pm.	
Mametz (Wood)	26th		Batt rested in Mametz Wood. Slight shelling in morning — 1 killed & 7 wounded. O.R. Message received from 33rd Division ordering Army Commander Corps & the to Divisions to Farewell to Gen. Pinney & 150 Bde on their share in the offensive from July 15th to Aug 25th. He was succeeded by the Corps Comd of the G.O.C. 33rd Division.	
	27th		Batt moved from Mametz (Wood) & proceeded by Motor buses to Viviers Mill Fricourt Circus Sheet 57, were covered by Motor buses to Viviers Mill to hot bath & clean change of underclothing. Batt bivouaced in old Camp near Becordel.	

Army Form C. 2118.

WAR DIARY
or
INTELLIGENCE SUMMARY.
(Erase heading not required.)

AUGUST 1916

Instructions regarding War Diaries and Intelligence Summaries are contained in F.S. Regs., Part II. and the Staff Manual respectively. Title pages will be prepared in manuscript.

Hour, Date, Place	Summary of Events and Information	Remarks and references to Appendices
N. RECORDEL 27th	[illegible handwritten entries]	
28th		
29th		
30th		
7-30 AM 30th RASCINCOURT		
8-15 AM 31st MOLLIENS-AU-BOIS		

WAR DIARY
or
INTELLIGENCE SUMMARY.

Army Form C. 2118.

AUGUST 1916

Hour, Date, Place	Summary of Events and Information	Remarks and references to Appendices
4 P.M. 31st MOLLIENS AU-BOIS	The G.O.C. 23rd Division (Major-Gen Babington) addressed the Battn on the conduct of the Brigade at MORLANCOURT and congratulated them on the top-hole way in which they had carried out their duties. The G.O.C. conveyed to the battn the appreciation that had been received from the Army Commander & Corps Commander.	

1.9.16.

Cecil L Porch Lewin
Cmdg 16/Kings Royal Rifles

Army Form C. 2118.

Instructions regarding War Diaries and Intelligence Summaries are contained in F.S. Regs., Part II. and the Staff Manual respectively. Title Pages will be prepared in manuscript.

WAR DIARY
or
INTELLIGENCE SUMMARY
(Erase heading not required.)

SEPTEMBER 1916   16 KRRC

VOL 11

Place	Date	Hour	Summary of Events and Information	Remarks and references to Appendices
TALMAS	1st	8.15 AM	Battn. marched to TALMAS when the men bivouacked for the night. The billets were very poor.	
BEAUMETZ	2nd	8.15 AM	Battn. marched to BEAUMETZ. A halt was drawn on route for dinners (~ 70 mins). The B? "Fallen Out" Stats are 32. This number was due to the fact that see, a number of the Battn. not being used to "hipper" from sore feet & one or two some received exhaustion from carrying the packs. The march was good on the whole, men were stuck to speedily well rather than fall out. Some hits fell out again soon after the commencement of the march from gas.) Billets rather poor.	
"	3rd	10 AM	Battn. rests at BEAUMETZ. Church parade in the 200yd? W of Church & afterwards a Gnl. march past C.O. The men were particularly smart in appearance & behaviour. Considering how dirty & tired and heavy marching.	
FORTEL	4th	10 AM	Battn. marches to FORTEL. Packs were carried by Motor Lorry - "Fallen Out" Stats nil. Billets were quite good.	
HERICOURT	5th	8 AM	Battn. marched to HERICOURT. Packs were again carried by Motor Lorry - "Fallen out" - Stats nil. Billets fair.	
TERNAS	6th	9.15 AM	Battn. marched to TERNAS. Packs were carried in the usual manner. The man one thin man was certified by M.O. as medically unfit to fallen out Sick - one thin man was certified by M.O. and subsequently referred to ADMS. as scarlet fever came march was was mate to FA. Subsequently referred fall out were taken on transport of Battn. y The names of known officers have	
			The numbers of known officers were as follows: Capt. Asst.-?T. Nils - A Coy. (in command) 2Lt. C.R. Liffler - D " G.A. Goddy - B "	

2449 Wt. W14957/M90 750,000 1/16 J.B.C. & A. Forms/C.2118/12.

Army Form C. 2118

WAR DIARY
or
INTELLIGENCE SUMMARY

(Erase heading not required.)   16 KRRC

SEPTEMBER 1916

Place	Date	Hour	Summary of Events and Information	Remarks and references to Appendices
TERNAS	7th	9 AM	Batt⁰ was to have marched to PENIN but orders were cancelled. Batt⁰ exercised in short route-march of 6 miles in full marching order. The march has very noticeably improved. 2nd Lt R.M. Murray-Anseley has reported for duty on posting to "C" Coy.	
HALLOY	8th	7·45 AM	Batt⁰ received orders at midnight 7/8th to entrain 8/9th starting 9 AM to billets at HALLOY. The trans. Coys were carried to the Ent. by Staff & Divisional Motors to save a tramp of about 7 miles. Batt⁰ reached HALLOY about remainder of Batt. & Transport proceeded by road into 1·15 P.M. Base Coys TcCoys were in huts & A Coy in billets — the accomodation was quite good.	
"	9th	6·30 AM	2 Officers, 2 NCOs per Coy proceeded with CO & Intelligence Officer & Form to Bn HQ. RIENVILLERS to prepare for & reconnoitre the line. Batt⁰ carried out training consisting of specialist work, steady drill Apt 12 men men went in devits to overhauling of kit & equipment. An order has been iss'd that 33 ORs to leave 17. Bn in Eng. by 1700 Hrs per day. Coys thoroughly overhauled Arms, Equipment, SAA & preparation to take over.	
GAUDIEMPRE	10th	9 AM	Batt⁰ marched to GAUDIEMPRE. The marching has much improved & falling out state was nil. The billets were very scattered from & considerable difficulty was experienced in housing. M.O's & 1136 Pte Carpenter to rejoin Coys. 2nd Lieut. B. Clutterbuck & Capt Jas L Lindsay & 2nd Lt Clutterbuck & 1136 ORC attached to 2nd French Routine Batt⁰ arrived at GAUDIEMPRE. Coy training into Evt was attention given attention	
"	11th		Batt⁰ carried out specialist training.	
HUMBERCAMPS		5·30 PM	Batt⁰ marched to HUMBERCAMPS where they relieved 2 R.W.F. after march a considerable time in the road wait for billets to be cleared.	

WAR DIARY or INTELLIGENCE SUMMARY

Army Form C. 2118.

10 K R R C

SEPTEMBER 1916

Place	Date	Hour	Summary of Events and Information	Remarks and references to Appendices
HUMBERCAMPS	12th		Battn. refitting in HUMBERCAMPS. The following officers having returned for duty were posted as follows:- Capt. Robinson — to "B" Coy (in command). 2/Lt. 2nd Lt. Dow — "A" Lt. H.C. Cholmondeley — "D"	
SOUASTRE	13th	6.45pm	Battn. marched to SOUASTRE where (less one Billet from the 1st Q. arrived) the Battn. proceeded to the line. Billets quite good.	
			Gas & Specialists carried on training. Morning devoted to afternoon. Battn. had to be provided from SOUASTRE. These included companies taken as specialists. Were not always possible taken below, 1cm it was known & specialists, 5 specialists officers at 222 F.C. R.E.	
		9pm	Working party of 2 officers & 100 men (A Coy) with 100 shovels & lieutenant officer to FONQUEVILLERS for signal work in line under officer 222 F.G. R.E. A similar working party (proceeded) from "B" Coy. — Same Place	
		10.30pm	2 officers 70 O.R. (170 shovels & 3 spikes) from C Coy had & report entrance place	
	11pm		Award. Short Ratt. received notice that 11 Military Medals had been awarded to the following men for conspicuous gallantry in the attack of 24th Aug. W) Deville Wood C.936 Capt. Glenn P. C.421 Sergt. Perry C.W. C.571 Rfm. Seville R.; C.729 Rfm. Green O.; C.347 Rfm. Welch J. C.141 Rfm. Mowbrey A.; C.424 Cpl. Hallam J.S.; C.667 Rfm. Maurice J.; C.316 Rfm. Hodgson A.J. S.2549 Rfm. Smith J.; S.12031 Rfm. Wootton C.	
	14th	10AM	Commanding officer inspected "D" Coy — fair marching order.	
		10pm	Working party of 3 officers & 150 men (officers) + 130 men from D Coy 20 men C (Coy) carried 150 shovels + 75 picks returned to same place, no same picture was out (25).	

Army Form C. 2118.

WAR DIARY
or
INTELLIGENCE SUMMARY

16 K.R.R.C.

SEPTEMBER 1916 *(Erase heading not required.)*

Place	Date	Hour	Summary of Events and Information	Remarks and references to Appendices
SOUASTRE	14th	10.30pm	2 Officers & 100 men (A Coy) reported at same place as earlier party. Sky clear. 100 Clouds - 50 Pickets.	
		11pm	2 Officers & 70 men (B. Coy) reported at same place.	
			All leave parties (Officers have a chocolate) except Bombers who were expected as far as possible. She parties were splendid on return while Officers etc. & on Pullman running.	
			2/4 Gillius proceeded on leave to England.	
	15th	9.30pm	1 Officer 20 men from A Coy reported to Rd of Sewers officers at Bde HQ SOUASTRE	
			1 Officer 20 men (A Coy) reported at The PONS, HEBUTERNE	
			1 Officer 20 men reconnoitred 222 F.C. R.E. for unloading wagons at HEBUTERNE.	
			4 Officers 200 men (A.B.C. Coys) reported at same place for carrying R.E. stores from wagons to Dumps.	
		11pm	1 Officer 75 men with 75 Shovels & 37 Picks reported at Artillery Rd FONQUEVILLERS	
		9.30pm	1 Officer 150 men reported at PONS, HEBUTERNE.	
		10.30pm	2 Officers Heavy working Parties (which include Specials 15 & some Cav. and a detachment of Officers' Servants) the men were not billeted for night but returned to Billets	
	16th		2 NCO's in Coy	
		9.15am	C.O. O.C Coys, M.G.O & proceeded to FONQUEVILLERS Sector to reconnoitre 15th bn.	
		7pm	1 NCO & 10 men (D Coy) reported to Bde Squad Officer at Bde HQ SOUASTRE	

Army Form C. 2118.

Instructions regarding War Diaries and Intelligence Summaries are contained in F. S. Regs., Part II. and the Staff Manual respectively. Title Pages will be prepared in manuscript.

WAR DIARY or INTELLIGENCE SUMMARY

(Erase heading not required.)

SEPTEMBER 1916   10th K.R.R.C.

Place	Date	Hour	Summary of Events and Information	Remarks and references to Appendices
SOUASTRE	16th	9 p.m.	4 Officers & 200 men from A.P.C. Corps reported to Officer 222 Fd. Coy. R.E. at Archel X Rds. FONQUEVILLERS as a working party for duty in YOUNG ST. & Z HEDGE.	
	17th	11 A.M.	Church Parade in orchard immediately in rear of Church.	
		7 p.m.	1 N.C.O. & 10 men A Coy reported to P.B.C. Signal Officer at Bde. H.Q. SOUASTRE.	
	18th		Very wet day. Cup front buttons. 2nd Lt. retained from BOULOGNE. Lieut Company proceeded on leave. 2 Batmen - 2 Lt took temporary command D Coy.	
		10.30 pm	4 Officers 200 men reported at POND, HEBUTERNE for carrying party. Raider proceeded to 4th Corps near BOULOGNE.	
	19th		Battn took over trenches RIGHT sector FONQUEVILLERS. Snipers & Observers Bombers & Signallers with 1 N.C.O. per platoon took over at 4 p.m. and Battn. relieved 10-2.30 p.m. Op. HQ.1 - Relief complete about 10-30 p.m.	
			Pilot Pole in Command B Cot: - Capt Webb Kaye - Capt Edwards - B Coy.	
			Cuthbertson C Coy, 2nd R. Cole. D Coy, A Coy Right, B Coy Centre, D Coy Left, 1 Coy in Reserve Disposition of Coys A Coy left, B Coy Centre, D Coy Right, 1 Coy in Reserve in "BLUFF" dugouts. Night of 19th quiet.	
LINE FONQUEVILLERS	20th		Part of Young Officers Class in FONQUEVILLERS under S.M. Lewis 9th K.R.1. The officers attending were 2nd Lts: Clemensha, Booth, Gerrard, Wyfe, Murray-Ridler. The situation too extremely quiet all day - Coys engaged in cleaning up trenches.	

Army Form C. 2118.

WAR DIARY
or
INTELLIGENCE SUMMARY

SEPTEMBER 1916   16 KRRC

(Erase heading not required.)

Place	Date	Hour	Summary of Events and Information	Remarks and references to Appendices
TRENCHES FONQUEVILLERS	21		Working parties of 4 NCOs & 24 men provided to 4 parties in each trench in reliefs of 6 hours each. Work built emplacement for 100th T.M. Battery. Working hours 9am-3pm & 3pm-9pm. Also 1 Officer & 50 men reported at HEBUTERNE POND for carrying party for RE. 3pm-9pm. All quiet in the remainder of our area in relief. Public Worship again. Batt in trenches & wounded, and Lt Col Pote.	
	22	10-3pm	100th T.M.Bty. working parties continued as on 21st & in addition 2 parties of 1 N.C.O. & 20 men for work on sump hole under RE. 37 men went on leave. Our line was at calm. 2 officers & 100 men supplies to RE at HEBUTERNE POND for carrying party. Public worship. In absence of Capt Wickham Capt Hinkman & 20 R proceeded. Rather quiet day. Lewis SP Scott wounded. Relief & stores carried on. 2nd Division. Bombers referrer & cleaned out all Boche carrier on 2nd Division with Bombers.	
	23"		Working parties for 100th T.M. Bty & RE as for 21st & 22nd. Training as known. 4 men been carried on in FONQUEVILLERS. Situation quiet with exception of a few light T.M. shells on Right Coy Front.	
	24"	8-30AM	Working parties of 1 officer & 50 men at FONCH. YUSSUF ST - THORPE ST. mts Southwark & 25picks to work in Avenelle trench under RE. Also normal working & parties of 1 NCO & 20 men each for RES.	
		10-3pm	2 officers & 100 men for RE Carrying party at HEBUTERNE POND. It was not found to carry out much work in trenches as no 1 was on other work in pursuance of which were on leave. 2nd Lt Tackle rejoined at him. 32 men (8 per Coy) returned from leave (brown) & Bn Tr. Prendering to Lt Col Pote proceeded on leave to England before. The situation on the line was quite normal except for an occasional shelling of A Coy (left) front with 6"-9" shells.	
	25"	8-30	1 Officer & 50 men work 50 shovel & 25picks reported to R.E. as on 24"for work in Avenelle Trenches.	

Army Form C. 2118.

WAR DIARY
or
INTELLIGENCE SUMMARY

(Erase heading not required.) 16 K.R.R.C.

SEPTEMBER 1916

Place	Date	Hour	Summary of Events and Information	Remarks and references to Appendices
TRENCHES & FONQUEVILLOP	25th	10 AM	Officers of 4th Khakhi Lancers came up here to look over - to take over billets. Alm't Specialist Officers handed over to A.P.M. 33rd Div. for transfer to line (F.S.C.M.) of 2 men N.Z. Rifleman (unknown returns from leave & surrender). Battn. visited sector.	
	26th	10 AM	Major Lieut. U & "I" Burnam visited sector. Battn. held reports to Town Major's Office at 3 pm (under 2nd Lt Majo. Jones) MAJOR Gen Pinney visited the sector in the afternoon. Battn. relief was complete about 10.30pm & the Battn. proceeded to SOUASTRE to the refuges where they were billeted in huts.	
SOUASTRE				
COULLEMONT	27th	2pm	Battn. moved to COULLEMONT. The billets here were quite good. Blankets were drawn for the men. Battn. rested for the day in COULLEMONT. Coys duplex time to clean equipment & for Maj-General's inspection which was cancelled. Battn. laundry, etc.	
	28th			
LUCHEUX	29th	9.30 AM	Battn. marched to LUCHEUX where the billets were quite good, but known returns from leave to England to ROUQUEMAISON. No billets, the men were not comfortable but after	
ROUQUEMAISON	30th	8.30 AM	Battn. moved to ROUQUEMAISON. "A company "swept up" accommodation was found for other ranks. A few deals of cleaning up. Then	

Cmdg LtCol
16th K.R.R.C.

WAR DIARY or INTELLIGENCE SUMMARY

Army Form C. 2118.

WO/12

10/23

16th (S) Bn. King's Royal Rifles

October 1916

Place	Date	Hour	Summary of Events and Information	Remarks and references to Appendices
Bouquemaison	1st		Bn. Church parade. Training under Company arrangements, and training of specialists received special attention to be paid to drill etc. in two helmets. A draft of eight O.R. joined for duty.	
	2nd		Training under Coy. arrangements. A detn. of 227nd of Coy. R.E. allotted to Bn. to assist in teaching, making of Blocks, Strong Points & Consolidation work. (A very useful idea, as Bn. was badly in need of such instruction). Specialists carried on as usual.	
	3rd		Training of Coys. & specialists carried on. Capt. R.O. Edwards, 1 Cdm., 1 dgt. & 4 O.R. proceeded to 7th Corps to take over duties in charge of Prisoner Camp.	
Bouquemaison	4th		Bn. had Bath at Boffles allotted. This two made a combined Route march & Bath. 2nd Lt. C.H. Cock took over Command of "B" Coy. Vice Capt. R.O. Edwards. Capt. & Adjt. E. Western returned from Leave to England, and resumed duties of Adjutant. 2nd Lt. C.H. Wilkins 1/6. Royal Sussex Regt. reported for duty, taken on Strength of Bn. & posted to "D" Coy. 2nd Lt. R. Syed admitted to F.A.	

Army Form C. 2118.

WAR DIARY
or
INTELLIGENCE SUMMARY

(Erase heading not required.) 1/6 (S)/Bn. K.R.R.C.

October 1916

Place	Date	Hour	Summary of Events and Information	Remarks and references to Appendices
BOURVEMAISON	5th		Training of Coys and Specialists as usual. 2nd Lt. Hitchcock granted leave to England; Lt. S.S. Scott performing the duties of Transport Officer in his absence.	
"	6th		Training of Coys & Specialists as usual.	
"	7th		Training of Coys & Specialists as usual. "B" & "D" Coys carried out attack practice with the use of S.A.A. & Bombs. A good volley was found which answered well for the purpose, & was quite safe for using live ammn.	
"	8th		Mr Church parade at 10 a.m. Div! Baths allotted to Bn. and used by 2 Coys.	
"	9th		Training of Coys & Specialists as usual. Div? Baths allotted to complete Bathing of Bn.	
"	10th		Training of Coys & Specialists as usual.	
"	11th		Training of Coys & Specialists as usual. Capt. & Adjt. Elmslie Capt. Weld & 2nd Lt. Cox, visited line in front of Hebuterne.	

Army Form C. 2118.

WAR DIARY
or
INTELLIGENCE SUMMARY

(Erase heading not required.) 16th (S) Bn. King's Royal Rifles

October 1916

Place	Date	Hour	Summary of Events and Information	Remarks and references to Appendices
BOUQUEMAISON	12th	—	Training of Coys & Specialists as usual. Lt. Col. Wyld, Capts Grave & Lindsay & Lt. Scott visited line in front of Hebuterne.	
	13th	9.30 am	Bn Parade. Practical Attack on Wood (Brig de Robermont) reconsideration of ground beyond. 2nd Lt. Lighton proceeded to Doullens on 4 days Course of Sniping.	
	14th	10 A.M.	Inspection of Bn by Divisional Commander (Maj. Gen. R.J. Pinney).	
		5 pm	Bn paraded for practice of Bugaloe.	
	15th	10 am	Bn Church Parade. Lt. Bennett & 2nd Lt M Beckley rejoined from 3rd Army School, Course. Lt. Stearn 9 days Sniping Course. Lt. Betcher, Sgts Tunicliffe & Sutcliffe proceeded to 3rd Army School Course.	
	16th	—	Training of Coys & Specialists as usual. Lt. Col. Wyld & Coy Officers attended a lecture on Tanks at LUCHEUX. ❌	
	17th	—	Training of Coys & Specialists as usual.	
	18th	—	Training of Coys & Specialists as usual. Received orders for Transport to move to TALMAS. Transport moved off under Bn arrangements 11.30 am	
CORBIE	19th	—	Bn moved by Bus (French Buses) to CORBIE. Bn paraded 9.30 am and fell in about 3 pm. (Raining the whole time.) Transport moved from TALMAS to CORBIE & arrived about 9.30 pm.	

WAR DIARY or INTELLIGENCE SUMMARY

Army Form C. 2118.

16th (S) Bn King's Royal Rifle Corps

October 1916

Place	Date	Hour	Summary of Events and Information	Remarks and references to Appendices
CORBIE	20th		Very heavy frost, but turned out a splendid day. Bn rested all day. C.O. attended a conference at Bde H.Qrs. On return to mess all Coy. experienced officers, and gave instructions as operations about to take place, and in which the Bn. should take a part.	
	21st		Bn. paraded at 8.30 a.m. and marched to MEAULTE. Bn. had Bde. Band on the march, the own band played for the first time on march. Arrived at MEAULTE about 1 p.m. Billeted in Village. The Bde. Comdr. Maj. Genl. Pinney saw the Bn. on the march, informed they looked very fit. Lt. Scott proceeded to England on leave.	
MEAULTE	22nd		Bn. marched to MANSEL CAMP. arrived about 12 noon. Took Bn. in Tents, very muddy & extremely cold. Received orders that Bn. would not be moving tomorrow. Capt. LINDSAY recalled from leave. Bde. in Div? Reserve, Div? taking over from 4th Div?	
MANSEL CAMP	23rd		Bn. resting C.O. Coy Comdr. & Batt. officers went up to view lines, we should have to take over, much too muddy for occupation as found out very later. Cap? Denny M.O. returned from leave. Cap? Pilcher M.O. returned to Corps group H.Q. Received orders to be ready to move by 8 a.m. Order to move cancelled. 3.30 p.m. 24th.	
	24th		Bn rested. Received orders to move to BRIQUETERIE CAMP weather and arrangements after yesterday today. Weather still very wet & extremely cold.	
	25th	8 a.m.	Bn. moved to BRIQUETERIE CAMP, rained very heavily. Bn. had to march across country, owing to congestion of the roads. Took me Bivouac nearly knee deep mud, had to set to work to try & improve things a bit, rather difficult job. Cap? Lindsay reported off leave.	
BRIQUETERIE CAMP			Transport remained behind wait [Bde arrangement] Bivouacked E of CARNOY MARICOURT Road.	

Army Form C. 2118.

WAR DIARY or INTELLIGENCE SUMMARY

16th (S) Bn Kings Royal Rifle Corps

October 1916

Place	Date	Hour	Summary of Events and Information	Remarks and references to Appendices
BRICQUETERIE CAMP	26th		Rested at BRICQUETERIE. Raining on and off all day, spent day trying to improve camp.	
	27th		Still raining during night. Found working parties of 8 Officers & 400 men during day working towards front line, laying trench boards for a track.	
	28th		Rather brighter, moved Bivouac nearer to Bde HdQuarters on little piece of ground, found working parties of 4 Officers & 200 men. Capt. Bowes, 2nd Lt Thacker to F.A. exit.	
	29th		Very cold & wet, found working parties of 8 Officers & 300 men. Lt Fardell took over pack mules, to be used for carrying rations forward to front line.	
	30th		Bde took over line 2nd Worcs. & 9 H.L.I. in front line, 16th Bn K.R.R.C. in front line in HOGS BACK, 1st Queens in GUILLEMONT E of LESBOEUFS. C.O. went forward in morning to look at line. Bde were occupying the Right sector of Div front, joined up to the French. Bn moved by companies, Lt Fenton at 10 min. interval to HOGSBACK TRENCH. Very heavy rainstorm during the whole of move. Bn relieved the 20th Bn. R.F. 2nd Lt Jay remained with transport, also Reserve L.M.G's Signallers etc. Relief complete by 5.45 pm.	
HOGS BACK TRENCH T.9.D.2.8. Pt H11.9.6.	31st		Rather finer, men busy trying to drain & improve Hun's trench & better holes from O.W. Hot butter were not to be worn in front system of trenches owing to difficulty of carrying out instructions re prevention of trench feet. Received shelling of Batteries near by otherwise quiet day despite that we observed Retaliation arrived of deck, neither difficult job, or make road on the road.	

Army Form C. 2118.

WAR DIARY or INTELLIGENCE SUMMARY

16th (S) Bn King's Royal Rifles

(Erase heading not required.)

Place	Date	Hour	Summary of Events and Information	Remarks and references to Appendices
HOG'S BACK TRENCH	Nov 1.		Capt. J.R. Smith rejoined Battn. 2/Lt. C.H. Halkins reported from Course.	
LESBOEUF	2.		2/Lt. T.R. Hartell sent to A. Sick. 2/Lt. T.R. Hartell sent to A. Sick. Battn relieved 2 Worcestrs. B Coy in front line. Snow T. Head with 1 Platoon A Coy in Posts Trench. Rest of A Coy in Support at Gun Pits. C & D in Reserve in Gr Trench Bn H.Q. in Sunken road, near Tank, S. of Les Boeufs	
	3.		2/Lt. M. Cork wounded. 1st Queens attack on Boritska Trench assisted by our intense r/f & M. Gun fire on immediate front. C & D Coys took places of Officers & S.O.R. Bn front R.E. in making Strong points. Attack failed — our men were not used	
	4.	7am	Front line evacuated being registration of Enemys Trenches by our Artillery. Positions reoccupied.	
		5pm	D & C Coys relieved B & A Coys respectively. Capt. A.H.M. Webb sent to S.A. Orders issued for attack next day. 2.11 Misty. Mostly reports missing. A & B Coys patrol captured a prisoner. 1/16, 8/1 R.I.R.	
	5.		General attack by 6th French Army in Conjunction with our 4th & 6th Armies 10th Bn attacked BORITSKA & HAZY Trenches 16th KRR & 1st Queens from front & 2 Worcestrs from Rt Flank. Zero Line 11a.m. Heavy Artillery bombarded all localities in rear of Military Boritska Trenches, Rolling barrage in front of flash attack opened at 25 yds per min. Preliminary art'y bombdt	

WAR DIARY or INTELLIGENCE SUMMARY

Army Form C. 2118.

(Erase heading not required.)

Place	Date	Hour	Summary of Events and Information	Remarks and references to Appendices
	6.		Batt. H.Q. remained in Sunken Road. 2 Lt Clonorsley was awarded leading his Platoon. A Lewis gun team remained between our Rt. flank and 2 Lincolns owing to the 1 Queens not attacking. Communication was however established with a Coy of the Lincolns under Capt. Bennett & Capt. Hon. L. Lindsay. Both companies of our line & consolidated positions. 2 Lt Lyston was wounded during consolidation. Casualties were comparatively few. 2 Lt Gray was severely wounded by shell outside Bn H.Q. Letters of hearty congratulation otherwise were received from the Divl. General, t. Bn. General, Special mention being made of Capt. E. P. Bennett 2 Lincoln Regt & Capt. Hon. L. Lindsay 11 KRR Regt. for the example of courage & resolution & for the splendid behaviour of the troops under their commands. With Grey meantime was silently between the civil village	
CARNOY	7	4am	Two prisoners walked into our lines in the early morning, apparently having lost their way. Battn relieved by 2 E. Lancs. Moved to Carnoy Hutts. Our total Casualties during period in line 173 all ranks — 5 Officers.	
		2pm	Last Company arrived at Carnoy hutts. Various huts were visited by G.O.C. Division to congratulate them on their recent success.	
CITADEL CAMP.			Battn left Carnoy Hutts for CITADEL CAMP, which was in a deplorable condition. Bn arrived about 6 pm.	
	8		Battn were issued with new warm clothing & techuis & gloves forgloves	

Army Form C. 2118.

WAR DIARY
or
INTELLIGENCE SUMMARY
(Erase heading not required.)

Instructions regarding War Diaries and Intelligence Summaries are contained in F.S. Regs., Part II. and the Staff Manual respectively. Title Pages will be prepared in manuscript.

Place	Date	Hour	Summary of Events and Information	Remarks and references to Appendices
CITADEL CAMP	9.	11.15 a.m.	Batn inspected by Brig: General. Advanced party moved by road to EDGEHILL STATION en route for HALLENCOURT AREA. 24. OR taken with S.A.	
AIRAINES	10	4 pm	Batn marched to BUIRE + entrained for AIRAINES, arriving about 8 p.m. + marched to CONDE-FOLIE, arriving about 11 p.m. Billets Very Good	
CONDE-FOLIE	11.	2.30 p.m.	Transport arrived about 2.30 p.m. The b/ld received orders to proceed to 4th ARMY H.Q. Following officers appeared in Part I Battn orders M. Module 7975 C.H.S. Trousdale; C.9184/3 W.R. Jeffs; C.676 Lt. Scott D.L.; C.309 Rfn Brown T.; C.138 Rfn J.T. Williams.	
	12	12 m-n	Col. W/d left for 4th Army H.Q. 135 O.R. of 18th Middx attached to 18th. Draft of 152 Rfm joined Battn. Capt. G. Wardlow (wounded) Command of the Batt.	
	13.		Capt Hon S. LINDSAY on a STAFF COURSE. Draft of 33 O.R. arrived. Stay spent in generally cleaning up	
	14		2/Lt Lellins + 6 N.C.O. went on a Bombing Course at Brigade 10. O.R. proceeded on leave. Coys: + Specialist Training as per programme drawn up. Scheme issued by Div. with.	

Army Form C. 2118.

WAR DIARY
or
INTELLIGENCE SUMMARY

(Erase heading not required.)

Place	Date	Hour	Summary of Events and Information	Remarks and references to Appendices
	15.		Batn. commenced Baths. Leave averaging 4 O.R. per diem opened. Batn. played 2 Worcesters in Divisional Cup Competition (Association) + won 4 - 1.	
	16.		Continued baths and Coy: Training as per programme.	
	17.		G.O.C. Division inspected Billets. Baths continued. Coy: + specialist training. Ranges for firing and Bombing Trenches were prepared.	
	18		Training as per programme.	
	19.		Voluntary Church Service provided for. Capt E.M. Gorner rejoined from Hospital.	
	20.		Training as per programme.	
	21.		do	
	22.		Major-General R.J. Pinney (G.O.C. Division) inspected Coys: at work.	
	23		2nd Lt C.E. Howard reported with draft 1 Lt 75 O.R. Capt Lindsay sent to Hospital. 2nd Lt C.W. Jenny rejoined from Hospital.	

Army Form C. 2118.

WAR DIARY
or
INTELLIGENCE SUMMARY
(Erase heading not required.)

Place	Date	Hour	Summary of Events and Information	Remarks and references to Appendices
	24		Coys Specialists training as per programme. Sleigh Bombing accident in Bn. Bombing Class. (Premature Mills No 23) 3 Seigns wounded.	
	25		Batt. played g. H.L.I in Div. Cup (Association) Lost 2 - Nil. Continued training as per programme.	
	26		Voluntary Church Service arranged.	
	27		Commenced Baths again. Training as per programme. 2 Lt S. Jay W.L.A	
	28		Training as per programme Baths cont'd	
	29		" "	
	30		" "	

Army Form C. 2118.

WAR DIARY
or
INTELLIGENCE SUMMARY 16th King's Royal Rifles
(Erase heading not required.)

Vol 14

Place	Date	Hour	Summary of Events and Information	Remarks and references to Appendices
CONDE FOLIE	1.12.16		Capt. Edwards & 53 O.R. reported for duty. Leave at rate of 3 O.R. per Btm still going.	
"	3.12.16		Batt. with 2 Lewis Guns 100th T.M.B. & M.G.Coy. & 101st T.A. attended Church Parade Service. (Blanks) by distribution of ribbons by the G.O.C. Division. M.M. to R.S.M. Trousdale, Sgt. Jeffries, Cp Scott & Rfm Morris.	
			Transport left by road for MORLANCOURT at 8.30 a.m.	
MORLAN COURT	4.12.16		Batt. moved by train from LONGPRE to MERICOURT at 5.15 p.m. & marched to MORLANCOURT arriving about 10.30 p.m.	
	5.		Lt Col. G.T. Lee reported for duty & assumed command of Batt.	
BRAY.	6.		Batt. moved to Camp 112 – 1 mile N.W. of BRAY-SUR-SOMME. Capt. Cockburn R.A.M.C. reported for duty. Batt. moved to Camp 16.	
	7.		" 20, between SUZANNE & MARICOURT.	
	8.			
	9.		Batt relieved 171 Reg. 254 Rd 127 Division French in Reserve line at BOIS DE CRANIERE. 100th Bn took over French Line relieving 37 Reg. XI Division.	

Army Form C. 2118.

WAR DIARY
or
INTELLIGENCE SUMMARY

(Erase heading not required.)

18th King's Royal Rifles

Instructions regarding War Diaries and Intelligence Summaries are contained in F. S. Regs., Part II. and the Staff Manual respectively. Title Pages will be prepared in manuscript.

Place	Date	Hour	Summary of Events and Information	Remarks and references to Appendices
	Dec 11 1916		Battn relieved & supplied. 1 left Battn front of 98th Bde at Pt Gaubert. Owing to 4th Division taking over left Battn of 100th Bde. Trenches here in awful condition. D + C relieving B + A respectively. Inlying relief.	
	13		2nd & 6th (pany arrived to shell in head. Owing to bad conditions sickness was rather high in Battn.	
	14		Battn relieved by 1st Cameronians. Buses met Battn and proceeded to Camp 21 between SUZANNE & MARICOURT.	
	15		Day spent in cleaning up.	
	16		Draft of 112 O.R. reported.	
	17		Voluntary Church service - well attended. Lt Manico sent to L.A. Lt Crafter reports for duty with R.T.C.	
	18		Battn moved to Camp 17 (relieving 2 A & S Highlanders) as Bn in Bde Res.	
	19		Coys engaged in Gas Helmet Drill + working parties.	
	20		" " in working parties. Lt. Lt Chadwick + 2Lt Edgar reports for duty.	
	21		4 Coy Commanders + I.O. visited new front line. - Regt Rel Section joined up with French on Rt at Ancherennes.	

Army Form C. 2118.

WAR DIARY
or
INTELLIGENCE SUMMARY

16th King's Royal Rifles

(Erase heading not required.)

Instructions regarding War Diaries and Intelligence Summaries are contained in F.S. Regs., Part II. and the Staff Manual respectively. Title Pages will be prepared in manuscript.

Place	Date	Hour	Summary of Events and Information	Remarks and references to Appendices
	Dec 22		Battn relieved 1st Queen's Regt in Rt Sub-Section. D. & C. Front B Support A Reserve. Trenches awful condition — no communication with Front line by day	
	23			
	24		Inter Coy relief	
	25			
BRAY-SUR-SOMME	26		Battn relieved by 14th A & S H (40th Division) & proceeded by bus to Camp 14 W of Bray-sur-Somme.	
	27		Battery path under Lt. F.E. Elliott proceeded to AILLY LE HAUT CLOCHER. Transport left at 8.30 a.m.	
AILLY LE HAUT CLOCHER	28		Battn proceeded by road to EDGEHILL Britain at 11.30 p.m.	
	29		AILLY LE HAUT CLOCHER. arriving at 3.30 p.m. 2nd Lts Mitchell sent to F.A. Transport arrived at 3.30 p.m. 2 heats H.E. Holloway & W Sullivan reptd for duty	
	30		General Cleaning up	
	31		Voluntary Church Service	

Bentham Capt
16 Bn
K.R.R.C.

Army Form C. 2118.

WAR DIARY
or
INTELLIGENCE SUMMARY
(Erase heading not required.)

January 1917   16th (S)/Bn. King's Royal Rifles

Vol 15

Place	Date	Hour	Summary of Events and Information	Remarks and references to Appendices
AILLY LE HAUT CLOCHER	1st		General Holiday.	
			Lt. Col. G. T. LEE proceeded on leave to England.	
			Capt. E. WENHAM assumed Command. Lt. L.C. Gidden took over duties of adjt. 2nd Lt. L.B. Forrest reported for duty.	
	2nd		Companies commenced training. Specialist classes formed. Programme drawn up.	
			Capt. (a/) G. Edmonds granted 3 days leave to PARIS.	
	3rd		Officers dug for lines.	
			Coy. & Specialist training carried on. 2nd Lt. C.H. Wilkins & 112 O.R. returned from musketry course (XIV Corps School).	
	4th			
	5th/12	10am	Bn. paraded for Bde. exercise with Contact Aeroplanes at GORENFLOS.	
			2nd Lt. C.G. Sternes proceeded on leave to England.	
	6th		Bde. Commander visited Bn. HQrs. to interview Candidates for Commissions.	
			"A" "B" & "D" Coys. held their Christmas Dinner.	
			Coy. & Specialist training carried on as usual.	
	7th		Voluntary Church parade. Deputy Chaplain General Bishop Gwynne held a Confirmation service at 2.30 p.m.	
			2nd Lt. C.A. Hayes & 2nd Lt. G.D. Brough reported for duty.	
			2nd Lt. C.H. Wilkins & 33 O.R. reported for duty to 33rd Divisional Works Bn.	
			"C" Coy. held their Christmas Dinner.	

Army Form C. 2118.

WAR DIARY
or
INTELLIGENCE SUMMARY

January 1917 *(Erase heading not required.)*

Instructions regarding War Diaries and Intelligence Summaries are contained in F. S. Regs., Part II. and the Staff Manual respectively. Title Pages will be prepared in manuscript.

Place	Date	Hour	Summary of Events and Information	Remarks and references to Appendices
AILLY LE HAUT CLOCHER	8th		Company & Specialist training carried on as usual.	
	9th		Company & Specialist training carried on as usual. 2nd Lt. R. Allen, H.S. Millard & W. Hoult. All Scottish Rifle Officers joined for duty.	
	10th		Bn. paraded for Route march.	
	11th		Coy. & Specialist training as usual. Lt. A. B. Bennard proceeded to England on leave.	
	12th		Coy. & Specialist training as usual. 1 Officer & 1 N.C.O. per Coy. attended a demonstration on "Henry Boy Bayonets" Coy. & Specialist training as usual. Lt. H.B. Smith 7/London Regt. joined for duty.	
	13th		Bn. paraded with the 2nd Bn. Worcester Regt. for Presentation of Medal Ribbons to Pte. T.R. at Ailly, by G.O.C. 33rd Div. Lt. Capt. E. Wenham. Capt. R. Smith received the M.C. 5 O.R. received the M.M. 2nd Lt. R. H. Garrard returned from leave.	

WAR DIARY or INTELLIGENCE SUMMARY

Army Form C. 2118.

January 1917.

Place	Date	Hour	Summary of Events and Information	Remarks and references to Appendices
AILLY LE HAUT CLOCHER	14th	10.15 am	Bn. paraded for Church parade.	
		11 am	Comdg. Officer attended Conference at Bde Hd Quarters. (Staff with Commanding Officers in the Trenches.)	
	15th		Coy & Specialist Training as usual. Capt. G.S. Edwards proceeded on leave to England. Lt. F. Chadwick to F.A.	
	16th		Coy & Specialist Training as usual. 2nd Lt. A.W. Mahony & 12 O.R. reported for duty.	
	17th		Coy & Specialist Training as usual. Bn. Bombers took part in a Bde Bombing exercise in Co. Operation with Lewis gun & Stokes mortars at FAMECHON.	
	18th		Bde Cross Country Run. Bn. represented. 1 Off. & 20 O.R. distance 2 miles. Transport moved under orders of 98th Bde to forming area at 8.30 am. Coys had final overhauling of their parades.	
	19th		Coys parade as usual. Lt. F.C. Einden proceeded to England on leave. 2nd Lt. A.G. Holloway took over duties of Adjutant.	
BRAY.	20th	6.30 am	Bn paraded & marched to LONGPRE and entrained for BRAY. Arrived at BRAY & marched to CAMP 112. 2nd Lt. C.E. Stevens reported from leave.	

Weather during 15th week, has been very cold, with snow.

Army Form C. 2118.

WAR DIARY
or
INTELLIGENCE SUMMARY

(Erase heading not required.)

January 1917

Place	Date	Hour	Summary of Events and Information	Remarks and references to Appendices
BRAY	21st		Voluntary Church. 5 Cands. O.R. reported for duty.	
CAMP 112			Bn. complimented by Brig.Gen. on the condition of the Transport at the inspection held by the D.A.D. & Q.M.G. 33rd Div. 2/Lt. G.T. LEE elects of Hateng of Bn. rd.L of (Medical board). 2/Lt. P. S. L. Spackley reported for duty.	
	22nd		Coy. & specialists carried on drill except on sound. Have snow. Found working party of 1/M.G./ 20 Pln. for unloading dues in BRAY.	
	23rd	12 noon	Battn. moved with Transport to SUZANNE and took over a Bivouac from the French, in a Wood S.W. of SUZANNE. Tents & Dugouts.	
SUZANNE	24th		Spent day in cleaning & improving Bivouac. 2/Lt. A.S. King reported for duty.	
	25th		Carried on Specialist Training. Coy's had inspection parade. Div. & B.de. Commanders visited Bivouac. 7 O.R. joined for duty.	
	26th		Coys. & Specialists carried on training. C.T.O., Coy. Commanders visited Front System, preparing to take over. Weather normal. Support line held by 2nd A.V.S.H. 12/Lt. A.W. Maloney proceeded to LE TOUQUET in charge of Lewis Gun.	
CLERY-SUR-SOMME	27th	7pm	Bn. took over LEFT SECTOR of Div. Front. Bn. relieved 2nd A.V.S.H. in Support line. Relief complete by 2.15am. 28th. Lt. A. B. Bernard rejoined from leave. Weather continued very cold.	

Army Form C. 2118.

WAR DIARY or INTELLIGENCE SUMMARY

January 1917

Place	Date	Hour	Summary of Events and Information	Remarks and references to Appendices
CLERY SUR SOMME	28th		Intermittent shelling of BOUCHAVESNES RAVINE during day. Otherwise quiet. "A" "C" & "D" Companies on working parties in ROAD WOOD. "B" Coy. in VAN TRENCH. Bn. Head Quarters in P.C. LAVAIRVE.	
		8am	Bn. found working parties of 1 NCO & 8 Bn. for Wells pumping.	
		9am	1 NCO & 20 men for work at MIDDLE DUMP B.30 central.	
		6pm	5 Officers and 200 O.R. for digging in ACCARIES AVENUE. Brig. General visited Bn. Head Quarters.	
	29th		2nd Lt. Speakerly proceeded to BOUCHON for course in Lewis Machine Gun. Night fairly quiet. Still freezing, very bright sunny morning. Enemy shelled the BOSCHAVESNES RAVINE very heavily during morning & afternoon with 8"s. A few 77 cm. fell or track near Bn. H.Q. Quarters during morning. "C" Coy. had two men killed at pumping station. Working parties were formed same as yesterday. 2nd A.C.O. Horner & 4 NCO's reported back from Div'l School. 2nd Lt. Gerrard & 4 Bn. reported back from Lewis Gun School BOUCHON.	
	30th		Light snow fell again during night. Found usual working parties. Comdg. Off. & Adjt. (at pres'nt visited Bn. H.Q'trs and arranged for relief. Coy. Commanders visited front line & Companies they are relieving.	

Army Form C. 2118.

WAR DIARY
or
INTELLIGENCE SUMMARY
(Erase heading not required.)

January 1919

Place	Date	Hour	Summary of Events and Information	Remarks and references to Appendices
CLERY -sur- SOMME	31st		Slight snow again during night, still freezing. Snow cleared up the new track to ACCARIES AVENUE very well. Pm. visited the 1st & 2nd Queens in the Right subsector; Bde front. Relief commenced at 6 pm. Specialists: Lewis Guns, Bombers etc. were relieved during daylight. "A", "C" & "D" took over front line, "B" Coy. in support. Relief completed without incident, by 10.15 pm.	

Graham (Capt on) Actg
for Lt Col
Comdg 1st Bn R W Kent Regt

Army Form C. 2118.

WAR DIARY or INTELLIGENCE SUMMARY

16th (S) Battn. King's Royal Rifles

Feb. 1917

(Erase heading not required.)

Place	Date	Hour	Summary of Events and Information	Remarks and references to Appendices
TRENCHES	1.		Battn. in the line.	
	2.		Bde. General visited Bn. H.Qrs. Artillery wire cutting on Battn. front.	
	3.		Lt. Col. A.V. Johnson. R.F. reported and assumed Command of the Battn. Wire cutting continued on Battn. front.	
	4.			
	5.		Battn. relieved by 1st Queens & moved back to Maricourt Huts as Bn. in Bde. Reserve. 2/Lt Spackley returned from L.G. Course.	
	6.			
	7.			
SUZANNE	8.		Battn. relieved by 1/5th S. Riffles & marched back to Bivouacs in Suzanne.	
	9.		Coys held inspection of Arms & clothing. C.O., All Officers, & N.C.O. attended lecture on "Trench System of Fighting Platoon" by Lt.Col Wabon 1st Queens.	
	10.		Lt. Col Galton returned from leave. Capt G.F. Howard proceeded to 4th Army School. Coys: specialed training carried out.	
	11.		C. of E. Parade service at 9.45 a.m. Battn. had Baths & Clean Clothing.	
	12		Part of Battn. issued with NEW Box Respirator. Capt. E. McGennes returned from leave. B Coy practising Fighting Platoon.	

Army Form C. 2118.

WAR DIARY
or
INTELLIGENCE SUMMARY.

(Erase heading not required.)

16th King's Royal Rifles

Feb. 1917

Place	Date	Hour	Summary of Events and Information	Remarks and references to Appendices
SOZANNE	13		All Officers + N.C.Os attended Camp 18 for instruction in use of new Box Respirator.	
	14			
	15		'B' Coy carried out attack on lines of Trench fighting Platoon system	
	16		Battn. relieved 1st Midx left subsector of R. Box Front - Clery Sector	
	17		Enemy's line bombarded on our front	
	18		Draft of 1 Off + 99 O.R. arrived at 'B' Echelon.	
	19		Draft of 2 Lieut. Page + 99 O.R. (Mine) Battn in Trenches. General Baird visited 15t H.Qrs. Capt. E Wenham proceeded on 1 months leave to England Lieut. F.C. Giddens assumed duties of Adjutant B" General visited Br. H.Qrs	
P.C. MERTON	20		Battn. relieved by 1st Queen's - moved back to P.C. Merton in support.	
	21		New General visited Co. Battn. used in fatigues	
	22		" "	
	23		" "	
CLERY SECTOR	24		2 Lt Moloney returned from L.G course Enemy bombarded our lines at 8.30 p.m Battn. relieved 1st Queen's	
	25			
	26		New General + Brig General visited Bn H.Qrs.	

Army Form C. 2118.

WAR DIARY
or
INTELLIGENCE SUMMARY.
(Erase heading not required.)

16th (S) Batn King's Royal Rifles

Feb 1917

Place	Date	Hour	Summary of Events and Information	Remarks and references to Appendices
TRENCHES (CLERY SECTOR)	27		Enemy bombarded our line – (owing a raid being carried out by Batn on our Rt) at 8.45 p.m.	
FRISE BEND	28.		Batn relieved by 1st Queens and moved back as Bn in Bde Reserve at FRIZE	

JM Johnson Lt Col.
King's Royal Rifles
Commanding 16th (S) Batn

Vol 17

No I. March 1917

WAR DIARY
or
INTELLIGENCE SUMMARY.
(Erase heading not required.)

16th (S/Bn) King's Royal Rifles

Army Form C. 2118.

Place	Date	Hour	Summary of Events and Information	Remarks and references to Appendices
FRISE	1st		Bn.HQ Bde Reserve. Supplied fatigue parties.	Ref. map Albert
Bray	2nd		2nd Lt. L.E. HOWARD and two O.R. proceeded to G.H.Q. M.Gun School LE TOUQUET. Supplied fatigue parties.	Albert Contour 1/40000
	3rd		Relieved by 20th Royal Fusiliers, Marched back to Château Camp SUZANNE.	
SUZANNE	4th		Voluntary Church parade.	
	5th		Spent cleaning up.	
CORBIE	6th	9am	Bn. marched to CORBIE. Having dinner on the way, arrived about 3pm and went into Billets on the CORBIE - BRAY Road. 2nd Lt V.S. NORTHAM reported for duty. Capt A.B. BERNARD proceeded to England on duty to interview the War Office.	CORBIE 1/40000
	7th		Day spent in general cleaning up & kitfitting.	
	8th		Bn. at disposal of M.G. Corps. 2nd Lt C.V. MILLER & 123 O.R. cadres reported for duty.	
	9th		Bn. at disposal of M.G. Corps.	
	10th		G.O.C. Division Major General J.R. PINNEY inspected Bn. in the afternoon. 2nd Lt C.E. HOWARD & 2 O.R. returned from M.G. Corps. Programme of Training sent to 13th Bde.	
	11th		Church Parade. Lt C. STERN proceeded to Telescopic Sight School. 2nd Lt F.J. PEACOCK & 2nd Lt. G.M. WELSFORD reported for duty.	
	12th		Bn. Route March.	

Army Form C. 2118.

WAR DIARY
or
INTELLIGENCE SUMMARY.

(Erase heading not required.)

Place	Date	Hour	Summary of Events and Information	Remarks and references to Appendices
CORBIE	13th		Coy. Specialist training as per programme. 66 O.R. reported 18th from Div. Works Bn.	
	14th		Coy. Specialist training. Insp. of Transport by Brig. General. 2nd Lt. C.H. Wilkin reported from Cadre, and Div. Works Bn.	
	15th		Coy. Specialist training. Capt. A.B. Renard reported back from duty leave. 38 OR pr Canada reported back for duty.	
	16th		Coy. Specialist training. All officers NCOs attended lecture by R.E. officer on "Consolidation & Defence of a village" Part of B. inoculated.	
	17th		Coy. Specialist training. Br. Band Battn. Capt. C.J. Edwards returned from 4th Army School.	
	18th		Church parade. Drafts put through Lachrymatory Gas Chamber.	
	19th	9.20 a.m.	Bn. Route March. Details Bathed. 500 Blankets disinfected.	
		2.30 p.m.	All officers NCOs meet C.O. for Trench sitting.	
	20th		Coy. Specialist training. 1000 Blankets disinfected.	
	21st		Coy. Specialist training. 250 Blankets disinfected. 2nd Lt. Peacocke sent to F.A.	
	22nd		Coy. Specialist training. Capt. E. Wenham returned from leave & took over duties of 2nd in Command, with All officers & NCOs per Coy. attached lecture by R.E. officers on R.E. subjects.	

Army Form C. 2118.

WAR DIARY
or
INTELLIGENCE SUMMARY.
(Erase heading not required.)

Title pages March 1917

Place	Date	Hour	Summary of Events and Information	Remarks and references to Appendices
CORBIE	23rd		Coy. & Specialist training.	
	24th		Coy. & Specialist training. Company Officers Capt. T.R.Smith & 120 O.R. attended instruction of Initial Ritual by Capt. Commander. Prior to the Corps Commander being too busy to come, the addressing of the instruction was instead taken by 2nd Lt. B.H. Maloy to Lt.Col. the Divisional Commander.	
	25th		Coy. & Specialist training. C.O. & 100 Officers & O.R. attended lecture on Bayonet fighting by Capt. Huntington.	
	26th			
	27th	5.15 p.m.	All officers & Sgts. per Coy. attended lecture on support by Comdg. Officer.	
			Coy. Specialist training. Pm allotted depths lecture of interlocking.	
	28th		Coy. Specialist training "C" & "D" Coys. on long range.	
	29th		Bn. Support scheme.	
	30th		Bn. Route march with Transport.	
	31st		Coy. & Specialist training "A" & "B" Coys. on long range.	

J.W. Moore
Maj.
Comdg. 10th (S) Bn.
King's Royal Rifle Corps

WAR DIARY or INTELLIGENCE SUMMARY

Army Form C. 2118.

Vol / 8

16th (S) Bn King's Royal Rifles

April 1917

Place	Date	Hour	Summary of Events and Information	Remarks and references to Appendices
CORBIE	1st		Bn Church parade. Orders received that Bn should be moving 2nd	
BERTANGLES	2nd	9.40 am	Bn marched to BERTANGLES arriving about 2 pm. Billets quite good. Eight men fell out from marching, caused chiefly out of their hostnails & hob nails. 2nd Lt. EDGAR returned from troops. Fairly heavy thunderstorm came on a/c arrival in billets.	
BEAUVAL	3rd	9.25 am	Bn marched to BEAUVAL about 10 miles arriving at 2 pm. First day, men marched. Billets good, two men fell out. Ten P.R. reported to Ed.? A.M.Pa. for ammunition. Camping for XII Corps Railway.	
BARLY	4th	9 am	Bn marched to BARLY via DOULLENS, about 10 miles arriving about 12.30 pm. Billets very poor. One man fell out during march roads very bad a/c leaving DOULLENS. 2nd Lt. PEACOCKE rejoined Bn from hospital.	
	5th	10.25 am	Bn marched to MONDICOURT about 12 miles arriving about 4.30 pm. Three men fell out. Billets fairly good. Received orders that Bde would not be moving the 6th.	? Map LENS 1/10,000
MONDICOURT	6th	—	Bn marched part of "A"&"B" Coys. billeted. Lt. C. E. STEARNS admitted to F.A. C.S.M. HASSALL 447 D.O. departed to Depth. Bn (ST. POL.)	
MONDICOURT	7th	8.55 am	Bn marched to SOUASTRE about 6 miles, arrived at 11.20 am. No men fell out. Men were chiefly in huts.	
SOUASTRE	8th		Bn marched to within ½ mile of BIENVILLERS, halted for about 1 hr. had to return to SOUASTRE owing to there being no accommodation at BIENVILLERS. Comdg Officer & 4 Coy Comm.Prs reconnoitred the line in front of "C" & "D" Coys SWITCH (SCARPE VALLEY). Three days iron rations & ammunition were shown to operations. Received the forthcoming operations, ie Z — 1 day.	

A 5834 Wt. W4973/M687. 750,000 8/16. D. D. & L. Ltd. Forms/C.2118/13

Army Form C. 2118.

WAR DIARY
or
INTELLIGENCE SUMMARY.
(Erase heading not required.)

April 1917

Instructions regarding War Diaries and Intelligence Summaries are contained in F.S. Regs., Part II. and the Staff Manual respectively. Title pages will be prepared in manuscript.

Place	Date	Hour	Summary of Events and Information	Remarks and references to Appendices
SOUASTRE	9th		Bn. remained at SOUASTRE. Received orders that Bn. were under Seventh Army district to move. All Government transport & extra clothing handed into Bn.e Store at BIENVILLERS. Also all spare kits were re-inventoried.	Map Ref. LENS 1/100.000
	10th		Coys at disposal of O.C. Coys. Training carried on.	
	11th		Coys at disposal of O.C. Coys. Heavy fall of snow.	
	12th		Orders received that the Bn. would be moving 13th inst.	
MERCATEL	13th	10-15 am	Bn. moved to MERCATEL area & took over Bivouacs & Shelters from 1st Cameronians. Orders received that Bn. were in Divisional Reserve. Bright. General visited Bn. at HdQrs. Bn. at TR. 2nd & St Bn. R.S. 3rd in TR.	
	14th		100 TR. B.A.B. C.XII. relieved 16th Bn. New RIFle Co'ds burnt. 2 HdQrs. & 100 TR. in fatigue. Coudy. Officers had conference of O.C. Coys. Contest at 18th HdQrs. Received information that Bn. were relieving 21st Division in the 7th Corps, and that Bn. would move 15th inst.	
MOYENNE VILLE	15th		Bn. moved to MOYENNEVILLE as Bn. in Brig.e Reserve. 1st Queens in support 2nd Norfolks & 9th H.L.I in line. 100th R.G. relieved Che 11.0 of the 110e Bn. in the Right Sector N.t CROISELLES. Bn. found village destroyed & occupied standing shelters new one. Ample material being found, the men were soon comfortable.	

Army Form C. 2118.

No 3

Instructions regarding War Diaries and Intelligence
Summaries are contained in F. S. Regs., Part II.
and the Staff Manual respectively. Title pages
will be prepared in manuscript.

WAR DIARY
or
INTELLIGENCE SUMMARY.
(Erase heading not required.)

April 1917

Place	Date	Hour	Summary of Events and Information	Remarks and references to Appendices
MOYENNE VILLE	16th		3 Officers & 150 O.R. on road fatigue under R.E. This fatigue was cancelled owing to bad weather.	
	17th		Comdg. Officer attended Conference at Bde. Hd Qrs Dro. 2nd/7th C.G. Howard & 2 Platoons for Observation Post.	
	18th		3 Officers & 150 O.R. on road fatigue under R.E.	
	19th		Comdg. Officers & 4 Coy. Comdrs went to look over line of Left Bde. 3 Officers & 150 O.R. on road fatigue under R.E. 350 O.R. Bathed at COURCELLES. 2nd Lt Garrard on duty Div. O.P. in relief of Lt Howard.	
	20th		"B" & "C" Coys relieved 2 Coys 1st Queens in Railway cutting T.27.c.4.0 & T.28.a. Comdg Officer Comdg, Coys & ratns, moved Camp on completion of relief. ST LEGER	
	21st		Comdg. Officer & 2 Officers per Coy made reconnaissance - preparatory to Bn. taking part in General attack in HINDENBERG LINE "A" & "D" Coys moved up to Railway Cutting ST LEGER. "B" Echelon of 1st Reinforcement consisting of 2 Coy Comdrs 2 2nd Lt's & 1 Coy Serjeant & 100 O.R. chiefly specialists under command of Major E. WENHAM remained at MOYENNEVILLE	
CROISILLES	22nd	8 pm	Order received for "B" & "C" Coys to move up to Sunken Rd N of CROISSILLES as supporting Companies to 1st Queens, & to come under the orders of O.C. 1st Queens.	
		11.15 pm	Bn Hd Qrtrs & "A" & "D" Coys turned to Sunken at 11.15 pm Pd. in silence.	

WAR DIARY or INTELLIGENCE SUMMARY

Army Form C. 2118.

April 1917

Place	Date	Hour	Summary of Events and Information	Remarks and references to Appendices
CROISILLES	23rd		The attack was carried out by the 100th Inf Bn on the right whilst the 98th Bn on the left. The 98th Inf Bn were to work down the HINDENBERG LINE from the north to the SENSÉE RIVER. The 100 B.J. Bn objective being the HINDENBERG LINE front & support trenches from SENSÉE River to Communication trench on contour 80. The 1st phase supported by "B" & "C" Coys. 16th KRRB carried out the attack. "A" & "D" Coys were in reserve. The 2nd Wave of 9th H.L.I. went to reinforce our forward positions holding the support line. 100 M.G. Coy & 3 sections 19th M.G. Coy were to cover the advance	Ref map S/8. S.W. 1/20,000.
		12.45 am	Bn HQrs & "A" & "D" Coys mobile allotted to the 100 B.J. Bde & kind by the 98th Bde. Position of 5"? jt quickly under 2 jt King field assembled in the Quarry T.18.d.10.8.	
		3.30 am	"B" & "C" Coys under command of Capt. E.M. GONNER and Capt. A.B. BERNARD moved to position of deployment in two ranks east at 50 paces interval following the rear wave of the 12th Queen at 100 yards. On arriving at position of deployment they lay down in one Coy on each side of road. These Coys reached objective S.A.A. tanks and their objective when the German front line	
		4.25 am	At 20 minutes before zero the whole moved forward and lay down with the leading wave on front running through T.O.7.C.4.4.	
		4.45 am	At zero the whole moved forward to the contact mine to within 80 yards of range when it lifted from German front line. The German front line was reached with little difficulty and a few wounded prisoners taken. It was reported that the 2nd Line had also been taken but they were enfiladed. A report came down to Bn HQ that this 2nd Line was a strong M.G post.	
		7.20 am	In front "A" Coy 2nd Lieut Lewis Gunners were sent up with a storage of gunmixture and about 1300 rounds.	

Army Form C. 2118.

WAR DIARY
or
INTELLIGENCE SUMMARY.
(Erase heading not required.)

April 1917

Place	Date	Hour	Summary of Events and Information	Remarks and references to Appendices
CROISS ILLES.	23rd	8.25 am	Message were received from "B" & "C" Coys that more bombs were needed, and that Artillery Barrage was wanted on German 2nd line.	Ref. Maps 51.B.S.W. 1/20,000
		8.45 am	The platoon of "D" Coy under 2nd Lt. HOLLOWAY went forward with 4 Bo. bombs.	
		11 am	Report received from 2nd Lt. Jacobs that more Lewis Gun ammt. was required. A party of "D" Coy under 2nd Lt. HOWATT moved up with 54 buckets.	
		12.15 pm	Telephone to further request, 40 boxes of bombs were taken up by a party of "D" Coy under Capts. OATES & PEACH	
		1 pm	The types of bombs were later up by a party of H.Q.Tr under Lt. CLEMENTS.	
		2.30 pm	Regiment took peace away to hast of bombs and failure of tanks to get up. The 9oth Bn. on the left were stills up, but had not got up, meanwhile a message received that a party of 1 Officer and 12 O.R's under 2nd Lt. FORREST	
		3.20 pm	were still in the German trench, which was across the line of advance between the Sunny & German Line. There were orders to retire in their 157 During the whole of the operation the position of Jumeny (Enemy) was under intermittent shell fire which caused a certain amount of casualties.	
		9 pm	The Bn. moved back to Summy Bernard W. of ST LEGER. Capt. E.M. CONNER A.B. BERNARD 2nd Lt. SPRECKLEY, were reported Wounded & missing 2nd Lt. GERRARD Killed, 5 other officers were wounded, the casualties OR's were about 260. The German barrage was very heavy at times, and our Counter were light, Consequently the amount of open ground the Coy. were particularly	

Army Form C. 2118.

WAR DIARY
or
INTELLIGENCE SUMMARY.
(Erase heading not required.)

April 1917

Instructions regarding War Diaries and Intelligence Summaries are contained in F.S. Regs., Part II. and the Staff Manual respectively. Title pages will be prepared in manuscript.

Place	Date	Hour	Summary of Events and Information	Remarks and references to Appendices
St LEGER	24th		G.O.C. Division visited Bn Hd Qrs. and thanked the Comdg Off. for the splendid work done by the Bn during the attack	Ref. Map S/B. S.W 1/20 000
	25th	4pm	Bn relieved by 9th Seaforths and moved thence about 9 pm. "B" echelon moved from MOYENNEVILLE at 2 pm & arrived BERLES-au-BOIS about 6.30 pm. Billets fairly good.	
BERLES au BOIS	26th		Bn commenced cleaning clothing 8 Officers & 33 O.R. moved for Canadian Reports for duty from Depôt. Bn. Officers' names. Lts. J.E. FRANCIS. CHADWICK. 2nd Lt. SULLIVAN-HOPE. HILL. THOMAS CORK. KINSLEY. Lt FRANCIS took over command of "C" Coy. 2nd Lt. CORK "B" Coy.	Ref. map LENS 1/100 000
	27th		Bn refitting. Bn had use of Baths. Bn Photo. Comdg Officers told Bn that the G.O.C. had said of the work performed. Coy Training. Specialists classes commenced. Short Range made. Bn finished Bathing	
	28th	10.30 am	Bn Church parade.	
	29th			
	30th		Coy & Specialist Training. "A" Coy. 50yd Range. Orders received that Bn is to move tomorrow 1st May.	

[signatures]

WAR DIARY or INTELLIGENCE SUMMARY

Army Form C. 2118.

16th (S) Bn. King's Royal Rifle Corps

May 1917

Place	Date	Hour	Summary of Events and Information	Remarks and references to Appendices
BERLES au BOIS	1st	9.40 am	Bn. marched to BLAIRVILLE. Then Bivouacked amongst the ruins. Draft of 6 to 7 O.R. joined Bn.	Map Ref. L E N S 1/100,000
BLAIRVILLE	2nd	12.55 pm	Bn. marched to MOYENNEVILLE. Lt TWL LIPSCOMB proceeded to England on leave. 2nd Lt A.S. KING took over duties of I.T.O. 2nd Lt FORREST & HOLLOWAY & 60 O.R. rejoined Bn. from Burial party duties.	
MOYENNE VILLE	3rd		General attack by I, III & VII Armies. 33rd Div - Corps Reserve. A Draft of 160 O.R. reported at midnight.	
	4th		G.O.C. Quiz held a Conference when all officers sleeps who were platoon leaders on April 23rd to discuss operations. C.O. & 2nd Lts U Boyd & A2 conference after. Coy specialist training. Commenced special training of all Bombing Rifle Grenade leaders of the under Bn. Bombing Officer.	
	5th		Coy specialist training carried on. "A" Coy on miniature Range.	
	6th		Bn. Church parade.	
	7th		Coy specialist training. B Coy on Range. Lt L.E. FRANCIS & 1 Sergt & 3 Army School.	
	8th		Bn. attacked with Gasoline.	
	9th		Coy specialist training. "C" Coy on Range. C.O. attended M.G. conference at AYETTE.	

Army Form C. 2118.

WAR DIARY
or
INTELLIGENCE SUMMARY.
(Erase heading not required.)

May 1917

Place	Date	Hour	Summary of Events and Information	Remarks and references to Appendices
MOYENNE VILLE	10th		Coy. afternoon Training. "D" Coy to Range. Platoon Bombing Instr. under Bn Bomb. Off. C.O. & Coy Officers 2nd & 4th & Coy Officers went to reconnoitre line of Rly. Posts. ST LEGER R.	Ry Map St. B. SW
	11th	2.30 pm	Bn. less "Bücheken" and "D" Companies move to ST LEGER to Bivs in R/W R... (relieving 9th Br Fusiliers) Bn in Billets	51. B. SW 1/20,000
ST LEGER	12th		1st Rly & "D" Coln moved in Busses W. of HAMELINCOURT. 2nd R H BEDGAR took over duties of Town Major MOYENNEVILLE	
	13th		Bn. remained at ST. LEGER	
	14th		Voluntary Church service Bn. still at ST LEGER. Cmdg Officers 1/5 Scottish Rifles visited Bn H. & ... was being relieved. At different intervals from Coys	
	15th		Bn. relieved by 1/5 Scottish Rifles, & marched back to MOYENNEVILLE	
MOYENNE VILLE	16th	7 pm	C.O. & 2nd & 4th Comd's invited lines on front of CROISILLES, and reconnoitred assembly places Spaces of assembly.	
		2.30 pm	Cmdg Officers & 2 Coy Cmdrs attended conference at Bgde H.Q. 9th Div re Manoeuvres on the 17th. Manoeuvre came on postponed operation would go ahead.	
	17th		Coys at Company Viva voce. drg Cmd's Committee	
	18th		Capt. Commands Hunter Met H. Riffen to Major & Regt. commanded units for 23-4-17. Bgde attached HQ Corps 4.9.32 Commanders present.	

WAR DIARY or INTELLIGENCE SUMMARY

Army Form C. 2118.

May 1917

Place	Date	Hour	Summary of Events and Information	Remarks and references to Appendices
MOYENNE VILLE	19th	9.30 a.m.	Bn. Bombing attack. Conference held with all Coy. & Operation Commanders. Orders received for operations taking place 20th inst. The retirement of the enemy was believed to be imminent if not already in progress to the BEAUMONT-DROCOURT Line. The 33rd Div. will carry out an attack on the 20th inst. with the object of securing the HINDENBERG Front and support lines, between the points where the 98th Inf. Bde. blocks are established in them, thus N. of the SENSÉE River, and the boundary of posts E. of and parallel to the Lupoyart Line with a defensive flank on the right (R.H., has on touch with the LEFT Division of the 5th Army. The Bde. will establish the defensive flank. It will be carried out by the 19th Inf. Bde. The centre attack by the 100th Inf. Bde. and the left by the 98th Inf. Bde. The attack to be made by the 19th I. Bde. will be carried out by the 2nd Worco. Regt. The Glasgow Highlanders and the 16th K.R.R.C. in that order from right to left. The 1st A. Queens will attend special orders will be issued in due course providing the garrisons of posts (Nos. 1 & 2) held by Right Res. 19th I. Bde. The frontages of attack, assembly areas allotted to the attacking battalions and division on attached sketch had to correspondence with verbal instructions already given on the ground to Comdg. Officers concerned.	
		9-15 p.m.	Bn. paraded moved to position of assembly under Maj. Mepham. Packs were carried in place of havresacks, each man carrying helmet, steel emergency ration, one preserved ration, one flare, 2 sandbags, extra rations in Rez., N hills very bright; every man other than a Bomber carried 170 rds. of S.A.A. 200 throwers were distributed amongst the Bn.	
		11.40 p.m.	Bn. arrived at position of assembly without casualties.	

WAR DIARY or INTELLIGENCE SUMMARY

Army Form C. 2118.

Place	Date	Hour	Summary of Events and Information	Remarks and references to Appendices
	May 1917		The CO Dr. Officers "B" Echelon & 1st Reinforcements remained at HAMELINCOURT	No 4
CROISILLES	30th	4.15 a.m.	The attack was carried out by the 1st, no under Objective being the HINDENBURG Front Support lines from the FONTAINE-CROISILLES Road inclusive to a point about 700 yds S.E. of that road. "C" Coy on the (2/Lt Bamford) on left, and "B" Coy under (Capt Chadwick) on right formed the first two waves, they were not extended into 4 waves of sections an extended order. Their objective being the HINDENBURG Front line and Strong point to left for 1/10,000 The 3rd & 4th waves "D" Coy on left under (Capt Smith) "A" Coy on right under (Capt Edwards) Objective being HINDENBURG Support line were formed up in line of column of sections in single file.	Ref map 51.B.3.N.W 1/10,000
		4.45 a.m.	At Zero-30 the fire was formed up ready to advance, on a frontage of 136+ open ammunition had been issued out. 2 L.M.Guns were attached	
		5.3 a.m.	As the attack on the front line was to be a surprise there was no artillery	Printed No 2
		4.3 a.m.	At Zero-12 The first waves advanced opening out to 25+ between 1st & 2nd waves + 70+ between 2nd & 3rd 25+ between 3rd & 4th. The advance was by the right and two adjusting to the left, the idea being to clear the FONTAINE-CROISELLES Road with the left of 1st Wave where this Front line crossed it. Enemy no resistance	attached
		5-5.a.m.	At Zero-10 The 3rd & 4th waves advanced 100y+ behind 3rd & 4th wave opening out to 25+ interval between sections on the move. The enemy was very nearly and the 1st Objective was reached without resistance. Our Artillery barrage commenced, The 18 Pounders playing on the Support line for 15 minutes and Valley in vicinity of Bn HQ Quarter (at where formerly)	

Army Form C. 2118.

WAR DIARY or INTELLIGENCE SUMMARY

(Erase heading not required.)

May 1917.

Place	Date	Hour	Summary of Events and Information	Remarks and references to Appendices
CROISILLES	10th		A party of 3 officers & 40 O.R. of the 1st Queens were allotted to Bn. for carrying purposes. Section of 222 # Coy R.E. and 2 Vickers Guns of 100th M.G. Coy also attached.	
		6.40 am	Message received from OC "C" Coy stating 6-15 am. Q. track south of Kings on left strong patrols in our hands.	
		6.30 am	Message from OC "B" Coy. 1st Objective gained in track south of H.L.1. on right.	
		7.17 am	Situation was "D" & "A" Coys driven back on front line, which was being held by "C" & "B" Coys. Both Commanders of leading Coys. Casualties – only one officer being left to with both Coys. Capt. J.C. Smith reported killed 2nd Lt. Edwards wounded 2nd Lt. Forrest } missing Prescott } Hamilton } wounded	
		7.30 am	Mules & Band Stokes moved up at Bn. H.Q. Quarries at H. 11.	
		9 am	Situation was Bn. holding HINDENBURG Front line & retain positions in front in track with H.L.1. On right and a detachment of "A" Coy on left. Position small. Heavy enemy artillery fire. Telephonic communication established. Lt. Beechan slightly wounded remained on duty.	
		10 am	Orders received to prepare for further advance some time later. Strength of Bn. at this time approximately 8 off. 260 O.R. Orders sent to Coys to reorganize & prepare to comply with this order.	
		11 am	R.E. detachment sent up to assist in consolidation.	
		12.35 pm	Report received that aeroplanes state HINDENBURG Support line was not occupied. Patrols sent out to verify. They reported the line was now held by the enemy.	

2449 Wt. W14957/Mgo 750,000 1/16 J.B.C. & A. Forms/C.2118/12.

WAR DIARY or INTELLIGENCE SUMMARY

Army Form C. 2118.

Place: CROISILLES
Date: May 1917

Place	Date	Hour	Summary of Events and Information	Remarks and references to Appendices
CROISILLES	2nd	3.25 pm	Info received that further advance would not take place and that existing line and posts were to be further strengthened.	
		4 pm	One Pl. 19. J. Bn. arrived on Trolley followed by one the shortly afterwards.	
		5.45 pm	Message received that an attack would be made by the 3 Bns through our position on the H. Support Line. These orders were sent up to Coys. with orders to assist in every way they could.	A/A 2 b
		7.15 pm	1 Pl. of the 19. J. B. advanced from line of deployment used by us in the morning. Estimated Casualty report sent in 5 Officers 350 O.R.	
		7.30 pm	Bn. Barrage started. Enemy retaliated on Trolley & Railway in vicinity of Bn. & J. Bn. HQ.	
		8 pm	About 60 prisoners passed Bn. Hd. Quarters. Lt. H.B. Smith reported killed & wounded. Very little news could be got from the firing of our line.	
		10 pm	Heavy rain. Enemy continued compans situation. HINDENBURG front captured. Some parts of Communication N. of FONTAINE Rd.	
		2.30 am	Parties of 2. R. F. in front of L. of C. Lt. F.C. Eaddis wounded Bn. HQ parties.	
	3rd	5.30 am	Situation fairly quiet from 12 M.N. until 5.30 a.m. when enemy put down a barrage of all calibres on our front line.	
		6 am	All quiet again	
		9 am	Situation that established. Bn. preparing salvage dumps.	

Army Form C. 2118.

WAR DIARY
or
INTELLIGENCE SUMMARY

(Erase heading not required.)

No 7.

Title Pages May 1917.

Place	Date	Hour	Summary of Events and Information	Remarks and references to Appendices
CROISILLES	31st	1 pm	Four Vickers Gun positions had been prepared. Situation normal	A/A 22 9 attached
		7.30 pm	Orders received from BnHQ. Reorganization of front Coys notified. The journey of distribution was made during the night. No trest was obtained. Coy started 30 g.s to the right taking over all posts held by the 19th G. Regt on our front. The 12th Queens relieved the	
		8.1.1	on our right and joined up with our officer killed 2. wounded 3. men 12. Estimated casualty list—	
		8.45 pm	The Rations arrived for the 22nd w/les. H. Jepson and Merchett 20. thanks to.	
			all got up to the front Coys. by 12 M.N. Intermittent shelling going on all evening.	
22nd	1.40 am	Message received from Bn. that relief was complete. Situation on the front quiet. Disposition of Coy.	
	6		"C" Coy. Lewis line of posts along the front of	
			H. Support line "B" Coy garrisoned at "A" & "D" Coy holding	
			H. Fort line. Raining.	
		5.30 am	Division was quiet, sniping continued from left.	
		12.30 pm to 5.20 pm	Patrols were sent out to see if the H. support line was occupied. on return they reported they could see no movement in the line & no Machine Gun or rifle fire. Further patrols were sent out to verify this, they found the line dead, dashes to Coy and after a lodgement were cancelled.	
		9.15 pm	Orders received that Bn. moved be relieved that night, movement of Enemy were brought in during day.	

WAR DIARY or INTELLIGENCE SUMMARY

Army Form C. 2118.

May 1917

Place	Date	Hour	Summary of Events and Information	Remarks and references to Appendices
CROISELLES	22nd	5.45 pm	Officers of the 6th Bn N.F. arrived to make arrangements re relief.	A.A.243 Copy attached
		5.40 pm	Transport arrived from Bde. Hdqrs re relief sent to Coys.	
			Sergeants clothing of Lewis & Gunnery pct arriving Guides sent to join 12 Coy arrived. Report received.	
		11-15 to 2.45 am		
	23rd	2.45 am	At 2.45 am the Batt. had completed G MOYENNEVILLE by platoons on relief and all arrived without casualties, relief complete by 5 am. Total Casualties sent in for operation period 20th to 22nd:
Capt. J. R. Smith Killed 20-5-17 Other Ranks Killed 23
2nd Lt. H.B. Smith " " Wounded 133
Capt. F.G Edwards Wounded " Wounded at duty 5
2nd Lt. W. Hogart " 21-5-17 Missing 5
Lt. Adgett F.C. Gidvin " 20-5-17 Wounded at duty 5
2nd Lt. L.B. Lorant Missing 20-5-17 ———
Lt. E.F. Pencock Missing 20-5-17 Total 229
Lt. H.K. Beedan Wounded
(Chg. Officer) Missing at duty 21-5-17	
	24th		Coys. Resting. Holiday up to P.
Coys at disposal of O.C. Coys respecting.
Visit by Bn Commdr. Brig G. Wright done Commandes during day Bn completion CQA. OR during operations 7.5.6 222	

WAR DIARY or INTELLIGENCE SUMMARY

Army Form C. 2118.

May 1917

Place	Date	Hour	Summary of Events and Information	Remarks and references to Appendices
MOYENNE VILLE	25th		Coy. at disposal of O.C. Coy. for refitting.	
	26th		Coy. at disposal of O.C. Coy. 1st 80 F.P. Jones. Moved pt. cannot. 23 hen hors.	
	27th		Reinforcements proceeded down to "B" Echelon near HAMELINCOURT. Bn. moved to JUDAS FARM area at 11 pm.	
	28th	9.30 pm	Bn. did not move. Voluntary Church Parades. Comm Offrs. attended Conference at 18th Bde Hrs. Bn. moved to CROISILLES & became Bn. in Bde Reserve.	
CROISILLES	29th	9.30 pm	"B" Coy. attached to 2nd Worc. and moved up to front line. had two casualties on way up.	
	30th	9 am	"C" & "D" Coys formed carrying parties for Trench Mortar Battery. Working parties formed by "A" "C" & "D" Coys.	
		4 pm	Comm.g Offrs. 16th Bn. Lincolns arrived 3.30 pm. to arrange relief.	
		6 pm	"B" Echelon moved to MOYENNEVILLE.	
	31st		Bn. relieved by 1st & 18th Lincolns (relief completed by 6.15 pm.) "B" Coy. were relieved last. Marched back to MOYENNEVILLE. Commenced down march 2nd Worcs.	

J.S.Johnston Lt. Col.

P 27

100th Inf Bde

Report on operations of May 20–22, 1917

On the evening of the 19/5/17, the Bn was in bivouac at MOYENVILLE. At 9.15 pm the Batn left their bivouacs for the posn of Assembly, arriving there at 11.40 pm.

Zero hour was fixed for 5.15 am. At 4.15 am the Batn moved to posn of Deployment & formed up with the 2 leading Coys in 4 waves. C Coy (2/Lt BROUGH) on left and B Coy (Lt CHADWICK) on right. Their objective being the Hindenburg front line from Fontaine Rd to a point about 400x S. of same. D Coy (Capt SMITH) on left & A Coy (Capt EDWARDS) on right formed 3rd & 4th waves. objective – Hindenburg Support line on same frontage. Coys were in this formation by Zero – 30'.

At 0 – 12' (5.3 am) 1st Coys advanced
— 0 – 10 (5.5 am) 2nd —"—

2/
The morning was very misty and the first objective was gained with practically no resistance. Very shortly after O the Enemy barrage came down, & the Valley near Bn HQ was heavily shelled.
At 6.40 am message recd, timed 6.15 am that we had joined with 4th Kings on left.
At 6.50 message recd that we were in touch with H.L.I on right.
At 7.12 am situation was:—
H.A Coys driven back on front line which was being held by B & C Coys. Both Commanders of leading Coys were Casualties, only one Officer being left with the 2 Coys.
At 7.20 Mules & limbers arrived at Bn HQ with bombs.
At 9 am posn was:—
Battn holding H front line & chain of posts in front, in touch with H.L.I. on right & Detachment of 98th Bde on left. Posn under heavy Enemy Art: fire. Telephone Commn with front line Established.
At 10 am Orders received to prepare for further attack on H. Support

3/ line some hours later. Strength at this time 8 Offrs & 260 OR.
Orders sent to & reorganize & prepare to comply with above —

At 11 am R.E. party was sent up to assist in consolidation —

At 12.35 pm report received that Aeroplanes state that H. Support line was not occupied — Patrols were sent out who reported that H. Support was occupied by Enemy —

At 3.25 pm orders received that further advance would not take place & that existing line & posts were to be further strengthened —

At 4 pm One Bn 19th Bde arrived at Quarry, followed shortly afterwards by a Second —

At 5.45 pm message rec'd that an attack would be made by these 2 Bns through our pos'n onto the H. Support line — these orders were communicated to our Coys in front.

At 7.15 pm the 2 Bns 19th I.B. moved forward thar advance beyond the line held by us being covered by our Lewis Guns pushed forward to front & left flank.

4/ At 7.30 pm Our Barrage Started, & Enemy's retaliation was severe on Quarry & Valley in rear.
At 12 m.n Situation in Bt front line normal. Sniping continual. Situation in front appeared to be confused.
Until 5.30 a.m 21st the Situation was quiet, when Enemy put down barrage on our position, till 5.45 a.m – By 6.am all quiet again.
At 9.am Situation quiet – Consolidation progressing & Salvage dumps established.
At 1.pm message received that posts for 4 Vickers Guns had been prepared – Situation normal.
On receipt of orders for reorganization of front, the following redistribution was made during the night. The Battn front was shortened by about 30 yds on the right – taking over all posts held by 19th I.B on our front. The final distribution was 3 Coys in Bt front line – 1 Coy & in posts in front.
Rations for 22nd were got up to the Coys by 12 m.n.
The relief was complete by 2.45 am 22nd.

5/ At 5.30 am situation was quiet, but sniping continuous from left. At 12.30 pm patrols were sent out to see if H. Support line was occupied. They reported that they could see no movement in the line — & no rifle or MG fire. A further patrol was sent out to verify this, who found that the line was held, and orders to effect a lodgement were cancelled. Orders were received at 2.15 pm that the Bn. would be relieved that night. Relief started at 11.15 pm & was completed by 2.45 am 23rd & the Battn. marched to MOYENVILLE.

Johnson Lt Col
Cdg 16 KRR

In the field
24-5-17

P.2/8

100th Inf Bde.   No. 7
                                  209

Herewith report on Operations
on 20 – 22 May 1917

                    [signature]
24/5/17   Lt Col 16 KRR

"A" Form.
MESSAGES AND SIGNALS.
Army Form C. 2121
No. of Message ....

Prefix ...... Code ...... m.	Words	Charge	This message is on a/c of:	Recd. at .... m.
Office of Origin and Service Instructions.	Sent		.... Service.	Date ....
....	At .... m.			From ....
....	To			
....	By		(Signature of "Franking Officer.")	By ....

TO { O C A/B Coy (1)

| Sender's Number. | Day of Month. | In reply to Number. | A A A |
| MA 216 | 20 | | |

19th I. Bde has been ordered to carry out an attack on HINDENBURG SUPPORT LINE this evening. 98th I. Bde will continue their attack at same time up to the limits of their original objectives of this morning. Attack on Rt will be carried out by 1st Cameronians & on the left by 20th R.F.

100th I Bde will cover advance of the TWO Batt'ns of the 19th from their present positions with L Gun and Rifle fire.

Zero 7.30 p.m tonight. At ZERO there will be a mixed barrage of Hows: + FIELD guns on H.S. LINE. At ZERO +10 barrage creeps away.

The Two Batt'ns will form up on same line of deployment as used by us this morning. Advance will start at ZERO -15.

Batt'ns will use their Emergency Rations for consumption to-morrow

On no account must more than 5 men per Coy be out of Trench at same time.

From ....
Place ....
Time ....

MESSAGES AND SIGNALS.

TO (2)

7. The B.G. looks with confidence to all ranks to maintain the ground which they have won to-day quite irrespective of the results of the attack referred to in these orders. He much regrets that it will not be possible for any relief tonight.

8. Let me know all the STORES you require as soon as possible. I shall be sending water up later.

9. B.O.C. wishes you to be very careful about the LEFT Flank. Send out snipers & L Guns to your front to cover the advance of the 20 R.F. These can be withdrawn after they have passed through.

From GALLIC
Place
Time 6.0 p.m.

16th K.R.R.
BATTN. OPERATION ORDERS.   No. 2.

Copy No. 5

1. The 33rd Division will attack a portion of the HINDENBURG FRONT & SUPPORT lines on the 20th inst.
   The objective of the 100th I. Bde is the HINDENBURG SUPPORT LINE between the CROISILLES - HENDECOURT ROAD on Right and the FONTAIN - CROISILLES ROAD on the Left. The attack will be carried out by the 2 WORCESTER REGT, 9th H.L.I. & 16th KRR. in that order from Right to Left. The objectives of the 16th KRR. are the enemy FRONT & SUPPORT LINES from the FONTAINE - CROISELLES ROAD inclusive to a point about 400 YDS. S.E. of that Road.

2. The attack will be made in 4 waves, first two waves being subdivided into 2 lines in extended order. The 3rd & 4th waves will be in line of column of sections in single file with 70 YDS between waves.
   Objective 1st & 2nd Waves FRONT Enemy Line.
   do.   3rd & 4th   do.   SUPPORT   do.
   The first two waves will start at ZERO - 12 mins. and the 2nd two waves at ZERO - 10 mins.

3. The capture of the HINDENBURG FRONT LINE should come as a surprise and will not be covered by Artillery Barrage. The attack of the Support Line will be preceded by a barrage from ZERO to ZERO + 15 mins.

4. Two Guns of the 100th M.G. Coy. & ONE HALF section of the 222 Fd Coy. R.E. will be attached to the Battn. during operations.

2 Officers & 40 O.R's 1st QUEENS are also attached
to the Battn. for carrying purposes.

5. The Battn. will be at its position of assembly by
12 midnight night 19th/20th May 1917.
Deployment from position of assembly on to line of
deployment to be completed by ZERO – 30 mins.

6. At the position of deployment the Battn. will be
disposed as follows:–
    First 2 waves 'B' Coy. on Right 'C' Coy. on Left
    Second do. 'A' do. do. 'D' do. do.
'B' & 'C' Coys. will each push forward 2 L. Guns
into shell holes within view of their objective,
in order to cover the advance of the leading waves
should their approach be observed.
'D' Coy. will relieve No. 2 POST occupied by
1st QUEENS on arrival at position of assembly.

7. Dress:– Battle Order with Pack in place of
Haversack. Pack will contain –
Waterproof Sheet, Emergency Ration, one
preserved Ration, one Flare, two sandbags,
and either RED or WHITE Very Light.
Every man – other than Bomber – will carry
TWO MILLS BOMBS in his pocket.

8. As soon as objectives have been gained
consolidation will be undertaken at once.
Bombing Blocks will be established where
necessary. During consolidation covering
parties and L. Guns must be pushed forward
& posts established along the line so
occupied.

9. On objectives being secured B⁴ H.Qrs will move from position of assembly to HINDENBURG FRONT Line.

10. A Contact Aeroplane will be up during the attack. Flares will be lit along the lines of the position gained when this aeroplane sounds his Klaxon HORN. Flares will also be lit along the front of position gained at ZERO + 1 HOUR.

11. Blue & white signal flags will be waved on reaching objectives.

12. Regimental AID POST will be established at position of assembly.

13. Only MAP 51B. S.W. 1/20.000 will be issued into the attack.

14. Prisoners will be sent back via FONTAINE-CROISILLES ROAD to CROSS ROADS N. of CROISILLES, where they will be handed over to 1st QUEENS.

15. Each Coy will send 1 Off. & 1 O.R. during day-light to position of assembly who will act as guides to their Coy.

16. Battn. will move up to position of assembly this evening. Order of March HdQrs, C, B, D, A. Head of Column at RAILWAY CROSSING at 9.15 p.m.

17. L. Guns and teams will go in advance of Battn. to a point W. of ST. LEGER & will be picked up by their Coys. on Route.

J.C. Giddens.
Lieut & a/Adjt.
16th K.R.R.

Copies to:
1 OC A Coy
2 " B "
3 " C "
4 " D "
5 HQ Qrs
6 FILE

"A" Form.
MESSAGES AND SIGNALS.
Army Form C. 2121

Prefix .... Code .... m.	Words	Charge	This message is on a/c of:	Recd. at .... m.
Office of Origin and Service Instructions.	Sent		............Service.	Date ....
....	At .... m.			From ....
....	To			
....	By		(Signature of "Franking Officer.")	By ....

TO	O.C. B & C. Coys.			

Sender's Number.	Day of Month.	In reply to Number.		AAA
A/A 229	21/5/17			

33rd Divl. Front will be
engaged tonight 21st/22nd May.
100th Infty Bde. will hold
the whole sector of the
Divl front from NEPPY LANE
inclusive to the CROISILLES FONTAINE
Rd. inclusive.

2. 1st QUEENS will take over
(A) the area from 9th H.L.I that portion of
the HINDENBERG front line from NEPPY
LANE to PLUM TRENCH inclusive and all
lines & posts held by units of the 19th
Infty Brigade on this front should there be
any.

CONTD

From			
Place			
Time			

"A" Form — MESSAGES AND SIGNALS.
Army Form C. 2121.

Office of Origin and Service Instructions: Battⁿ Orders

To: ...ilit... ...

TO: Coy'...

Sender's Number: AA 229

---

2 (B) 16ᵗʰ K.R.R.s will close to their following frontages to their present lines from PILKEM TRENCH (inclusive) to the Krommes Fontaine Rd inclusive. S will take over all frontage from between these points now. (...)

(3) All movements to take place after dark tonight. Relief to be completed by daylight May 22ⁿᵈ
All dumps of S.A.A. rations, bombs &c will be noted and receipt for same being taken. Options of any kind be reported to Battⁿ H.Qrs by means of the expression "CONTENT".

Guides from each of the 19ᵗʰ I.B. will meet our relief parties or officers in charge of same at about point de Bune Road (C. Coys H.Qrs)

(4) "C" Coy will take over all advanced posts from 19ᵗʰ I.B. A.B & D will hold front line. Touch must be kept with
1ˢᵗ Queens on right & look out kept for
9ᵗʰ I.B. on left.
Bombing posts will be made & ...
(if) necessary.

From:
Place: 9ᵗʰ I.B.
Time:

G Denham
8.70 p

MESSAGES AND SIGNALS.

Army Form C. 2121.

Prefix	Code	m	Words	Charge	This message is on a/c of:	Recd. at	m
Office of Origin and Service Instructions.			Sent		Service.	Date	
Secret			At	m		From	
			To			By	
			By		(Signature of "Franking Officer,")		

TO { O.C. "A" "B" "C" "D" Coys

Sender's Number.	Day of Month.	In reply to Number.	
* A.A. 243.	22.5.17		AAA

The Bn. will be relieved tonight 22/23rd. inst.

(1) by two Coys 5th N.F. (time about 10 pm.)
"B" Coy 5th N.F. relieving "C" Coy 16 KRRC
"C" " — " " "A" "B" & "D" Coys 16 KRRC
Platoon guides to be supplied as per my
A.A. 242.

(2) All dumps of S.A.A. Bombs etc to be handed over. Receipts obtained.

(3) During progress of Relief, O.C. "C" Coy, will send out protective patrols, these should be withdrawn on completion of Relief.

(4) On relief Coys will march back by platoons to MOYENNEVILLE.
Via ST LEGER. HAMELINCOURT.

(5) Completion of Relief to be reported to Bn. H Qrs by expression
"NO LONGER REQUIRED TONIGHT"

From
Place
Time 6.35 pm.

The above may be forwarded as now corrected. (Z)

Army Form C. 2118.

WAR DIARY
or
INTELLIGENCE SUMMARY

(Erase heading not required.) 16.(S)/Bn. King's Royal Rifles

June 1917

Vol 20

Instructions regarding War Diaries and Intelligence Summaries are contained in F.S. Regs., Part II. and the Staff Manual respectively. Title pages will be prepared in manuscript.

Place	Date	Hour	Summary of Events and Information	Remarks and references to Appendices
MOYENNE VILLE	1st	9:45 am	Bn. marched to BERLES au BOIS — arrived about 1:40 pm. Three men fell out on march. Bn. occupied Billets on the previous manner of resting at BERLES.	Ref. Map LENS
BERLES au BOIS	2nd		Lt. Col. A.V. Johnson proceeded to England on leave. Major Newton resumed Command. Bn. refitting, cleaning, Inspection of Clothing by C.O.	1/10,000
	3rd		Church parades. Draft of 104 O.R. joined for duty. 30 being returned casuals.	
	4th		A & B Coys. had Basha Remembers at the Coys. disposal. Programme of Rifle Training sent to Bde. 50ᵗ Range put in working order.	
	5th	7 pm	Bn. parade under R.S.M. Sheerby and "B" Coy. Specialist training commenced. "C" & "D" had Baths. A Coy on 50ᵗ Range.	
	6th		"A" & "B" on 300ᵗ Range. "D" 50ᵗ Range. C Coy Training.	
	7th		Coy. Specialist Training. Demonstration in afternoon to all Officers in MAORI Pattern Wire Entanglements. 3/Lt Rutherby proceeded to England.	
	8th		Coy. Specialist Training. Lecture to party of Officers N.C.O.'s N.C.O's on Co-operation of Artillery & Infantry.	
	9th		Coys. appeared at disposal of the Coy. 4:49 hrs. Coy on 50ᵗ Range. Inspection of Billets by Col. B. Officer.	
	10th		Church parade. 2/Lt Sullivan proceeded on leave to England. 2/Lt Aylward took music Battery.	
	11th		Coy. operations at disposal of O.C. Coys "C" & "D" on 300ᵗ Range in afternoon. 3/Lt Cron & 4 N.C.O. on Bns. Course of Bayonet Fighting.	

WAR DIARY
INTELLIGENCE SUMMARY

Army Form C. 2118.

June 1917.

Place	Date	Hour	Summary of Events and Information	Remarks and references to Appendices
BERLES au BOIS.	12th		Coy. specialist Training. Field Firing Range carried out by Companies in afternoon on Field Firing Range near RANSART. 2nd Lt. Hill proceeded to LE TOUQUET on a L.M.G. course. Lt. Col. A.V. Johnson returned from leave & resumed command.	
	13th		Coy. specialists at disposal of Coy. Capt. Francis returned from Army Course.	
	14th		Coy. specialist training. 2nd Lt. Kingsley returned from Coy. Course. 2nd Lt. Forbes & 41 O.R. reported for duty.	
	15th		"A" & "B" Coys. on 300x Range "C" & "D" training. Bn. Held Sports.	
	16th		"A" "B" & "C" Coys. had Baths. 2nd Lt. Cue & 4 ORs joined. BW Bayonet class	
	17th		Church parade. "D" Coy 122 Hrs. Bathed	
	18th		Bn on Field Firing Range. Coy. attended Demonstration by Tank 2nd Lt. Mulvany returned from leave. Batt. Company movement held	
	19th		Bn. getting ready for moving to forward area. 2nd Lt. C.V.G. Everett & 3 OR. joined for duty. Bn paraded 6.00 a.m. & marched to MOYENNEVILLE. Two coys Camp "A". No Men fell out 2nd Lt. J. Reed & 29 O.R. joined for duty. 9 O.R. being men returned from Light Railway Coy.	
MOYENNE VILLE 3pt.	20th		Training carried on 9 OR to VII Corps L.G. School for Course of instruction 1 Officer (2nd Lt R.G.R. Day) & 50 O.R. to 222nd H.Q. Gy. R.E. for duty whilst Division is on line 1 Officer (2nd Lt. Forbes) & 36 O.R. to be attached to 121st Fd. Coy. R.E. for working on line

Army Form C. 2118.

WAR DIARY
or
INTELLIGENCE SUMMARY
(Erase heading not required.)

June 1917

Place	Date	Hour	Summary of Events and Information	Remarks and references to Appendices
MOYENNE VILLE	22nd		Coys at training. Found fatigue party of 1 Off & 50 O.R.	Ref. Map LENS 1/10,000
	23rd		Bn in Divisional Field Firing Range from 10am - 6.15pm. RANGART. 2nd Lt Sullivan returned from leave to England. 1 Off & 50 O.R. on fatigue. Reinforcement officers are here:	
	24th	10am	Brigade Parade for presentation of Indian Colours by the Corps Commander: Lt Cecqueio – 27th Sullivan M.C. L/Sgt Coad Coy Sgt M Carey d Bar L/M.M. Sgt Lloyd Sgt Kenner, Trpton, Tyler, Cpl Jane Battersworth, Pioneer Benson, Sgts Reed Cpl Coad Meadows Murray Bartley, Cramps Ferguson Griffiths Military Medal. Bn moved up into R.W. Reserve, relieving 2nd Col M.K.& Johnson Bn over from 2nd & 9th R.W.F. Relief completed at 7pm. 1st Reinforcements of 'B' Ration under Major E. Denham moved to position W.17 HAMELINCOURT. Majority of Bn on working parties.	
CROISILLES	25th		Orders received from Bde that stress Bn & Reserve Bn 3rd & Ist would relieve front line Bns on Wed 26 inst. 18 K.R.R. with 15 O.R. Front Line from Left Bn. CO Coy Commanders reconnoitred line. Bn & H.Q. General Quarters Bn H.Q Pte —	
	26th		Bn took over sector of Trenches FONTAINE-CROISILLES from 17 Bn Recon 42nd Div Bns. Relief completed by 1.15am. 2nd Lt W.E. Fields & 5 O.R killed, 13 O.R wounded. Enemy shelled tunnel heavily during early morning & intermittently during day. Bomb General standed near dug out during morning. B.g.Carnage on dugout. 1st Carnage on dugout 1st Carnage on support in preparation to Raid 31st Green.	

2353 Wt W3541/1454 700,000 5/15 D.D.&L. A.D.S.S./Forms/C.2118

WAR DIARY or INTELLIGENCE SUMMARY

Army Form C. 2118.

June 1917

Place	Date	Hour	Summary of Events and Information	Remarks and references to Appendices
CROSSILLES	27th		Orders received that line was to be raided. Party of 19th Middx sent up to man saps. Received development in inspection trench. R.E. C.o.y 1st Division detailed for to confer with C.O. about covering Raid. Orders received that O.P.'s were to be manned night & day. Attack no sniping was to take place from them.	Reg. hist. 51.13. S.W. 1/20,000
		11 pm	A Company on Brown up, to hold new MEBUS leading to Tunnel Trench. "C" Coy returned a few casualties from artillery fire. Reported in billets supporting attack. 1 O.R. killed & O.R. wounded.	
	28th		Intermittent shelling. Officer of 1st Queen mistook mistook road line. Brig Gen? mate No.1? Mr Stanton with C.O. R.A. Officer made his way up & was preparing to some artillery being thickish. Twenty flares during evening.	
	29th	12.50	Coy of 1st Queen mine ½ of "A" Coy relieved forward trench to line Road T 27 B.	
		7.30am	Bishops + Co 1st Queen scraps with Co. 8.50am T.M.O. Artillery barrage	
		11 am	O.C. Queen Raiding party reports attack unsuccessful. Very little retaliation by artillery.	
		1 pm	Enemy shelled front support line heavily, weak led waited for.	
		6.30pm	C.O. + Coy Officers 15th O.L.I. visited line preparatory to taking over.	
→	7.30pm		"B" Echelon & spare men Coy. Transport moved back from MOYENNEVILLE & spare men BOIS arriving there at 6.30pm	
BERLES au BOIS				

Army Form C. 2118.

WAR DIARY
or
INTELLIGENCE SUMMARY.
(Erase heading not required.)

June 1917

Place	Date	Hour	Summary of Events and Information	Remarks and references to Appendices
CROISILLES	30th	3.30 a.m.	Enemy shelled front & support line very heavily for ½ an hour.	
		10.50	First relieving company of D.L.I. arrived.	
		3.10 pm	"A" "B" & "C" Coys relieved. "D" Coy. have to wait till dark	
			Bn. took over Camp F. MOYENNEVILLE	
			"D" Coy. arrived back about 3.30 a.m. 1st July.	
			1 Officer & 6 O.R. wounded during day.	

J.S. Drummond Lt Col
Cmdg 16 R.F.

WAR DIARY
or
INTELLIGENCE SUMMARY

Army Form C. 2118.

No. 1. July 1917. 16th (S) Bn. King's Royal Rifles Vol 21

Place	Date	Hour	Summary of Events and Information	Remarks and references to Appendices
MOYENNE VILLE	1st	11.20 a.m.	Bn. marched to BERLES au BOIS, arrived about 3.30 p.m. Lt. N.K. Beledon seconded to Gen. H.Q.	Ref. Map LENS 1/100,000
	2nd		Coys at disposal of O.C. Coys for cleaning up. Orders for move received.	
	3rd	8.30 am	Bn. marched to FORCEVILLE. 33 fell out during the march owing to the heat	
FORCEVILLE	4th	4 am	& chewing feet being tender coming out of the line. Packs were carried on limbers. Bn. marched to MIRVAUX. No one fell out. This was due to marching in the	
MIRVAUX			early morning, packs were carried on the man. The use of kethylated spirits & Picric acid greatly improved the mens feet. Bn. arrived about 9 am.	Ref. Map AMIENS
	5th	4 am	Bn. marched to Rest area BREILLY, arrived about 10.30 am Bn. stopped	1/100,000
BREILLY			for Breakfast on the way. No one fell out. Billets were found to be very good.	
	6th		Coys at disposal of O.C. Coys for general cleaning & kit fitting.	
	7th		Coys at disposal of O.C. Coys. Training groups & Ranges for Rifle Bombing & L.M. Gun located. Com. Dy. Officers inspected Billets. 2nd Lt. A. BOTTOMS, B. STRATTON, E. HARRISON, E. KARN, C. HODGES, D. SMITH, and 50 O.R. arrived from ST. POL. for duty with Bn.	
	8th		Bn. Church parade	

Army Form C. 2118.

WAR DIARY
or
INTELLIGENCE SUMMARY.

(Erase heading not required.)

July 1917

Instructions regarding War Diaries and Intelligence Summaries are contained in F. S. Regs., Part II. and the Staff Manual respectively. Title pages will be prepared in manuscript.

Place	Date	Hour	Summary of Events and Information	Remarks and references to Appendices
BRESLE	9th	7 to 8 9 to 6	Specialist classes commenced. "A" Coy. attend Range. "B", "C" & "D" Coy Training.	Ref map AMIENS 1/100,000
		12 noon	2nd Lt. CLEUGH & 3 O.R. joined for duty. 2nd Lt. BROUGH, leave to England.	
	10th	"	Specialist classes. "C" Coy Range. "D" Coy Training. "A" & "B" Training.	
			2nd Lt. MATHER proceeds RIENCOURT for Sniping Course.	
	11th	"	Coy & Specialist Training as programme.	
	12th	"	Coy & Specialist Training as programme. Div' Comdt inspected Coys at training.	
			Capt. JOHNSTONE 2nd A. & S. HIGHLNDRS joined for duty.	
	13th	"	Bn. Route March. Specialist training as usual.	
	14th	8.30am	Coy & Specialist training as programme. 2nd Lt. MIDDLECOTE returned from T.M. Course.	
	15th		Bn Church parade. 2nd Lt. MATHER from Sniping Course.	
			LT. NOTLEY 2nd LT. APPLEBEE & 1 O.R. joined for duty.	
	16th		Bn. Bathed at AILLY. Coy & Specialist Training carried on.	
			2Lt. HOPE returned from Course at Army School HUMBERCAMPS.	
			Brig Gen 92 visited Coys at training.	
	17th		Coy & Specialist Training. 17th July 27 Div' Horse Show	
	18th		Bn Holiday. 2nd Day of Div' Horse Show.	
	19th		Coy & Specialist Training.	

WAR DIARY
or
INTELLIGENCE SUMMARY.
(Erase heading not required.)

Army Form C. 2118.

July 1917

Place	Date	Hour	Summary of Events and Information	Remarks and references to Appendices
BRAY	20th	8.30 a.m.	Bn. marched to SOUE for Gas demonstration by Div'l Gas Officer. C.O. Adjt. took part in Gas exercise from 8 a.m. to 8.30 a.m. 2/Lt TALBOT reported for duty. 2/Lt. TALBOT reported for duty. 2 Officers & 16 O.Rs. Shooting Comp. also a Bayonet Remainder training	Ref. Map AMIENS 1/100,000
	21st		in Camp	
	22nd		Bn. Church parade	
	23rd		Coy & Specialist training. Div. Comdr. visited Bn at training	
	24th		Coy & Specialist training. (2/Lt F. BROUGH returned from England)	
	25th		Bn. parade. Coys under R.S.M. at Drill. Officers taken on Tactical scheme by Comdg Officer. Brig G.O. visited Bn. Warning orders for move received. 2nd Lts. INIGO-JONES, MANNING, CURRY & 21 O.R.	
	26th		Coy & Specialist training reported for duty	
	27th		Bn. route march.	
	28th		Bn. Bathed at Ailly. Coy & Specialist training. Inspection of Billets. Bn. Church parade. Orders received for Bn Cdrs/Coy Cdrs to go to LONGPRE	
	29th		at 1 A.M. Wednesday Aug 1st.	

Army Form C. 2118.

WAR DIARY
or
INTELLIGENCE SUMMARY.

(Erase heading not required.)

W.B.W.

July 1917.

Instructions regarding War Diaries and Intelligence Summaries are contained in F. S. Regs., Part II. and the Staff Manual respectively. Title pages will be prepared in manuscript.

Place	Date	Hour	Summary of Events and Information	Remarks and references to Appendices
BRAY SUR SOMME	30th		Coys at disposal of O.C. Coys. 100 O.R's & Officers of "A" Coy. 2nd/Lt. CHEETHAM in Command proceeded to AMIENS	Reg Insp. AMIENS 1/00 p.m.
	31st	2.30 p.m.	LONGPRÉ for entraining duty. General cleaning up of Billets. Transport marched to LONGPRÉ at 6 p.m. Bn less "A" Coy paraded 7.30 p.m. & marched to LONGPRÉ	

[signature]

Army Form C. 2118.

No. 1

WAR DIARY
or
INTELLIGENCE SUMMARY.

(Erase heading not required.) 16th (S) Bn Kings Royal Rifles

Vol 22

August 1917.

Place	Date	Hour	Summary of Events and Information	Remarks and references to Appendices
LONGPRÉ	1st	1.20 a.m	Bn less "A" Coy entrained for DUNKERQUE, arriving there about 10 a.m. On detraining marched to TETEGHAM area and billetted. Heavy rain falling most of the journey, arrived about 2.30 p.m. Bn noted "A" Coy reported Bn. Still raining.	Ref. map AMIENS 1/100,000
TETEGHAM	2nd	8 am	Bn noted.	
	3rd		Bn marched to GHYVELDE, arrived about 12 noon. Then billetted in Huts. Officers in Village. Remainder rest part of day.	Ref. map DUNKERQUE 1/100,000
	4th		Coys at disposal of O.C. Coys. Cleaning up. Capt. Chadwick leave to England.	
	5th	10 am	Bn Church parade. Lecture to Officers & NCOs by Div. Gas Officer. 5.30 p.m on new German Gas shell.	
GHYVELDE	6th		Coys at Training. Specialist classes continued. 13 O.R. joined Bn. for duty. 2nd Lt. ELSWICK HARRISON to Gas Course. 2nd Lt. INIGO JONES to Course of Bn. Air Craft defence.	
	7th		Coys & Specialist Training as programme. Bathing in afternoon.	
	8th	8.30 am	Bn Route march. Comm Dg. Officer & Capt FRANCIS went to reconnoitre	
	9th	7 pm	new line at 7 pm. 2nd Lt. KINSLEY leave to England. Coys & Specialist Training as programme.	

Army Form C. 2118.

WAR DIARY
or
INTELLIGENCE SUMMARY.
(Erase heading not required.)

August 1917.

Place	Date	Hour	Summary of Events and Information	Remarks and references to Appendices
GHYVELDE	10th		Coys Specialist Training.	Coy Prop of DUNKERQUE /100,000
	11th		Coys Specialist Training. Drop of Bullets by Coy Pig Officers.	
	12th		Capt KING proceeded to FLIXECOURT for course as a Gas Army School.	
			Bde Church Parade.	
	13th		Bn Route March.	
	14th		Coys Specialist Training. 2nd Lts MORANT & BIGGS joined for duty.	
	15th	8 a.m.	Bn. leave the Company musketry on beach. 2nd Lt ELNICK HARRISON to Field Punt.	
		3 p.m.	Lecture to all Officers in Machine Gun Work in Cinema Hall.	
	16th	9 a.m.	B'de Field operations. Bn. took right center of attack. Operations took place on sand dunes. Shelter enemy artillery barrage taken by smoke bombs. Contact aeroplane took part in operation. Operations finished very satisfactory.	
			2nd Lt KARN & 26 O.R. joined R.E. to work which was in hand.	
			Capt CHADWICK returned from leave to England.	
	17th		Coys at disposal of O.C. Coys. Cleaning up preparation to move.	
			Bn. less Capt CHADWICK, 2nd Lts BROUGH, INIGO-JONES & 100 O.R. detailed for Depth. Pct. and to remain at GHYVELDE, moved to AUSTRALIA CAMP	
COXYDE	18th	5 a.m.	W. of COXYDE — arrived at about 9.30am. No one fell out. Bn Billetted in Huts which are quite good.	

Army Form C. 2118.

WAR DIARY
or
INTELLIGENCE SUMMARY.

(Erase heading not required.)

August 1917

Place	Date	Hour	Summary of Events and Information	Remarks and references to Appendices
COXYDE	19th		Voluntary Church Service. 2nd Lt. C.H. WILKINS to England on leave. 2nd Lt L.W. CHEETHAM Ref. map took over duties of Adjt. 2nd Lt. MANNING & 60 O.R. from "C" Coy. to work with 49th Fd. Ambs. DUNKERQUE during night	1/40.000
— " —	20th		Artillery slightly shelling of roads near camp during night. Coy. at specialist training	
— " —	21st		" " 2nd Lt H.R. KINSLEY returned from leave	
— " —	22nd		" " Lt. A.G. HOLMS R.A.M.C returned from leave	
— " —	23rd		" "	
— " —	24th		" " Some shelling of vicinity of camp during evening	
— " —	25th			
— " —	26th		Voluntary Service – C.O. and By Comdrs visited support line, THE REDAN, NIEUPORT. Major E. WENHAM to England on leave. Received warning order for more considerable shelling by H.V. Guns round camp during afternoon & from 9pm to 1am 27th. 0/0 casualties –	
			Marched to GHYVELDE, being relieved by 2nd Manchesters. Arrived 12noon.	
GHYVELDE	27th		Falling out state Nil. 1 Off & 160 o.r from 49th Div Arty fatigue, 10 o.r from XV Corps H.A. fatigue, & minimum reserve from 33rd Bwe Depot 19th rejoined. 2nd Lieut G.H. COE & 3 o.r joined for duty –	

Army Form C. 2118.

WAR DIARY
or
INTELLIGENCE SUMMARY.

August 1917. (Erase heading not required.)

Place	Date	Hour	Summary of Events and Information	Remarks and references to Appendices
TETEGHEM	28		Marched to TETEGHEM area, arriving about 12 noon. Wet & very windy. Falling out state Nil. Divl General saw Batt on march. 1 Offr & 28 o.r. rejoined from PE field.	Ref map. DUNKERQUE 1/100000
— " —	29		Very wet. Warning orders for move received.	
— " —	30		10 Offrs & 64 o.r. with Batt Transport less Cookers left by road for WORMHOUDT	HAZEBROUCK
— " —	31		Batt marched to DUNKERQUE and entrained at 8.30am. Arrived WATTEN 12.30 pm. Marched to billets at LA COMMUNE, picking up transport en route.	5A 1/100000

J Richmond Lt Col
Cmdg 10 H.L.I

Army Form C. 2118.

WAR DIARY
or
INTELLIGENCE SUMMARY
(Erase heading not required.)

No. I

Instructions regarding War Diaries and Intelligence Summaries are contained in F. S. Regs., Part II and the Staff Manual respectively. Title pages will be prepared in manuscript.

September 1917 16th (S)/B Kings Royal Rifles

Place	Date	Hour	Summary of Events and Information	Remarks and references to Appendices
LA COMMUNE	1st		2nd Lt. H.A. CRAM & 7 O.R. proceeded to LA PLAINE to XV Corps Signalling school course. Coys at disposal of Lt. Cops. Hon. Fr. V. O'Reilly W. HUDDLESTONE reported for duty. Voluntary Ch. E. Service. R.C. Church parade at BAYENGHEM. 2nd Lt. C.H. WILKINS returned from leave.	Ref map HAZEBROUCK 5 A. 1/100,000.
	2nd		Coy Alt Training. Specialist classes commenced.	
	3rd		Coy & Specialist Training. 8 Officers under R.S.M. Rowbury & three commenced 7 days course of instruction on Lewis gun.	
	4th		Coy & Specialist Training.	
	5th		Coy & Specialist Training.	
	6th	6 A.M.	Coy Commdg Officers. 24 O.R. For General reformed from Depot 2nd Lt FRANCIS 2nd Lt HOLLOWAY went to reconnoitre line ZILLEBEKE area. Coy Specialist Training. 2nd Lt. lectured at EPERLEQUES. Major E. WENHAM from leave.	
	7th		"A" & "B" Coys on long range in morning. "C" & "D" Coys in afternoon.	
	8th		Lt.Col. A.V. JOHNSON & 2nd Lt. HOPE to England on leave. Major E. WENHAM assumed command of Bn.	
	9th		Church parade in morning "A" & "B" Coys. on long range in afternoon.	
	10th		"C" & "D" Coys on long range. Capt. FRANCIS leave to England. 2nd Lt. HOLLOWAY to Corps.	
	11th		Coy & Specialist Training. Capt. FRANCIS leave to England. Infantry Course at MILLIAM. Comm. Officers, all Officers & Platoon Sergts reconnoitred ground for R.N. Field Operation.	

WAR DIARY or INTELLIGENCE SUMMARY

Army Form C. 2118.

Sept. 1917.

Place	Date	Hour	Summary of Events and Information	Remarks and references to Appendices
LA COMMUNE	12th	7.45 a.m.	Bn. paraded for Bde. Field Operations. Coy. & Bn². Commanders present. Bde. was exercised in the attack & consolidation in depth.	Ref. Map HAZEBROUCK 5 A. 1/100,000
	13th	10 a.m.	Bde. Scheme was repeated. 2nd Army & Bn². Commanders present during the exercise, and at the Conference held afterwards at the end of exercise. Transport marched past Army Commander on way back to billets. Warning orders for move received.	
	14th		Bn. carried out Coy. Field Firing scheme on Range at GUEMY.	
			New Chaplain Rev. GRIFFITHS reported for duty tonight 1932.	
LEDERZEELE	15th	9.15 a.m.	Bn. marched to LEDERZEELE area. arrived about 1.15 pm. Billets very scattered but good. 5 men fell out	
STEEN VOORDE	16th	8.15 a.m.	Bn. marched to STEENVOORDE Area. arrived about 12.45 pm. killed good but central trying march trying to obtain at CASSEL HILL, 7 men fell out. Capt. CORK from Leave.	
FONTAINE HOUCK	17th		Bn. marched to FONTAINE HOUCK area. arrived about 1.15 pm. billets good but scattered. 5 men fell out. Weather during the marching was good, but the pavé roads trying.	
	18th		Bn. rested. Comdg. Officer attended Bde. Conference at Bn. HQ. 2.30 pm. 4 parties	
LA CLYTTE	19th	1.15 pm	Bn. marched to MURRAMBIDGEE CAMP LA CLYTTE area. arrived 4.30 pm. very trying march, very warm & hard road. 7 men fell out. Men in Huts & shelters.	
		11 am	Comdg. Officer & Coy. Officers & NCO Officers for any attended demonstration in the use of	

Army Form C. 2118.

WAR DIARY
or
INTELLIGENCE SUMMARY.
(Erase heading not required.)

September 1917

Instructions regarding War Diaries and Intelligence Summaries are contained in F. S. Regs., Part II. and the Staff Manual respectively. Title pages will be prepared in manuscript.

No 3

Place	Date	Hour	Summary of Events and Information	Remarks and references to Appendices
LA CLYTTE	20th		Coys at disposal of O.C. Coys. Specialists on usual. Lt. Col. A.Y. JOHNSON & 2nd Lt. HOPE returned from leave to England. 2nd Lt. THOMAS to England on leave. Intermittent shelling during night but none fell in the Camp.	Ref. Map HAZEBROUCK 5 A 1/100,000
	21st		Coys Specialists as usual. Con.Dg.Officers Expense as 19th & 9th Pros 2nd Lt. SULLIVAN & CHEETHAM attd H.Q. reconnoitred Tracks up to forward area.	
	22nd		Coys at disposal of O.C. Coys. Cap?? COOK, NOTLEY and KING with two NCO's (minimum reserve) proceeded to BERTHEN area to Bde Report 13v. Con.Dg.Officers attended Conference at Bde H.Q. 9am.	
KRUISTRAAT HOEK AREA	23rd	7.45 am	Bn marched to KRUISSTAATHOEK Area and bivouaced in field. Con.Dg.Officer & Cap? CHADWICK proceeded at 9.15am to reconnoitre lines. Cap? KING proceeded to England on leave. Bn postponed to move into line. Cap? FRANCIS returned from leave to England.	
ZILLEBEKE AREA	24th	3.30 pm	Bn moved up into BW Reserve to TOR TOP. Bn leading line N of MENIN Road. 2nd Lt. STRATTON & 50 O.R. reported to Pier for carrying purposes. 2nd Lt. HOPE & MORANT & 75 O.R. reported to O.C. 222 Field Coy. R.E. Several casualties received from shell fire on journey up. MAJOR. WENHAM & 2nd Lt. BROUGH moved back to BERTHEN Area to Bde Report 13v. Transport & "B" echelon remained in KRUISSTAATHOEK area.	

No 4

WAR DIARY
or
INTELLIGENCE SUMMARY.

Army Form C. 2118.

September 1917

Place	Date	Hour	Summary of Events and Information	Remarks and references to Appendices
ZILLEBEKE AREA	25th	10 am	"C" Coy under (Capt. FRANCIS) ordered to report to O.C. 1st Queens.	Ref. Maps. Sheet 28. France & Belgium 1/40,000 French Sheet
		11.30 am	"A" Coy under (Capt. CHADWICK) ordered to report to O.C. 2nd Worcs.	
		3 pm	"B" Coy under (2nd Lt. INIGO JONES) ordered to report to O.C. 1st Queens.	
		5 pm	"D" Coy under (2nd Lt. MATHER) ordered to occupy LUCKY DUG OUT and trenches in vicinity (S.W of DUMBARTON WOOD) Orders to O.C. D.Coy to report to O.C. 9th H.L.I.	
	26th	6+8 pm	Liaison officer 9th H.L.I. came to Coy "D" Coy up guide not being availed.	
		10.30 am	Verbal communication from Bdes re relief.	
	27th	3 pm	"A" Coy report relief complete. Bn 10.9th left TOR TOP for KREUSSTATHOEK area, where Coy arrived during night 27/28th.	
		4.30pm	Relief TOR TOP Bdr Coy ordered/prefigured 2nd Lt. STRATTON, party attached to 272 Field Chem. Coy. R.E. under 2nd Lt. HOPE & MORANT from RAILWAY DUGOUTS and all Bn HQ Pers were constantly employed in carrying to the forward area, and suffered considerably from shell fire. Reports by Coy Commanders 25th to 27th inst.	forest
	28th	11.30	"A" Coy. Capt. F. CHADWICK. Proceed to report to O/c 2nd W/Worcs. at TOWER DUGOUTS (J 14.d.9.3) went via STIRLING CASTLE - JASPER AVENUE - INVERNESS COPSE. A few casualties en route. On arrival found that dugouts were occupied. Party for this dug out lay in vicinity.	

2353 Wt. W2514/1454 700,000 5/15 D.D.&L. A.D.S.S./Forms/C. 2118.
(6.t. J.14. D.4.6.)

WAR DIARY or INTELLIGENCE SUMMARY

Army Form C. 2118.

No 5.

September 1917

Date	Hour	Summary of Events and Information	Remarks and references to Appendices
25th		Vicinity. Coy Commander reports to continued and reported remainder of Coy when HQ Coys moved out during night 25/26. Enemy shelling continuous & heavy, caused considerable casualties. Orders from O.C. 2nd Hoers. Were to be ready to move up to support in case of enemy counter attack. The Coy was employed in carrying S.A.A. shells from JACKDAW DUMP to Moro H.Q.Pro.	Trench maps
26th		During afternoon of 26th received orders from P.C. 2nd Moors to move up & take up a position between TOWER H.Q.Pro. and front line in conjunction with C Coy 2nd Moors in counter attack as expected. Moved forward through heavy barrage in Worm formation, in artillery in support but by enemy aircraft. No counter attack.	Sheimbuy forest
27th		Coy took up position decided in itinerary night 26/27, at times being heavily shelled, suffered considerable casualties. Moved back to J.14.d.46 early 27th. Carrying parties found during morning. Afternoon taking over V.S.A.A from JACKDAW Dump to Moro H.Q.Pro. afternoon of 27th Coy relieved by C Coy 11th W.YORKS located East to KREUSSTHOEK Area. "B" Coy. 2nd L-RINIGO JONES.	
28th		During afternoon moved from TORT.P. to support the 1st Queens to a position on the Right of Old MENIN Road. 2 Platoons Any received strong points with 2 in reserve. In accordance with orders from T.C. 1st Queens. 2 Platoons moved forward and	
	10p.m		
29th	2.30 a.m	occupied a trench on the right off the road in the front line in accordance with orders received.	

WAR DIARY
or
INTELLIGENCE SUMMARY.
(Erase heading not required.)

Army Form C. 2118.

No 6

September 1917

Place	Date	Hour	Summary of Events and Information	Remarks and references to Appendices
			Coy Commanders reports continued.	
	24th	5.30 am	received. The Coy. two to attack on the right of the road. Front line reorganised with a view to this, and guide sent back to the rear platoon.	
			Fresh attack orders received, to form a second front to the 1st Queens in the attack.	
		5.45 am	As a result of this attack, the Coy. occupied reorganised a line of shell holes about 150 yds. to the front.	
	27th	3 p.m	A further attack was carried out and the strong point taken and reopened until relieved "C" Coy. Capt. L. FRANCIS	
	28th	10 am	During morning moved from TOR TOP to Pge K2 Ster 1st Queens. At 11 am relieved "A" Coy 1st Queens in reserve line, leaving 30 men at Pge HQ 9th as carrying party.	French map
		11 am	Orders received from FC 1st Queens to act in support to that Bn in an attack in the N. of The Shrewsbury Forest	
		12 MN	MENIN Road. with the object of retaking the ground lost there in the morning.	
	30th		Arrived at the front line in conjunction with "B" Coy K.R.R. & about 40 officers 145 of the 1st Queens. moved forward to the attack at ZERO keeping close to the barrage. All objectives were quickly taken on the MENIN Road and about 30 prisoners taken. N. of the road we were held up by a strong point, but a hut was made about 100 yds. short of their objective. During the morning several local enemy counter attacks were driven off, by rifle & L. Gun fire. the bayonet also being used. An enemy aeroplane smoke was seen flying low by I.M. Gun fire.	
		3.40 p.m	A phalanx of Germans appeared as reinforcements, and a further attack	

WAR DIARY or INTELLIGENCE SUMMARY

Army Form C. 2118.

September 1917

Place	Date	Hour	Summary of Events and Information	Remarks and references to Appendices
	26th		Coy Commanders reports continued. Attack. was made on the strong point where 2nd Lt. PRESTON 1/Cameronians. The two successful partys 5 O.R. was killed between + 30 O.R. killed or wounded. The whole did N.G. the head Coy moved forward + occupied final objective. + Officers + 77 O.R. and the machine guns were mopped up during the gallant consolidated supposed small local counter attacks beaten off, work	French map
	27th	3 pm	Considerable loss to the enemy. 5 pm. Enemy put a heavy barrage on the support line followed by an attack on the right flank, this was taken up by our artillery. (Capt. FRANCIS was put in charge of the attack on the front held by the 1st Queens.)	Shrewsbury Forest
		10 pm	Relieved by K.O.Y.L.I. D. Coy 2nd Lt. H. MATHER.	
	28th		During afternoon moved up from TOR TOP to LUCKY DUGOUT and thence in readiness for heavy shelling. Owing enemy received orders to report to O.C. 9th H.L.I. no guides available. Many of O.C. & liaison officers moved from 9th H.L.I. & guides Coy up. Took up position in shell hole Sgt in touch with one "A" Coy. At dusk we moved forward about 200 yds and dug in. Orders received from O.C. 9th H.L.I. to move up into support	
	29th		behind front line finally 2 Coys reinforced the H.L.I. the other 2 Coys reinforced the Notts. Relieved by Sherwood Foresters. Midnight 27 Lind.	

Army Form C. 2118.

WAR DIARY
or
INTELLIGENCE SUMMARY.

September 1917

Place	Date	Hour	Summary of Events and Information	Remarks and references to Appendices
KREUS ATHOEK AREA	29th		Total Casualties period 24/27th. 2nd Lt. FOOKES, STRATTON, MANNING. DAY. Wounded. O.R. Killed 33. Wounded 152. Missing 31.	
		9 am	Transport left for BRAYINGHEM area & then received F.O. to entrain at OUDERDOM for above area. Bn. paraded at 3.15 pm. & marched to OUDERDOM entrained at 5.15 pm. Arrived EBLINGHEM 10.10 pm. Arrived at Billets in SERCUS about 12.15 am. Billets centered, fairly good.	
SERCUS	29th	6 pm.	Major WENHAM and 16 officers & men from BERTHEN area proceeded to cleaning up Capt CORK, Y.C.S.M. WATERS proceeded on Course at 2nd Army School WISQUES.	
	30th		Voluntary Church parade. 2nd Lt. BROUGH proceeded to L.M.G. Course LE TOUQUET.	

J. Johnson Col
Cdg 16th R.R

Army Form C. 2118.

No. I

WAR DIARY
or
INTELLIGENCE SUMMARY.

(Erase heading not required.)

October 1917

16(51)82 King's Royal Rifles

Vol 2

Place	Date	Hour	Summary of Events and Information	Remarks and references to Appendices
SERCUS AREA	1st		Coys at disposal of OC Coys. general cleaning and refitting. Brig'r Comm'r F. called.	Ref map HAZEBROUCK
	2nd	10 am	Bn paraded for ceremonial drill in morning. Attended 2nd Rgt rehearsal of parade for inspection by Commander in Chief. S.A.	
		3.30 pm	for inspection by Commander in Chief. 2nd Lt. THOMAS returned from leave to Eng'd.	
	3rd	11 am	Bn paraded for B'de Inspection by Commander in Chief. M.M. presented to Cpl. F. CLARKE 1/1/07/1911, and Cpl. T. HARTLEY. Congratulary message received from C.in Chief through Brigadier on general appearance steadiness of men at the inspection.	
	4th		Coys at disposal of the Coys. Capt CHADWICK proceeded to England for Comm Offrs course at Aldershot. Warning order received for Bn to move to TATINGHEM	
TATINGHEM	5th	10 am	Bn marched to TATINGHEM. Dinners on march. arrived about 4.15 pm Falling out poor but Billets very good. Warning order for move received	
NEUVE EGLISE	6th	6.45 am	Transport moved off by road. Bn marched to WIZERNE and entrained for BAILLEUL at 1 pm arrived 8.30 pm, and marched to NEUVE EGLISE arriving about 6 pm. Billets good. Transport arrived following day. Voluntary Church parades. Transport arrived about 2.30 pm	
	7th		Capt KING returned from leave to England.	
	8th		Coys marched to BAILLEUL for Baths to change of clothing. Lt S.S. SCOTT rejoined Bn from England. took over command of "A" Coy.	

WAR DIARY or INTELLIGENCE SUMMARY

Army Form C. 2118.

No 2

October 1917

Place	Date	Hour	Summary of Events and Information	Remarks and references to Appendices
NEUVE EGLISE	9th		Coys at disposal of Pl. Coys. C.O. Coy & platoon Commanders went by lorry to reconnoitre the Southern defences of ARMENTIERES at 9 a.m. 2nd Lt EDGAR rejoined Bn from T.M.B.	Ref. Map HAZEBROUCK 5.a. 1/100,000
	10th		Bn allotted 30x range. Very wet.	
	11th		Bn allotted 100x range.	
	12th		Coys at disposal of the Coys C.O. O Coy Commanders reconnoitre line in front of MESSINES. Conference of all officers in evening. 2nd Lt HOLLOWAY reported back from Coy. Course.	
	13th		Bn allotted 30x range. Major WENHAM & Signalling Officer reconnoitred line	
	14th		Voluntary Church parade. Bn relieved the 2nd R.W.F. in the left sector of Bde front, leaving Bgd H⁰ Qrs at 6.15 p.m. relief completed without incident by 12 M.N. Fairly heavy shelling during night. "A" Coy R.T., "B" Centre, "C" left. "D" Coy support.	
	15th		Good deal of shelling at dawn. Very heavy. Most cleared up Coys of got quieter. "C" Coy. had 5 men killed & 10 wounded by shell fire early morning. Brig M G² visited Bn. Nº Qrs. in afternoon. Coys employed in improving front line	
MESSINES Sector	16th		Fairly heavy shelling during night, principally between Bn. H.Qrs & left front company 9th H.L.I. Officers came up to reconnoitre line. Artillery carried out shoots against line of Steel Keep, occupied by Germans on our front. Slight attestation on FANNY Farm about Bn. H⁰ Qrs. Work carried on improving line and wire in front	

Army Form C. 2118.

WAR DIARY
or
INTELLIGENCE SUMMARY.

(Erase heading not required.)

October 1917

Place	Date	Hour	Summary of Events and Information	Remarks and references to Appendices
MESSINES	17th		Fairly heavy artillery barrage on our support line from 12 M.N. to 4.30 a.m. Fairly quiet during day. Brig. & G² visited Bn. H.Q. during morning. Enemy trench mortar fired on "C" Coy. H.Q. Artillery retaliation asked for, but had little effect. Work continued during improving front line. A good supply of R.E. material taken to front line. Quiet day. C.R.E. visited Bn. H.Q. Channel work to be done to improve line.	Ref. Map.
Sect.	18th			WARNETON Sheet and Belgium & France
	19th	4 p.m.	H.L.I. advance parties came up & took over same etc. Bn. advance parties moved back to support Bn. to take over. Bn. H.Q. 9/9th H.L.I. arrived about 9.45 p.m. Relief reported complete by 9.45 p.m. Bn moved back to Support Bn. H.Q. Bn. Old post damaged. Slight shelling during night. Bn employed in finding working parties for R.E. concealed. 1 casualty. Bn employed in finding working parties for "D" Coy at disposal of O.C. 9th H.L.I.	1/4 am
	20th		Quiet night. Intermittent shelling day & night. G.S.O. visited Bn. H.Q. during morning. Comdg. Officer & Adrell. Officer visited Rt. Bn. H.Q. Bn. front line. Canal working parties found. Weather very unsettled.	
	21st		Rather more shelling during night. Quieter during day. C.O. & Coy Comdrs. reconnoitred way to R? front Bn. H.Q. Bn. Coy Officers 12nd A & S.H. came up to reconnoitre line. Relief by Bn. in view of Tuesday	

Army Form C. 2118.

No 4

WAR DIARY
or
INTELLIGENCE SUMMARY.

October 1917

(Erase heading not required.)

Instructions regarding War Diaries and Intelligence Summaries are contained in F. S. Regs., Part II. and the Staff Manual respectively. Title pages will be prepared in manuscript.

Place	Date	Hour	Summary of Events and Information	Remarks and references to Appendices
MESSINES	22nd		Quiet night. Shelling in neighbourhood of J/B H.Qrs. during morning. Advance party of 2nd A.R.S.H. moved about 4 pm. Relief by NZ H.Qrs. arrived 7.15 pm Relief complete at 8.45 pm to cancelled. Bn moved back to NEUVE EGLISE arrived about 10 pm and occupied same billets as before.	Ref. map WARNETON Sheet and Belgium & France 1/40,000
	23rd		Bn rested. Relieved orders. Warning orders received to move to YPRES. Be employed under HQ Canadian Corps. working Lyster Railway) on the 24th inst. 2nd Lt CLEDEN proceeded to R.T. Crewe at ST POL to NOTLEY joined flying corps	(To YPRES
	24th		Bn embussed at 12.30 pm for YPRES. Transport moving by Rd Bn took over Camp N.E. of YPRES from 1st Canadian Transpt billeted in VLAMERTINGE Lieut officers left behind at NEUVE EGLISE for instruction in R.E. work & L.M. Gun.	
YPRES I.24.d.74	25th		Bn employed finding working parties in relief. Also in improving Camp which was in a bad state owing to the rain. 2nd Lts. HARRISON, CROWE, DOWLING, EDWARDS joined Bn for duty 23rd inst.	
	26th		Except rest of working parties in vicinity, nothing	
	27th	"		
	28		No change to Camp.	

Army Form C. 2118.

No 5

WAR DIARY
or
INTELLIGENCE SUMMARY.
(Erase heading not required.)

October 1917

Place	Date	Hour	Summary of Events and Information	Remarks and references to Appendices
YPRES I.2.d.7.4	29th		Working parties as usual. 2nd Lt BOTTOMS left for LEWIS GUN CRSE LE TOUQUET	Ref. Map Belgium
	30th		Working parties as usual	France
	31st		do — Marching orders received for relief tomorrow back to NEUVE EGLISE	1/40,000

Army Form C. 2118.

WAR DIARY
or
INTELLIGENCE SUMMARY.

(Erase heading not required.)

16th. Bn. King's Royal Rifles

November 1917

Place	Date	Hour	Summary of Events and Information	Remarks and references to Appendices
YPRES	1st		Considerable rain during the night. Early morning, men dropped in the camp having working parties as usual. Bn. moved by lorries to NEUVE EGLISE at 2 p.m. arrived about 4 p.m. BILLETED in this ALDERSHOT CAMP. Very good camp.	Ref. Map S.28. Belgium & part of France 1/40,000
	2nd		Bn. had 5 casualties during tour at YPRES, all slightly wounded.	
	3rd		Bn. at disposal of I.C. Camp for general cleaning up.	
	4th		Coy. at disposal of the Camp Baths in afternoon. 2nd/Lt CRAM granted leave to England. Church parade in morning. 30 O.R. & 140 O.R. found for working parties.	
	5th		Capt. COOK rejoined from 2nd Army Course. 2nd/Lt GOLDSACK returned from leave to England. Capt. at disposal of I.C. Camp. Comdg. Officer & 2nd/Lt 2nd i/c. Coy Comdrs. & the Officers for Coy. went to WULVERGHEM to witness demonstration of practical working by Class of Officer Instrs. Comdg. Officer & Major WENHAM went on to support line to arrange relief with 1/5th Scottish Rifle.	
NEUVE EGLISE	6th		Bn. paraded at 11 a.m. for presentation of Medal Ribbons by Brig. Comdr. D. Recipients as under. Capt. FRANCIS. M.C. Rfn. TRACEY. Bar to M.M. M.M. to Rfn. JACKSON. CLEMENTS. LEVETT. BOND. WALTERS. GLEAVE. Sgt. TINDALL. Cpl. PAYNE. 4Cpl. COVENTRY. BRENNAN. Cpl. GIBSON. Comdg. Officer attended conference at Bde. Hd Quarters.	

WAR DIARY or **INTELLIGENCE SUMMARY**

November 1917

Place	Date	Hour	Summary of Events and Information	Remarks and references to Appendices
NEUVE EGLISE	7th		Btn relieved 1/5 S.R. in Support line on MESSINES RIDGE 4.15 p.m. relief complete by 8 p.m. Quiet night.	Ref. List S. 28
	8th		2nd Lt. CHEETHAM granted leave to England. Enemy shelled vicinity of Bn H.Q. during day. 3 Officers 130 O.R. for digging the support line, 5 Offrs & 120 O.R. employed in carrying material for same. Major WENHAM supervised the work. Work carried on from 5.30 pm to 4 am.	Belgium part VI Tranel 40.000
	9th		Very poor progress made in spite of rain and mud. Quiet night. 6 Officers & 200 O.R. employed carrying R.E. material from BELL'S FARM to SMYTHE's dump during day. Support line parties carried on at night. Brigdr G2 visited Bn H.Q. during day. Captain of Coy lend in afternoon.	
	10th		A few S.A.A. fired into MESSINES during last night. Day carrying parties as usual. C.O. went up to arrange details of relief with 9th H.L.I. Support line parties worked from 5.30 pm to 1 am. Only enemy to Raid by 1 Queens Coy Offr at 2.15 am. 2nd Lt. APPLEBY, BIGGS, TALBOT & TRUBY to report from "B" Echelon to 9th H.L.I. for duty (Temporary). Quiet night.	
MESSINES	11th		No retaliation for Raid during night. Considerable shelling in vicinity of Bn H.Q. and "A" & "B" Coys during day. 1 O.R. killed 6 O.R. wounded "A" Coy. C.O. of Australian 18 visited Bn H.Q. during day. Relief of Bn by 13th Bn front relief commenced 5 pm. reported complete at 10 pm. Casualties 4 O.R. wounded in support line.	

WAR DIARY
INTELLIGENCE SUMMARY

November 1917

Place	Date	Hour	Summary of Events and Information	Remarks and references to Appendices
MESSINES	12th		Disposition of Coys in line: "D" Right, "A" Centre, "B" Left, "C" Support.	Ref. map S.28 Belgium & France
			Quiet night. 2nd Lt THOMAS proceeded to 2nd Army School. 2nd Lt COE granted leave to England. Front line in a very bad state owing to rain, much over the knee in places. "D" Coy. on night of 12th cut off by they, "A" Coy had in places, left of "B" Coy very bad. Men kept busy in trying to clear & repair. Enemy quiet except for a little T.M. machine gun fire during day.	
	13th		Quiet. Brig'r G.O.C. visited Bn during afternoon. Intermittent shelling, mostly about GAPAARD during night. Bn 2 Cas. waited line during afternoon. Australian M/G moved into Bn to arrange about taking over. Ration party shelled coming up, 2 ours killed, 2 OR wounded, obliged to return, arrived remainder come up with the first found at 12 M.N. During night orders received re relief by Australian 18th Bgde of 14/15. Fairly quiet night. Slight shelling of front line, left of right coy "D" Coy hit. 1 Killed 2 wounded. C.O. of Australian Bn arrive to discuss details of relief.	1/40.000
	14th		Relief commenced at 5 p.m. reported complete 9.15 p.m. No casualties. Bn marched back on relief to ALDERSHOT Camp. Casualties during Tour in line OR 2 killed 13 wounded.	

WAR DIARY
or
INTELLIGENCE SUMMARY.
(Erase heading not required.)

Army Form C. 2118.

November 1917

Place	Date	Hour	Summary of Events and Information	Remarks and references to Appendices
NEUVE EGLISE	15th		Coys at disposal of O.C. Coys cleaning up & inspecting. Warning order received that 100th & 9th Bde would move to LOCRE area 16th. Memo from BGC received complimentary Bn on the work done during the tour in the line, especially the good work done in the support line. Bn? Comdr also spoke of the men cheerfulness under very bad condition.	Ref. Map S 28. Belgium & part of France 1/40,000
LOCRE	16th	8.15 am	Bn marched to LOCRE area. Billeted in BIRR HUTS, very good quarters. Arrived about 11-15 am. Falling out state kit. 2nd Lt BOTTOMS returned from L.M.G. course.	
	17th		Bn rested at LOCRE. 2nd Lt ERRETT granted leave to England.	
	18th	9 am	Bn moved by motor Buses to BRANDHOEK area arrived at 10 am billeted in TORONTO Camp. huts & tents, very dirty condition.	
BRAND HOEK	19th 20th 21st		Bn employed in cleaning up Camp & area. 2nd Lt KARN granted leave to England. Coys at disposal of O.C. Coys. Cleaning Camp continued. 400 Reported. Coys at disposal of Bn Coys. 2nd Lt. MATHER, MORANT, TALBOT proceeded to VIIIth Corps Rifle School. 2nd Lt. CROWE to VIIIth Corps Bombing School.	
	22nd 23rd		Coys at disposal of Bn Coys. MAJOR WENHAM returned confirmed up B.W to H.E.Ypres. Coys at disposal of Bn Coys. Bn Hqrs Gas Respirators tested at Bn? Gas Chamber. 2nd Lt SURREY Brinkworth D.B.&T. A.D.S.S. from Cheetham 2nd Lt CHEETHAM Off. team from England. Moved to POTIJZE area as Bn in support.	

Army Form C. 2118.

No 5

WAR DIARY
or
INTELLIGENCE SUMMARY.

(Erase heading not required.)

November 1917.

Instructions regarding War Diaries and Intelligence Summaries are contained in F. S. Regs., Part II. and the Staff Manual respectively. Title pages will be prepared in manuscript.

Place	Date	Hour	Summary of Events and Information	Remarks and references to Appendices
BRAND HOEK	24th	7.40 p.m.	Bn. marched to Hussar Farm. POTIJZE area. Arrived about 10.40 a.m. Billeyput Farm Hk.	
POTIJZE	25th		Bn. lick over shelters, Tents etc. Voluntary Church parade. 2 O/R, 100 O/R found for working on building huts.	Reg. Inf. 329
	26th		Bn. at 2 hours notice to move into support. From 2 pm. Reduced to 4 hrs. 27th	Belgium
	27th		Bn at 2 hours notice. Bn. employed on working parties. 2nd Lt. BOTTOMS, proceeded to England on leave. 3 Casualties received from shell fire in working parties.	part of France
	28th	9 Hrs.	340 O.R. on working parties. Major WENHAM & Coy. Commdr. reconnoitred support line, 1 casualty. Coy. Runner slightly wounded Shrapnel C.O. visited Bde. H.Q.Prs. re. taking over line. Brig. Comdr. Maj. G. PINNEY visited Bn. H.Q. Prs.	1/40-vvv
	29th		2nd Lt. COE returned from leave to England. Bn. relieved the 1st Cameronians in LEFT SUPPORT "A", "C", "D" "B" Coy. 3 Coys. at HAMBURG. 1 Coy. at BOETHOEK. Relief complete Bn. H.Q. PASSCHENDAELE Sector. Bn. H.Q. 9 m. BOETHOEK.	PASSCHENDAELE Sheets 20 & 28
PASSCHN DAELE	30th	9.30 p.m.	Bn. H.Q. 9.30 p.m. Casualties Nil. ABRAHAM HEIGHTS, PASSCHENDAELE. Quiet till 10.30 a.m. when Hd. Brasheller for 30 mins. Occasional heavy shell ing at intervals during day. O/C Coys reconnoitred front line. O/C & 2nd-in-comd B/n H.Q. 2/Lt. S.U.C. COE killed by shell. Left for front line 5.30 pm Re. R.I. A/O D Coy PASSCHENDAELE. B Coy CREST FARM. Hd Qtrs. HAMBURG. M. Bretherwick Lieut Col. 16 K.R.R.	1/10-vvv

WAR DIARY or INTELLIGENCE SUMMARY

Army Form C. 2118.

No. 1

16th (S) Bn Kings Royal Rifles

December 1917

Places	Date	Hour	Summary of Events and Information	Remarks and references to Appendices
PASSCHAN-DAELE	1st		Coys took over positions as follows. "D" left front Coy finishing 7 posts N.E. of Church, with 2 platoons in cellars in support. "C" Coy right front Coy finding 14 posts E & S of church, with one platoon in support. Coy H.Qrs. Coy H.Qrs. in dugout nr PASSCHANDAELE Road. Major R. WENHAM remained with "C" Coy H.Qrs. 100 yds S. of church. "A" Coy in Reserve in trench 300 yds W. of "D" Coy. "B" Coy found garrison of CREST FARM. Bn. H.Q. Bn remained at HAMBURG. Orders were received night of 20/1st that enemy were likely to make a raid. Coys helpful from 6.30 am till 7.30 am. PASSCHANDAELE village was heavily shelled other intermittently during day particularly in the vicinity of Church. Orders received during day that the 8th Bn were coming out an attack on our left. "D" Coy were to raise by Rifle & L.M.G. fire a fire barrage. All movement in our line to be reduced to a minimum. No movement by day was possible at all, owing to being under observation by the enemy and all communication was by runner. ZERO was fixed at 1.55 am. Coys notified. Relieve for 3 days was brought up on the mn of H.L.I. brought up Coys dumps during the night. Two prisoners were	PASSCHAN-DAELE parts of sheets 20 V 28 1/10.000
	2nd	1.45 am	taken by "D" Coy dead to Bn H.Q. Pm. They stated a relief was in progress 2pm Enemy barrage came down 2 min. after own terminalg intense. Brit Bgn. 2pm No communication possible. Coys & Bn H.Q. impossible from 2 am until 4 pm. Our firing was intermittent from 4-20 pm to 5 pm. It became initial. A S.O.S. sent up, no our left which probably caused the 8th proposed down again. In the afternoon. News came in from Coys "A" Coy had suffered largely. Heavy casualties. Opt. MYS. Coy went down badly but all were back again up. This shewed that attack had been abandoned,	

WAR DIARY or INTELLIGENCE SUMMARY

Army Form C. 2118.

December 1917.

Place	Date	Hour	Summary of Events and Information	Remarks and references to Appendices
PASSCHAN DAELE	3rd		Intermittent shelling round PASSCHANDAELE Church during night. Orders received re relief. "A" & "D" Coys went to be relieved by 9th Bn. K.R.R.C. "C" & "B" by 9th H.L.I. Comdg Offr went to interview H.C. 8th K.R.R.C & 1st D.V. re details of relief. Guides reported from Camp at 6 am. PASSCHANDAELE shelled fairly heavily during morning. Situation ─── for Brigr Gl visited Bn. H.Q. during morning. Shell shelling at dusk, after it became normal shelling ──── when men came up. "B" C & "D" Coys relief completed by 1 am. Maj Menten arrived at Bn H.Q. This ──── no sign of a relief for "A" Coy. Unless movement from Btn H.Q. "A" Coy did withdraw & relief is completed by 4 am. No casualties Bn. H.Q. The remain where they are but Companies in ──── in shelters.	PASSCHAN DAELE Part of Sheets 20 & 28 1/10,000
HAM BOOM FARM	4th		Slight shelling in vicinity during day, also good deal of enemy activity. Working parties found from all Coys on Communicating Trench & Company "C" Camp. Changed position with Coy of 1st Queens. Adjt of 1st Middx arrived to discuss details of relief nights 5/6. Quiet night.	
	5th		Slight shelling during day. 2nd Bn CLEVEH to England on leave. Carrying parties found for Land ── manual. Relief commenced 11.15 pm. Reported Camp cote 12-15 am. All hands in Camp near YPRES by 2-45 am. No Casualties. Very quiet relief.	
	6th			

WAR DIARY or INTELLIGENCE SUMMARY

Army Form C. 2118.

No 3. December 1917

Place	Date	Hour	Summary of Events and Information	Remarks and references to Appendices
YPRES area	6th		Orders received to entrain at ST JEAN ST. at 10.30 a.m. for BRANDHOEK	
		9.45	Marched to ST JEAN. (Transport moved by road.) Entrained, arrived BRANDHOEK 11.30 am marched to TORONTO CAMP but was again ordered before Total Casualties during time in line Officers 2 Killed 1 wounded O.R. Killed 23 wounded 45. Many relieved Nos 6 3. Several cases of Trench feet caused by the men being unable to move owing to deep & little conditions of the line	Of Inst.
BRANDHOEK	7th		2nd Lt ERRETT returns from leave to England. 22nd Lt CROWE from Bombing course. Coys at disposal of R E Corps for cleaning up & refitting.	S.28. Belgium
	8th		2nd Lt KARN from leave to England. 2nd Lt CROWE & 1st CR June 1171st Tunnelling Coy for work on Dugouts in the line. Coys at disposal of R E Corps	part of France
	9th		Voluntary Church parade. 2nd Lt SORRY returns from leave to England. Orders received for Bn to move to WINNEZEELE - STEENVOORDE Area.	1/40 000
	10th	8.30am	Bn marched to WINNEZEELE arrived there about 1.30 p.m. Billets good, but scattered. 2nd Lt EDGAR & 8 O.R. proceeded to VLAMERTINGHE on draft for Corps Salvage Coy.	
WINNEZEELE area	11th		Coys refitting. Musketry class for NCO's commenced. Capt BALSHAW proceeded to 9th Corps Signalling School as instructor.	

Army Form C. 2118.

To W.

WAR DIARY
or
INTELLIGENCE SUMMARY

(Erase heading not required.)

December 1917

Instructions regarding War Diaries and Intelligence Summaries are contained in F. S. Regs., Part II. and the Staff Manual respectively. Title pages will be prepared in manuscript.

Place	Date	Hour	Summary of Events and Information	Remarks and references to Appendices
WINNEZEELE Area.	12th		Coys at disposal of D.E. Coys. Marning orders received for moving to YPRES, for working on roads under C.R.E. 8th Corps.	Ref Map S.28
	13th	9.30 am	Bn marched to GODVAERSVELDE Station. Entrained 1.15 pm. arrived YPRES 2.15 pm. & marched to Camp, SALVATION CORNER. Coys very good. Nissen huts & dug outs. 2nd Lt Sullivan proceeded to England on Court Martial duty.	Belgium but in France
YPRE'S area	14th		No working parties required. Cleaned up camp. C.R.E. 8th Div. arranged with Bn H.Qrs to arrange working parties. 2nd Lt Bottoms returned from leave to England.	France 1/40,000
	15th	5.15 am	"A" & "B" Coys with 4 Officers 4 Officers moved off by lorry to work under 490th F. Coy. R.E. & D.L.I. "B" & "C" Coys 4th off moved off at 5.30 pm. in lorries for work under 112 F. Coy. R.E. All returned by 1 pm. no casualties.	
	16th		"A" "B" & "C" Coys found working parties. "D" Coy. Battal. Voluntary Church parade. 2nd Lt Harris & 31 O.R. returned from work on Br 2 Reinft Camp.	
	17th		"A" "B" & "D" Coys worked as detailed. "C" Coy Battal.	
	18th		"A" "C" & "D" Coys worked as detailed. "B" Coy. Battal. 2nd Lt Holloway returned from leave to U.K.	
	19th		"B" "C" & "D" Coys worked as detailed. "A" Coy. Battal.	
	20th		"A" "B" & "C" Coys worked as detailed.	

Army Form C. 2118.

No 5

WAR DIARY
or
INTELLIGENCE SUMMARY.
(Erase heading not required.)

December 1917

Place	Date	Hour	Summary of Events and Information	Remarks and references to Appendices
YPRES	21st		Bn relieved by 1st Camerons. Entrained at YPRES for GODWAERSVELDE arrived there at 12-5.15 pm and marched to WINNEZEELE arrived there 3 pm.	Ref Map S 28
WINNEZEELE	22nd		Cox over. Billets came up before 2nd Lt APPLEBY & BIGGS proceeded on leave to U.K. Belgium Bn had no casualties whilst working in the forward area.	part of
	23rd		Coys at disposal of OC Coys cleaning up & refitting. H/9/c 13 V.C. Coys Roped Voluntary Church parades. 2nd Lt CLEUGH returned from leave to U.K.	France
	24th		"A & D" Bathed, Training carried on as per programme	1/40.000
	25th		General Holiday. Voluntary Church parades. 2/Lt HODGES returned from leave to U.K.	
	26th		Capt CORK Lt BROUGH proceeded on leave to U.K. "A" Coy had two divines in school. Training carried on per programme. Lecture to Officers N.C.O on CAMBRIA fighting by Divl Comander. Lt Col A.V. JOHNSON proceeded on leave to U.K. Major WENHAM assumed command of Bn. "C" Coy had two divines in school.	5.20 pm
	27th		Training carried on per programme. Hon Lt & 2/Lt Mr HUDDLESTONE proceeded to U.K. to take up appointment as Equipment Officer in the Tank Corps. 2/Lt GOLDSACK proceeded to LE TOUQUET for small arms & L.M.G Course. Lt Col HOWARD to VIII Corps School from Intelligence Course. "B" Coy had two divines in school.	

Army Form C. 2118.

WAR DIARY
or
INTELLIGENCE SUMMARY.
(Erase heading not required.)

No 6

December 1917

Place	Date	Hour	Summary of Events and Information	Remarks and references to Appendices
WINNE ZEELE	28th		Coys at training. There were Coys employed in cleaning camp in afternoon.	Ref. Map S29 Belgium
		10.15 am	Lecture by Corps Commander to Officers deemed necs of 18th. on system of training. Lt. Col. LEVY (Comdr 8th Corps School) lectured to Officers. New Rifle and gun demonstration (New system of training) with Platoon from	Blagny turned part of France
		11.20 to 6 pm	the School, in Class room drill and simple tactical operations.	1/40.000
		4 pm	Coys at training. 2/Lts MATHER, TALBOT & MORANT return from VIIIth Corps School. 2/Lt TALBOT & MORANT proceed to England on leave. Lt. LIDSCOMBE return from special leave to England.	
	29th		Morning Church parade. Frost continues. 2nd Lt. SULLIVAN return from leave to England.	
	30th		Coys at training. Specialist classes commenced lecture on Intelligence to Coy Comdrs. Platoon Officers & Sergts. by G.S.O.3. in schoolroom. Capt. CHADWICK returns from Senior Officers Course at Aldershot and resumed duties in second in Command temporarily.	
	31st		Forecast received, Bn move to forward area about 4th prox.	

Eberham Major
K.E. 16 Kings Royal Rifles

WAR DIARY
INTELLIGENCE SUMMARY

Army Form C. 2118.

January 1918   16-7B. King's Royal Rifles

Places	Date	Hour	Summary of Events and Information	Remarks and references to Appendices
WINNE ZEELE	1st		General holiday. New Year greetings received from 8 Corps, Division & Bde.	Ref. Map IS 28 Belgium & part of France 1/40,000
	2nd		Training carried on per programme. Bde. Boxing Tournament at STEENVOORDE in afternoon. Bn. done very well. Bn. Concert in evening. Brigadier attended. 2nd Lt Smith "D" Coy from leave to U.K. 2nd Lt. Sharp to Gas Course at STEENVOORDE.	
	3rd		Training carried on per programme. Brigadier discussed points of interest re Training. Tour in the line etc. to the Bn's & Coy Commanders of the Bde. Orders received for move to BRANDHOEK on the 4th. Congratulatory telegram sent to Lt Col A.V. Johnson re award of D.S.O. appearing in Gazette.	
BRAND HOEK	4th		Batt'n entrained at 9am for TORONTO Camp, arrived there about 9.30am. Transport moved by road at 8am. Heavy going owing to state of roads with sharp 4 points. 2nd Cve refresh. from Machine Gun Course at PONT REMY and proceeded on leave to U.K. Orders received for move to YPRES 5th inst.	
YPRES	5th	2pm	Batt'n marched to YPRES arrived about 4pm. Billeted in cellars, fairly comfortable. Transport remained at BRANDHOEK. B'lay willed to town unless others of C.R.E. 50th Division. Orders for further working parties received.	
	6th		Bn cleaned up. Billeting and 30 Officers & 130 O.R's in working parties in forward area 4 Brig KRR's vacated 16th 4th 9ths	12 Mfrs.

WAR DIARY or INTELLIGENCE SUMMARY

Army Form C. 2118.

January 1918

Place	Date	Hour	Summary of Events and Information	Remarks and references to Appendices
YPRES	7th	6 a.m.	5 Offrs & 130 O.R. working in forward area. Remainder of Bn. Bathed in morning, working parties in afternoon. 2nd Lt. Sunny rejoined from Gas Course.	Dy. trap Gas 1125 Belgium
	8th	6 a.m.	5 Offrs & 130 O.R. working in forward area. Details bathed. Lt. Holmes (M.O.) left Bn. for England on completion of Contract. New M.O. Lt. Taylor joined Bn. immediately. 2nd Lt. Smith O/Coy evacuated to Field Ambulance. Thaw & snow during day.	0/party France
	9th	6 a.m.	6 Offrs & 180 O.R. working in forward area. All Woodmen proceeding into line attacked French Fort. Treatment hut at POTIJZE during morning. Working party attacked in afternoon and pushed Bn. as at present on way up. G sub.	140,000
		3 p.m.	Bn. less 2nd Lt. Pullinan & 150 O.R. who formed attacked "B" Echelon observed at POTIJZE, moved up to support and to relieve 9th H.L.I. Relief slow slowly owing at the time. Relief was completed by 8.15 p.m. with 2 casualties. Two men of "B" Coy being wounded by shell fire on way up. Bn. bivouaced in shelters near HAMBURG. (Bn. 2nd in command Stales (IRKSOME) Camping party of 1 Off, 46 O.R. found for 9th H.L.I. & front line. Lt. C.H. Wilkins O/adjt. proceeded on leave to U.K.	
HAMBURG	10th		2nd Lt. L.W. Cheetham resumed duties of O/Adjt. Intermittent shelling during night. Coy. Comd's "A" & "B" Coys reconnoitred line of advance for Counter attack. 2nd Lt. Thomas & 1 Sooting wounded by shell fire. Shots badly being killed. Slight shelling in vicinity of HQ during day. "B" Coy. bombing party for H.L.I. "D" Coy. — ditto — had 12 queries.	

WAR DIARY or INTELLIGENCE SUMMARY

Army Form C. 2118.

January 1918

Place	Date	Hour	Summary of Events and Information	Remarks and references to Appendices
HAMBURG	10th		"A" Coy & "B" Coy. were kept ready to move at 10 minutes notice until Coys. 1 & 2 of "D" Coy. killed. Fairly quiet night.	Ref Map PASSCHEN DAELE parts of sheets 20 & 28 1/10,000
	11th	10 pm	Bdg. g.a. wanted Bde. H.Q. Gas. "C" Coy found fatigue party for 171st Tunnelling Coy. Very heavy shelling N. of PASSCHENDAELE from 1 pm to 2.30 pm. Vicinity of HAMBURG shelled during afternoon. Boundary reported. Enemy patrols of 4 H.L.I. & 1st Queens. Left 11.5 pm returning at 10 pm. Quiet night. Lt. Col. Johnson Capt. Cooke & Lt. Brough returned from leave to England. Wounded at CROIX EDMOND.	
	12th		Test S.O.S. carried out at 7.30 am. Orders for relief by 4th Suffolks received. Quiet day. Carrying party to 1st H.L.I. 40th Queens left at 5 pm. Relieved by 4th Suffolks, relief reported complete by 7.45 pm. Bde. proposed truck to WHITBY CAMP by JUDAH TRACK all reported on by 10.15 pm. no casualties. 2nd Lt. SANDFORD joined Bn. for duty. Total casualties during time in line 2 killed 11 wounded, including 2 offrs.	
POTIJZE	13th	9.30 am	Bn. moved by light railway to BRANDHOEK. Thence to TORONTO CAMP WEST arriving about 1 pm.	
BRANDHOEK	14th		Coys. at disposal of O.C. Coys for cleaning up & refitting. Major Wenham proceeded to England on leave. Capt. Chadwick took over duties of 2nd i/c. Brandfours, 2/Lt. N.R.N. left to join 2nd Lts. Morris and Talbot returned from leave. 2/Lt. Nam left to join 10th Bn. E. Yorks. Bn. attended Baths in afternoon.	

Army Form C. 2118.

WAR DIARY
or
INTELLIGENCE SUMMARY.
(Erase heading not required.)

January 1918

Place	Date	Hour	Summary of Events and Information	Remarks and references to Appendices
BRAND HOEK	15th		Camp at disposal of OC Coys. Both allotted in morning. 2nd Lt Clough to 9th Coy to advance at TERDEGHEM.	Ref. Map Sheet 28
	16/13		Coy at rest about 1 P.M. Coys Storms occupied his underclothes damaged in Camp. Lt Taylor MO journeyed on leave to England. Lt Staggers DSR attached for M Medical duties. Few received for rest at forested area.	Belgium & French [part?]
	(7th)	8.30 am	Bn proceeded by light Railway from BRANDHOEK to ST JEAN, many coloured new journey. Bn moved up to support line at SEINE and relieved 1st Cameronians. Quiet until relief reconnaissance carried out today. Bn only lost Pte ... ... 194 Pte ... Rifle	1/40,000
		4.30 pm		
SEINE	18th	2.30 am	Brig.de GT 19th F. Bull trailed to No. 2 Cor. Occasional Concussion shell at 8.30 am	Ref map
		10.45 am	Co Stay Counter reconnaissance defence positions. Working parties of 5th Middlesex and 23/div found by Bn. Return moved about 2 to 2.30 pm. Quiet night.	Boesinghe DAEYE
	19th		All Kings party used as in previous day. Heavy shelling in vicinity of "A" & "B" Coys. no casualties. Command of this front to CC no Transport Command by 1/10c "D" Coy.	[part 1] sheets 20 & 28
			Capt Chadwick received command of B. American Officer attached to Bn. Bn moved up to front line at 5 pm to relieve 1st Cameronian in left sector of Bde front. Disposition of Coys. "A" Coy. left front "B" Coy right front. "C" Coy Support (Caes Farm). "D" Coy Reserve (HAALEM). Relief completed by 9 pm. Wounded: 1st Middlesex Ltd.	1/10,000
on SEINE				

Army Form C. 2118.

WAR DIARY
or
INTELLIGENCE SUMMARY.

(Erase heading not required.)

January 1918

Instructions regarding War Diaries and Intelligence Summaries are contained in F. S. Regs., Part II. and the Staff Manual respectively. Title pages will be prepared in manuscript.

Place	Date	Hour	Summary of Events and Information	Remarks and references to Appendices
PASSCHAN-DAELE	20th	5.15 pm	C.O. & 2 other officers visited front line Sentry groups on our front both keeping a lookout on them. N. 7 PASSCHANDAELE. 2/Lt TALBOT proceeded to lecture to Henry Battalions for 3 days. Capt Andrews arrived from leave to England. Quiet night. Coy 4 Canadian officers wounded for instruction, weather fine.	App. Map "PASSCHA-DAELE" 20/17 S 1/10.000
	21st		Reinforcements Pte 4/9930 Cpl J. [?]30 am Baths Camp, being Brigade day. Reliefs completed by 7.50 p.m. No casualties. Relieved by 1st Middlesex.	
			On move from 6 LOW FARM thence by Hope Railway to YPRES (Chateau brickworks) and marched down with no time before Canadian during this rel. 25ft. & request from [?] to England. The attention of tank of in live area due to the bad weather.	
YPRES	22nd		Camp at disposal of Lt. Coy for cleaning up etc. Baths allotted to "A"B & "C" Coys under orders 4/9 982 2/ Bn. S[?] Capt S.C. Scott proceeded on leave to England.	
	23rd		Proceeded to "A" Coy 4/14.0 O.R. for working parties "D"Coy 4/497 or Baths	
	24th		Working parties as previous day, interior work carried out. 2nd Lt Sullivan proceeded to England & report to Second Army 2nd Lt Talbot return. 2. 2. Lt Officers showing no increase	
	25th		Received Trench Tray Exchequer, before moving up to the YPRES Hillock from 10 am to 12 noon. 2/Lt A.M. SMITH badly wounded.	

2353 Wt W2544/1454 700,000 5/15 D. D. & L. A.D.S.S./Forms/C. 2118.

WAR DIARY
or
INTELLIGENCE SUMMARY

Army Form C. 2118.

January 1918

Place	Date	Hour	Summary of Events and Information	Remarks and references to Appendices
YPRES	25th	4pm	Bn moved from YPRES by light Railway to IBERIAN & took over in relief of 1st Cameronians, who relieved Bn. Changed 12 hour army to Brandenburg Line. Disposition was as follows. "C" Coy. Right front, "D" Coy Left front, "A" Coy Support (front line), "B" Coy Reserve (HAALEM). Full relief 16 Caurville. C.O. visited line 11 pm. Very quiet night.	Ref. Map PASSCHAN DAELE part of Sheet 20 & 28
PASSCHA-NDAELE	26th	9 am	Great Comd't visited Bn HQ. Hm. Very quiet. Very hazy.	No ops
	27th		Bn Comd proceeded to reconnoitre training ground to be given Bn on leaving ESQUERDES area. Bn taken a lorry. Officers details left at 12 midnight by C.O. D'Coy. Within return from leave to England.	
	27th	9 am	Brig Comd't made Bn HQ. am. Very quiet day. Bn relieved by 1st Middlesex relief complete by 9.25pm in cameleon	Ref. Map France
BRAN D HOEK	28th 3.45		Bn moved back by light Railway from Low Farm to BRANDHOEK and left via TORONTO camp (Huts). Bn reported all in by 11.30pm. Total Casualties 1 OR. kd. Bn entrained at BRANDHOEK for WIZERNES arrived about 8.30pm marched to ESGUERDES. Billets good. Horsing all into his	Sheet 36 D N.E
ESGUER DES	29th		Bn rested cleaned up	

Army Form C. 2118.

WAR DIARY
or
INTELLIGENCE SUMMARY.
(Erase heading not required.)

January 1918

Place	Date	Hour	Summary of Events and Information	Remarks and references to Appendices
ESQUERDES	30th		Coys at disposal of V.C. Coys for clearing up & everything. Training was recommenced by Cos. steps by Coys.	Ref Map of France Sheet 36.D N.E.
	31st		Major Benham returned from Leave to England & Major Jt. Wood proceeded on leave to England. Coys at disposal of V.C. Coys. Maj. Benham resumed command of No. 1 Coy & Chadwick assumed charge of command.	

Benham Major
O.C. 116 Fd Coy R.E.

Army Form C. 2118.

WAR DIARY
or
INTELLIGENCE SUMMARY

(Erase heading not required.) 16th (S) Bn King's Royal Rifles Vol 28

February 1918

Place	Date	Hour	Summary of Events and Information	Remarks and references to Appendices
ESQUERDES	1st		Coys at disposal of Coy Commdrs for Training. Bombing practice Trench dug by "C's'D" Coys	Ref/Mob
	2nd	7.30 pm	Company bombers. 2nd Lt M. SULLIVAN returned from England after reporting to Public Office France. Bn marched to "X" Range "A" & "C" Coys to 12.30 pm "B" & "D" 12.30 pm to 4 pm. Sheet 36D Range very good practice was had at 300x in Rapid & deliberate fire at 200x in N.E. snapping shooting was fairly good considering the small amount of practice "X" Range the Bn has had lately at the long ranges. ✓ 24 ORs	
	3rd		Voluntary Church parades. Lt.Col A.V. JOHNSON D.S.O returns to Bn from Acting Brig'r and assumes Command. 2nd Lt. EDWARDS proceeds on Musketry Course Maj. WENHAM assumes 2nd i/c of Bn.	
	4th		Coys at Training. 12 N.C.Os commence 6 day course under BdeP.T.&B. Instructor. Senior NCOs parade daily under R.S.M. for Drill. Specialist Classes carry on. Bugles & 13 noticed Bn. N.S.97 Snipers have use of Civil Range 700x in village.	
	5th		Bn. allotted Baths at SETQUES Training carried on.	
	6th		"X" Range allotted to 18th "B" & "D" Coys 9 am to 12.30 pm. "A" & "C" 12.30 pm 6.4 pm Shooting improved especially the rapid. Draft of 52 O.R. & 13 fd-Corpls joined 18th from 13 Rnd under 2nd Lt Mc LEAN. 2nd Lt. Mc LEAN posted to "D" Coy	

WAR DIARY or INTELLIGENCE SUMMARY

Army Form C. 2118.

No 2

Instructions regarding War Diaries and Intelligence Summaries are contained in F.S. Regs., Part II. and the Staff Manual respectively. Title pages will be prepared in manuscript.

Month: February 1918

Place	Date	Hour	Summary of Events and Information	Remarks and references to Appendices
ESQUERDES	7th		Coy. & Specialists training carried on.	Ref: map
	8th		Bn. carried out John Platoon Rifle Comp: a bed down by "Army Rifle Assn." France in "X" Range. No 2 Platoon "C" Coy. being the winners.	France Sheet
			Capt. CHADWICK M.C. left Bn. to join 13th Rifle Bde. on posting as 2nd i/c	36 D
	9th		Coy. & Specialist training carried on. C.S.M. PEACH "D" Coy. to England for 6 months.	N.E.
			being relieved by Sgt. THWAITES from 6th Bn. for Army Interprices Heavy M.G.s	
			2nd Lt. MORANT reported to 100th Inf. Bde.	
	10th		Voluntary Church Parades.	
			Pioneers Coy for duty.	
	11th		Coy. & Specialist training carried on. "X" Range allotted to "C" Coy. for practice	
			of the Platoon Comp: 2nd Lt. HOLLOWAY proceeded to LE TOUQUET on G.H.Q. Course	
			M.L.M.G. Lt. LIPSCOMB B3 Transp. Offices appt: Bn: T.O.	
	12th		Bn. attends Bn. parade for Aeroplane demonstration cancelled owing to bad	
			weather. Coy. & Specialist training carried on. Capt. CORK Lt. WILKINS (Adjt.)	
			2nd Lts. MATHER & HODGES proceeded to BOULOGNE to look over Camouflage Works.	
			Capt. J. HANNAY "D" Coy. Lt. J. REID "A" Coy. 2nd Lt. J. GRAY "C" Coy. 2nd Lt. RICHES "D" Coy.	
			2nd Lt. E.W. JEFFERY "C" Coy. 2nd Lt. C.G. WILDER and B3 O.R. joined for duty.	
			Officers posted to Coys as against their names	

Army Form C. 2118.

No 3

WAR DIARY
or
INTELLIGENCE SUMMARY.

(Erase heading not required.)

Instructions regarding War Diaries and Intelligence Summaries are contained in F. S. Regs., Part II. and the Staff Manual respectively. Title pages will be prepared in manuscript.

Title pages February 1918

Place	Date	Hour	Summary of Events and Information	Remarks and references to Appendices
ESQUERDES	13"		Coy Specialist Training carried on. "C" Coys Platoon Competition	Ref. map of France
			on 'A' Range. They went but in Buyers, but Coys in shooting 2nd Bn moved being 1st	
		10.30am	Comd. Officer inspected Drafts. They were mostly employed their Trngs. at	Sheet 36.0.
			Bn. paraded at Gas hut during afternoon for testing of Box Respirators	
	14"		Coy Specialist training carried on. Divisional Comdr. visited Bn. during morning	N.E.
			Brig.W. PAH. Hays dined with Bn. in evening	
	15"		Coy Specialist Training carried on. 2nd Lt MATHER proceeded on leave to England	
	16"	9.30am to 12.30pm	Bn. paraded for demonstration by low flying Aeroplanes near HALLINES. Pull in Working men practiced in firing at them. They also fell on bombing targets when being assailed by tear lights. A/G demonstration Bn. was formed up of demonstration of Gas cloud attack. Gas was released from cylinders. Bn. wore respirators when adjusted & worn for about 10 minutes Bn. then marched back	
	17"		Representatives of 50th Div. apportd to take over training area etc.	
	18"		Coy Specialist training carried on. "B" Coy Field Firing Movement in evening	
	19"		Bn. attacked "C" Range. "A" & "C" Coys from 9 to 12. "B" & "D" Coys 12 to finish Coys proficient rapid firing at 300x	

(A5893) D.D.&.J., London, E.C. Wt. W50J/M1673 350,000 4/17 Sch. 92a. Forms/C/2118/4

Army Form C. 2118.

No 4

WAR DIARY
or
INTELLIGENCE SUMMARY.

(Erase heading not required.)

February 1918

Instructions regarding War Diaries and Intelligence Summaries are contained in F. S. Regs., Part II. and the Staff Manual respectively. Title pages will be prepared in manuscript.

Place	Date	Hour	Summary of Events and Information	Remarks and references to Appendices
ESQUERDES	19th	5pm	Lecture by Div. Gas Officer to officers & NCOs on "Gas Schol".	Ref Map France
	20th		22 O.R. Forming returned from L.M.G. course.	
			Coy Comma & programme. Maj. Neuham and 4 Coy. Commanders from 1st to YPRES	Ref Map Sheet 36.D. N.E.
			on advance party to reconnoitre barrage relief for taking over supply line in	
			Right Batt. Sector Cafe front from S.O.? Division.	
	21st		Batt. moved by train from WIZERNES to BRANDHOEK and C.T.E. bus	
BRAND- HOEK	22nd		Hutts in TORONTO CAMP (W).	
			Bn moved by light Railway from BRANDHOEK to POTIJZE, arrived there about	
			11.30 am. & rested in MAIDEN Camp until 5.30pm. Advance for Coy. & men. and	Ref Map Trench Map ZONNEBEKE
			M.G. took over Stones etc. Maj. Wenham & 4 Coy. Commanders reported to	28N.E.1
			Bn moved up at 6pm by light Railway to BORRY Farm in two trains.	
			1st at 4.15pm "A" & "B" in 1st train, "C" & "D" in 2nd train. Guides of 5th N.F. met them.	
			then conducted them to Supp[t] line. Very quiet night. Relief complete by 9pm. by 1/10,000	
ZONNE- BEKE			Dispositions of Coys were 15th H.Q.Bs. (SEINE) in MEBUS named "INDIA" with 3 Coys.	
			"A" & "D" in vicinity, "C" about 570x away at "THAMES"	
			Transport and "B" Echelon remained at Ridge Camp BRANDHOEK with advanced	
			"B" Echelon at H.Q. Stacking POTIJZE.	

WAR DIARY or INTELLIGENCE SUMMARY

Army Form C. 2118.

No 5

(Erase heading not required.)

February 1918

Place	Date	Hour	Summary of Events and Information	Remarks and references to Appendices
ZONNEBEKE	23rd	6.15 am	Quiet day. Working parties went forward as follows 107/450 O.R carrying from SEINE DUMP to CREST FARM. 2 Offrs 450 O.R. for trenching in front of pub in front of system from DEFY CROSSING to 22 P.S.T. from 6.30pm to 9pm. At 11.30pm the enemy put Barrage on our Front Support Posts. S.O.S. was sent up on our right. #42 went to Trenchfield assembly position. Enemy then opened at 1-4-5A.m. and Coys returned to Shelters. No casualties. heard that a raid had taken place on front	Rel. Inst. Trench Map ZONNEBEKE 28 N.E.1 1/10,000
	24th		of Bn on our right. Occasional shelling during remainder of night. Occasional shelling in vicinity of SEINE during morning, one shell fell near "C" Coy Hd Qtrs wounding 2nd Lt CLEUGH and 9 O.R. Working parties from Bn yesterday. "D" Coy continued wiring at night. Bn Comdr visited 18th H.L.I during the day.	
	25th		Raining. Working parties no record. Occasional shelling during day. M.G.9th H.L.I came arranged lines for 106 & 163 officers right of/26th Coy Comanders made a front line Coy trenchmortar posts to be taken over at dusk.	
	26th		Heavy shelling from 12 M.N. to 2 A.M. in vicinity of SEINE. Working parties to war! Bn relieved 9th H.L.I Relief started 6pm. Reported complete 8.30pm. 1 Casualty (Wounding) "B" Coy into O.R. Wounded during morning. 2nd Mtrs took over Support line last night. C.O. 4, 2nd ½ C. Infect 7th 2nd Line	

WAR DIARY or INTELLIGENCE SUMMARY

Army Form C. 2118.

No 6

February 1918.

Place	Date	Hour	Summary of Events and Information	Remarks and references to Appendices
ZONNEBEKE	27		Disposition of Coys were "A" Coy Right Coy. "B" Left Coy. "D" Coy Support. "C" Coy Reserve.	Ref map
		2.9 pm	DARING Covering Party proceeded to front line of posts by night.	Trenchup
			Occasional shelling during day. Readjustment of Coys Hrs. placed much of DURHAM	ZONNEBEKE
			Fort sub sector in area of "B" Coy making 3 Coys in front line & Coy in support	28 N.E.1
		10 pm	Patrol sent out tonight to "BIRMA" to examine C.O.V. 2 – 4/6 Area reached Right	1/10,000
		to	of Left of "B" Coy front, with a view to observing posts, found ground on Left mostly	
		12 pm	Light much tho. Burst of shelling about 3 am. near Left Coy. 10th Pro 15th RoundHd	
28th			S.O.A. dump blown up. Heavy shelling to our right from 3 am to 4 pm.	
			Bng Os Hadin 8th 10th Pro and discussed about arranging posts. Post in R.F.J. Pm front	
		10 pm	to be relieved tonight by 15 commences tonight. C.O. & Off. from R.E. sent out and selected	
			wire listing posts from 2nd Mrcs. Evening prty from "A" Coy.	
		10 pm	Patrol of 2 Officers & 12 O.R. sent out in direction of "BIRMA" but were unable to	
		to	much that owing to being fired on by our machine gun fire.	
		1 am.	from "BIRMA", & N. end of BoIW Wood. Reported ground west of 1.	
			Much quiet tonight. Bright Moon & Frosty.	
			A few Gas Shell fell in vicinity of Bn HQrs about 9.30 pm	

Army Form C. 2118.

No. I

WAR DIARY
or
INTELLIGENCE SUMMARY

(Erase heading not required.) 16th (S) Bn Kings Royal Rifle Corps

March 1918

100/33

Vol 29

Place	Date	Hour	Summary of Events and Information	Remarks and references to Appendices
YPRES	1st		Quiet night. 8th Coy Commander 91st Brigade came round line at	Ref. map
ZONNEBEKE SECTOR		4:30 am	C.O. accompanied them round & returned about 7.30 am	Sheet 28 N.E.
			Quiet day. S.O.S. shot up N. of PASSCHENDAELE at 10.30 p.m, all quiet on outpost.	
			Patrol went out to BIRNA during night, found nothing to report on.	
	2nd		Fine morning, quiet day. Relieved by 2nd Worcs relief commenced at 1.7 pm	
			reported complete by 9.30 pm. The Batallion then marched to BORRY FARM	
			entrained on Light Railway lost YPRES at 11.45 pm (billets as before)	
	3rd		2nd Lt R.W. Edwards proceeded on leave to ENGLAND	
			Battalion returned up Volunteer Church parade	
	4th		Battalion bath	
	5th		Battalion employed on work in Corps line & Divisional Line & its approaches & R.E.	
			paraded 7-15 am returned about 3 pm. 2nd Lt H.G. MATHER returned from leave to UK	
	6th		Battalion paraded at POTIJZE during morning for Trench fort treatment.	
YPRES			2nd Lt H.G. MATHER took over command of D Coy vice Capt. O.S. KENT & B Echelon ordinary	
			move to ENGLAND for 6 months Coy of duty. Intelligence Officer & one Officer per Coy	
			reconnoitred route of Bttn on our right during morning, then proceeded	
			to SEINE to take over. Scheme out, preparatory to relief	

Army Form C. 2118.

WAR DIARY
or
INTELLIGENCE SUMMARY.
(Erase heading not required.)

No 2

Instructions regarding War Diaries and Intelligence Summaries are contained in F. S. Regs., Part II. and the Staff Manual respectively. Title pages will be prepared in manuscript.

March 1915

Place	Date	Hour	Summary of Events and Information	Remarks and references to Appendices
YPRES	6th		Returned to Support line in Reply to St. PIERRE St. L. Railway at Wieltje	Rly. Ref
		5.30 pm	1 & 2 pm detained BORRY FARM demanded to SEINE relief coffers 8.30pm	Sheet 28
			Assembled. Capt. LE FRANCIS proceeded to CALAIS to meet Salvage book. Mess. N.E.	
			Commdg Officer proceeded to Brigade H.Qrs & took over Acting Brigadier the / DENHAM	
ZONNEBEKE SECTOR			took over command of Bde SEINE area shelled with Gas & H.E. at 10.30 pm	
	7th	1 hr	½ of "A" Coy killed & 2 wounded, several gas cases	
			Considerable shelling at intervals during night, a good deal of gas found in area of "B" Coy on left. Coy Commanders Officers of GSO visited Bn	
			H.Qrs during morning. Shelling continued at intervals during day.	
			Before the following working parties "D" Coy on Reserve bomb dump R.E.	
			"C" Coy found company guards for 171st Tunnelling Coy R.E. "A" & "B" Coys working,	
			digging new portion front line	
	8th		Not carried on as usual. Message received from Bde stating Corps Commander	
			wishes his appreciation intimated conveyed to all ranks for the good work done	
			by Corps and on the 5 inst. Enemy shelling heard in front of B.H.Q.	
			from 4 am till 4.30 am, quiet then until 10 pm when it started again.	
			Quieted down somewhere Steenwerck of night front.	

Army Form C. 2118.

WAR DIARY
or
INTELLIGENCE SUMMARY.

(Erase heading not required.)

March 1918.

Place	Date	Hour	Summary of Events and Information	Remarks and references to Appendices
ZONNEBEKE	9th		MOT carried on as usual. 2nd Lt. E.W. JEFFERY & 3 O.R. slightly gassed whilst on company parts. At 2pm a S.O.S struck the front of 9 Bn 4.O.S.R. Killing the Sentry & Runner & wounding 4 others, of whom 2 died later. I ordered everyone up inside, knocked a lump of the concrete off outside telescope all gunbursts of fittings from all entrance, find all shelled only come onto no other damage done. Quiet then until 9.30 when SEINE DUMP area heavily shelled. Warning received that Enemy mined positions on our front was to be exploded. MOT carried on as usual. Personal shelling of SEINE Dump heavy. (Chlorhine) General Counter mortar Bde. H.Q.rs. Capt. LEFRANCIS returned from CALAIS.	Report N.E. Sheet 28
	10th		Bt Coy met 9" H.L.I. Coys in front line to arrange relief. Comdy Offr returns from Brigade dressing command of Bn. Relieve 9" H.L.I. in front line. 2" Horse Lt.R. in support line. The relief complete by 9.10 PM. During relief enemy retaliation SEIN E area heavily. NCO Y/e 9 guides for 27"H.R.Cs was killed 2 O.R. wounded. 2 O.R. gassed. 2" Horse Lt.R. had several casualties, all gassed by 8.30 pm. Lt. C.E. HOWARD proceeded to R.E. Corps to be attached for 3 days course of instruction. Disposition "A" Coy R.F. Front "C" Coy Centre "B" Coy Left Front. "D" Coy. Reserve. Bn H.Q.rs DARING CROSSING. (INHALE)	

A.D.S.S./Forms/C. 2118.

WAR DIARY or INTELLIGENCE SUMMARY

Army Form C. 2118.

No. 4.

March 1918.

Place	Date	Hour	Summary of Events and Information	Remarks and references to Appendices
ZONNEBEKE	11th		Quiet night. C.O. & 2nd/Lt. went round support posts. & Coy. H.Q.P.O. at 10 a.m. Bright visited Bn H.Q. Noon. Day quiet general [illegible] shells fell around SEINE. 18 O.R. Field Casuals rejoined Bn. Slight shelling of area at 10 p.m. Gas & H.E. This continued all night.	Ref Map Sheet 28 N.E.
	10th		5 am to 7am Artillery active on both sides. SEINE heavily shelled also Left Front Coy Support Posts. 2 Killed & 1 wounded. Left Coy "B" first standing Patrol of 1 Officer & 15 O.R. to go out to Contour 38 Nord of BIRMA from front to daylight. 2nd Lt. Monro, who working on new posts Brandy officer. Came to the R.S. Maj. E. WENHAM assumed command of Bn. Brig [illegible] visits Bn in afternoon. Intermittent shelling all day. Co. went round front posts 10pm.	
	13th	2am	S.O.S. went up N & S of 18 Front Bn. Barrage came down all along Bn front. Died down for a short time. 6 am. LEFT front Bn "B" reoccupied new posts, numbered 26 & 27. 2nd Lt. H.E. HOLLOWAY 4th & 5 Standing patrol wounded by shell fire. Slight shelling during day. 2nd Lt. W.H. MCLEAN proceeded on Bombing Course Co.	
	14th	5am	Enemy Machine guns very active. Patrol got in touch with 18c on our Left Front 27 Front. Standing Patrol had nothing to report.	

Army Form C. 2118.

WAR DIARY
or
INTELLIGENCE SUMMARY.
(Erase heading not required.)

No 5

March 1918

Place	Date	Hour	Summary of Events and Information	Remarks and references to Appendices
ZONNEBEKE	14	9.30am	Slight shelling. Bright warm B.H.Q during morning. Coy Comdr Go recce B.H.Q and checked route to relief by 2nd Bn troops. P.O, 2nd Bn troops made R.H.Q barrage sheet 28 N.E	Sheet 28 N.E
			Guides over for relief. Quiet day. Relief commenced 8pm, reported complete at 9.40pm.	
			Coy in relief proceeded to BORRY FARM. Reserves accommodated for YPRES dismounted.	
			trans Siding as before, except Bn H.Q & to tramway shelters 1483 EZ	
YPRES	15th		by R.E. All reported in by 12 noon. No casualties	
			Batt noted L. Barker. 2nd Lt J.Reid 6 days leave reporting back from leave to U.K.	
			Court-martial noted summary of evidence taken & forwarded to 1st P.W.O	
	16		Coys carrying fatiguing up to 4 officers & 92 O.R. joined "B" Echelon from	
			2/6 Batt. Coys Royal Rifles. R/Cpts E.F. SARGENT & 2nd Lt A.A. KERR posted to	
			"B" Coy. 7th Lt R.H.M. LEA to "C" Coy. 2nd Lt F.B. HOLBOROW to "D" Coy.	
	17		Voluntary Church parade. Bn worked on army zone proposed 7.15am worked	
			from 9am to 1.30pm. dugout work at arroup 2pm. Lt DUHN W.S.R American	
			Army attached to Bn for 5 days. YPRES shelled during day.	
	18		Bn paraded for trench fort fatigues during morning at POTIJZE.	
			Advance parties sent up to support line SEINE to Culto new strong pts.	
			Bn moved up to support line SEINE by Rail to BORRY FARM. Relief by	
		7pm	trench to SEINE. Relief reported complete by 10. 50pm. Quiet relief	
			- no casualties	

WAR DIARY or INTELLIGENCE SUMMARY

Army Form C. 2118.

March 1918

Place	Date	Hour	Summary of Events and Information	Remarks and references to Appendices
ZONNEBEKE	19th		Disposition of Bn. in support were B.H.Q. SEINE (INDIA) A Coy. THAMES "B" & "C" & 2 platoons of "D" Coy. SEINE, "D" Coy. HQ & 2 platoons CORDIAL FACTORY.	By map Sheet 28 N.E.1 1/10,000
		1-10am	From 1-10am until 3.15am enemy shelled SEINE area heavily with H.E. & Gas. 2 OR killed several gas cases. Bn. Respirators had to be worn.	
		6.30pm	About 6.30pm shelling commenced again for short kind. Retaliation asked for during early bombardment. Bn. was much quieter. "A", "C" & "D" Coys worked on Reserve posts under R.E. "B" Coy on trolley Tram Line J-7/J/L N. CHEETHAM returned from 34th Division Lewis Gun School	
	20th	1.30am	SEINE heavily shelled with gas, several casualties. 4.30am Heavy bombardment on our left. S.O.S. sent up of PASSCHENDAELE. Bn. stood to for great part. Stood down when during day on our left. Day much quieter, renewed shell storms and some gas near HAMBURG. Lt. Col. A.Y. JOHNSON D.S.O. returned from leave & took carried on as usual. B. Echellon party Paris & went to Tramway School, and	
	21st	4.10am	Heavy shelling all round SEINE lasting till 6.30am. Good deal of gas. Retaliation asked for. 2 OR. "C" Coy. Killed 1 Wounded severely gassed Lt. A.Y. JOHNSON B50 gassed 13th about 11am. Tonight visited B.H.Q during morning. 2 OR. mined guides. LT. C.H. WILKINS gladly proceeded to LE TOUQUET for week end of officers Rest House. 2nd Lt. L.W.CHEETHAM 2nd Lt. L.W.CHEETHAM took leslie of death	

2353 Wt. W3544/454 700,000 5/15 D.D. & L. A.D.S.S./Forms/C.2118.

Army Form C. 2118.

WAR DIARY
or
INTELLIGENCE SUMMARY.

(Erase heading not required.)

March 1918

Place	Date	Hour	Summary of Events and Information	Remarks and references to Appendices
ZONNEBEKE	22nd	2am	A raid was carried out by the Batt. on the GASOMETERS which was supported by heavy artillery bombardment to which the enemy did not reply. During the remainder of the day it was very quiet, hostile shelling being practically nil.	Ry. MAP SHEET 28 NE.i.
	23rd	9am	Batt. relieved g[th] H.L.I. in front line. B Coy left, C Coy centre, D Coy right. A Coy Reserve. Batt. HQ. INHALE. Very quiet relief, being complete by 9.30pm. No casualties. Offr. Survey to hospital from Gupta School, Lt. Williams proceeded to LE TOUQUET for one week rest. Very quiet day. — Commanding Officer proceeded to 100th Brigade to take command and Major Wurden assumed command of the Batt. — Major Girard joining "B" Echelon. — Lieut Dunn U.S. Army Inf.	
	24th		At 4am heavy gas hostile bombardment of the SEINE AREA which lasted until 8am. Hostile shelling more active during the day resulting in 2 O.R. of "A" Coy being killed. Owing to re-adjustment of the line, D Coy moved from front line to Reserve, and HQ @ INDIA. Relief by Coy of 20[th]Worcesters.	

2353 Wt. W3544/1454 700,000 5/15 D. D. & L. A.D.S.S./Forms/C. 2118.

WAR DIARY or INTELLIGENCE SUMMARY

Army Form C. 2118.

No. 8

March 1916.

Place	Date	Hour	Summary of Events and Information	Remarks and references to Appendices
ZONNEBEKE	25		Hostile shelling practically nil during the day. "D" Coy providing party of 13 or for 141st Tunnelling Coy R.E., and whole Coy working on new posts in the front line at night. Standing patrol of 1 Off. & 15 O.R. sent out from "B" Coy. to HILL 38. 2/Lt. A. Kerr in charge of patrol went forward and was shot in BUSY WOOD, and reported missing. Patrol returned and went out again under 2/Lt. Statham but no trace could be found of 2/Lt Kerr. Divisional General visited Batt. H.Q. at 9.30 a.m.	Ref. Map. SHEET 28 NE.
"	26		"D" Coy. moved to THAMES, and "A" Coy H.Q. to INDIA. — Very quiet day. Batts. relieved. At night by 9th H.L.I. and proceeded by track to BORRY FARM. Thence by light railway to YPRES. "S.O.S." was sent up on the left whilst the Batt. was proceeding to BORRY FARM. Last ½ Batt. arrived at YPRES at 12.15 a.m. — YPRES being shelled. No Casualties. 2/Lts. Wilde and McKean returned from VIII Corps School.	
YPRES	27		Batt. Bathing. — Shelling at intervals during the day. 3 O.R. of "D" Coy. killed in the morning. — Commanding officer returns from 100th [?] Brigade and takes over command of the Batt.	

No. 9.

Army Form C. 2118.

WAR DIARY
or
INTELLIGENCE SUMMARY.

(Erase heading not required.)

March 1918

Place	Date	Hour	Summary of Events and Information	Remarks and references to Appendices
YPRES.	28th	—	Coys. at disposal of Coy. Cmdrs. for cleaning up. - Representative from each Coy. visit the Divisional Reserve line prior to Batt. working in neighbourhood. YPRES shelled at intervals during the day.	Ref. Map. 28 N.E.
"	29th	—	Batt. working in the Divisional Reserve line in the morning - Major E. Wenham proceeds to LE TOUQUET for one week rest.	
"	30.	—	Commanding Officer proceeds to Divisional HQ. and present at Court Martial. Batt. left YPRES at 7.30 p.m. to proceed to front line in relief of 2nd Worcesters. Entrained at SAVILLE ROAD JUNCTION, detraining at BORRY FARM. Very wet and dark. - A + D Coys. proceed first. Batt. takes over two batt. of line in front Sector. A + D Coys front line. B Support. C Reserve. Accommodation good. Standing patrol of 1 Off. + 15 O.R. Established soon after relief.	
ZONNEBEKE	31	9.30 a.m.	Divisional and Brigade Commanders visit the Commanding Officer and at 12 noon the Corps Commander visits the Commanding Officer. Commanding Officer + Coy. Cmdrs. of "The Queen's" came to reconnoitre new Sector. Light shelling of area during the day.	

Granville. / CR.

A. Nightingale Lt Col
July 16 R.W.K.
Comdg 1/6 R.W.K.

100th Brigade.

33rd Division.

1/16th BATTALION

KING'S ROYAL RIFLE CORPS

APRIL 1918.

WAR DIARY
OR
INTELLIGENCE SUMMARY

Army Form C. 2118.

16th (S) Bn. King's Royal Rifle Corps

April 1918

Place	Date	Hour	Summary of Events and Information	Remarks and references to Appendices
ZONNEBEKE	1st		Light shelling at intervals during day. Lt. C.H. Wilkins again returned to Bn. from LE TOUQUET. It. It. Cunliffe & 34 O.R. joined Bn. in the line. Quiet night. "B" & "D" Coys carried on ordinary work, "A" & "C" Coys on saving.	Ref. Map. Sheet 28 N.E.
	2nd		Occasional shell alarms otherwise quiet. Brig Gl. visited Bn. 4.30 p.m. in morning. Warning orders received that Bn. was to prepare to move in 16 hours. Quiet night. Work carried on as usual.	
	3rd		C.O. & Coy Officers of 4th Brigade aeroplane in morning to reconnoitre trenches by Bn. in company with Bn for relief on the night 4/5th. Remainder of Bn. on ordinary duty. Bn Bay Ld. North Redoubt killed during shelling.	
	4th		4.0 2 p.m. Co. Commanders returned from 17th Training Bn. Bombt carried on & increased during the night. Quiet noisy night Relief by 4th Fusiliers started 6.15 pm. Battn Report complete without incident by 12.45 am. Coys marched to BORRY FARM or while entrained in light Railway for WARRINGTON CAMP, VLAMERTINGHE, arrived there about 5.30 am way slow owing	
VLAMER TINGHE	5th		to much traffic. Bn. in BRANDHOEK. All details joined Bn. from various sources including R.Q.S. Dump at MENIN	
	6th		Bn cleaning up, Lewis guns Lewis guns, 25 Lewis guns & Coy functions on 25.94. Imp & E Workout	
	7th		17th Marched to POPERINGHE and entrained at 10.15 am for TINQUES, arrived about 3.15 pm. Marched to PELLERS. PE HIM about 14 miles. Rather heavy going.	Ref. Map LENS Sheet 11
PERNIM	8th		Had E Workout. Had received reinforcement & pouring in the 16th Bn. Carried on training A. & B. Coys in attack. Coy'd. 107" manner	1/100,000
	9th		Bn. Ground ordered. All Officers with 112 Res. paraded to IZEL LES HAMEAU for lecture by Major O. Harwood Reports. The Rus Highland Infantry after recent mid to Great Front. Bt. Pattell to arrange the 16th	

Army Form C. 2118.

WAR DIARY
or
INTELLIGENCE SUMMARY.

(Erase heading not required.)

No 2

Instructions regarding War Diaries and Intelligence Summaries are contained in F. S. Regs., Part II. and the Staff Manual respectively. Title pages will be prepared in manuscript.

April 1918

Place	Date	Hour	Summary of Events and Information	Remarks and references to Appendices
PENIN	10th	9.15am	Bn returned to march to SUS St LEGER. got about 2 miles on the way, when new R/F orders received to turn about & move back to PENIN & entrain by night to move up north. train received at 8.30 pm. to march to AUBIGNY dentrain for CAESTRE. Transport to move by road. Canteen & water carts accompanied Bn.	R/F orders Jour II 1/Inf. OOA
AUBIGNY	11th	1 am	Bn marched to AUBIGNY entraining there about 12 am entrained & moved off about 9 am. arrived at CAESTRE about 10am. 2nd Lt H.A. Crow rejoined Bn.	
CAESTRE		3.30 pm	A,B & C. moved by motor lorry to pass W. of METEREN remainder of Bn bivouacked into a camp just W. of BAILLEUL, about ¼ of a mile from the REVELSBERG when received to move to a camp E of BAILLEUL on the REVELSBERG	
REVELSBERG			Bn. arrived there about 3pm. tea was served. Dinners were received 12 md & Laundry after that. Bn moved off to relieve the S. LANCS in line "A"N"D" in support "B" & "C" Coys in line. "A"N"D" in support.	
NEUVE EGLISE	12th		from N NEUVE EGLISE, "B&C" Coys moved off to Hannut Farm 2nd Lt Cram & about 1000 men Rackyne Hoste, Hay, Headden, Rickets, Jeffery Gilluck Grey remained at Road Monnet Norbes, Ricks, Jeffery Gilluck Grey remained at REVELSBERG. Heavy shelling from 6 pm stand to at night 2nd Lt Grey reported to Bn HQ & set in for duty as Lieson officer. General Scheme were new orders to move at short notice.	R/F map Sheet 28 N Belgium
	13th		Relief of st Stand carried out about 5 am. a heavy barrage opened on our night barrage surprised a party was sent out to form a defensive flank 2nd Lt Crawford & 20 MK goes out from "C" Coys line as a patrol they report that them at T28.6.5.8 was strongly held by the enemy the patrol being pinned down A message received from S. Land to say that from at some tenor of the captured by the enemy at 6.15 am enemy field developed on front	

Army Form C. 2118.

WAR DIARY
or
INTELLIGENCE SUMMARY.
(Erase heading not required.)

April 1918

Place	Date	Hour	Summary of Events and Information	Remarks and references to Appendices
NEUVE EGLISE	12th		Officer reports of enemy being in front. Covering party went out & fired & gun.	By Map Belgium & France Sheet 28 20.070
		6.40am	6.40am Cap. Francis & others OK. I.15am Cap. Francis sent message by runner to say that strong party of enemy in Building whose alt? being fired upon by rifles & M.G. fire. 7.30 am Message received from Bde. ordering Bn. 16th CRLR to attack ROMARIN in conjunction with S. Fence. Gars shelling had down front facing ROMARIN.	
		10am	10am Informed by S. Fence that Regiment may not be able to attack ROMARIN.	
		10.30am	10.30am Enemy still again in vicinity, counted dead.	
		1pm	1pm Irish again C.O. S. Fence made the HQ'rs & discusses attack on ROMARIN. Cap Collins	
		2pm	2pm from Irish 13th & 9th 2.30pm message from Bde that ROMARIN attack cancelled. 3pm message received from 2nd Worc. mcd. that "D" Coy to say that	
		3pm	considerable enemy retiring over the xxx ridge not moving. 3.15pm message received from 75th B/de stating that 2000 enemy had been observed	
		3.15pm	N.W. from STEENWERKE and TROIS ARBRES 4pm. Heavy enemy barrage on our line Bde on right just back. Enemy seen advancing attack back till 8pm. Enemy well held. "C" Coy fell back a little Right flank of line will bent to Forward of 75 m & and up 7m Minimum Reserve C reinforced about 1st Brigade had line intact from Rd? Quel + very heavy mist. 6am heavy mist & had sent that Bellefield engaged loss on our right but fallen back 2 platoons of "D" Coy sent to reinforce all Corps on right also falling back. Very heavy fire of bullets	
	13th	3am	Call directly on next remnt. to 13th Coy Yeoman support Flank & 17th H & gave Still held on right 2nd Yd xxx on our left make a ditch through barrage & get to 13 & bn? went directly in front of us is on eye. Enemy seen — no sign of 73rd Coy on Wr left. Practicably cut off. Co. & myself bombarded. Last through enemy Headquarters at ECLISE V2 A.D.S.	

WAR DIARY or INTELLIGENCE SUMMARY

Army Form C. 2118.

April 1918

(Erase heading not required.)

Place	Date	Hour	Summary of Events and Information	Remarks and references to Appendices
Micmac Reserve	12th	(?)am	Maj Watson reported to Bn. H.Qrs. & was received orders to dig a defensive position on Mont de Lille, and get in touch with the 2nd Wores. Guide on my Capt Littler met us	Map
RESERVE		11am	Lieut got into touch with HQ 2nd Bn. on right. Enemy continued shelling vicinity of Camp - MONTREUIL	Ref
			S.15.a.1.2. Enemy patrol tried to work round left flank but was dispersed & retired on Estamine	Belgian
			up to Bn 4/9th orders there C.Coy's moved north to S.Sgt. under the 2nd Mgr.	France
		5.30pm	Reported Bn. at 2nd Mgr. returned to end It Howard & 7th NF (C.V.D.hays) at 2.7th Gilbert M.G.	Sheet
			Picker to move up to KORTEPYP. WATERLOO Road relief up ultimation on this night	28.
			of Bn front, extending telewing ground between NIEPPE Po. & KORTEPYP Rd.	
			Remainder of Brune took up position in front of Bn. H.Qrs. 2nd Mnt.F Belletry on C Coy	1/20,000
	13th		during night very cold night. Bn moved back during night & took up position	
			in Camp close to KEERSEBROM. Battn. moved back hometyied from at S.7.A.9.5	
		6am	Lieut Cokaer over to him had breakfast. Slight shelling during day. Transport had	Guiveek transport had
			to move out to S.3. A during afternoon where they formed remainder of Transport.	
			7th Grey tried to get into touch with present 125th & 19th Inf but found they had been	
			ordered the Co. & O.C. 4/9th king arranged to council put us over from Cupe	
HURST FARM	14th		Fairly quiet night. Thirty morning Bth moved back to S.4. C.9.5.	
			Brune moved Corp. Ce got in touch Lieut Smith Transport received orders to jour	
		11am	Bn. Bth moved New Strew up position in Camp at S.15.A.S.3.	

WAR DIARY or INTELLIGENCE SUMMARY

Army Form C. 2118.

April 1918

Place	Date	Hour	Summary of Events and Information	Remarks and references to Appendices
Hill 70 FR	14th	Noon	Received orders from Bde. that 10th T.M.B. Bazalon 2nd Lines, 16th K.R.R's and a proportion of 1st Bde. H.Q.rs. would be employed in excavating a line about Hill 70 Sh. d. S.5.c.	Ref. Map
			The 9th H.L.I. worked on the right. The "B" Echelon under Maj. Wenham worked in	Belgium
			front on the Left. The Advance took the form of a line of posts on the forward slope	4 part
		2.45pm	having direct with a supporting line on the reverse slope 30 yds in rear. Work commenced and good progress made.	France
		6pm	Men went back to camp. Had to stand to about 7 pm afterwards in our posts,	Sheet 28 SW
			there being no attack by the enemy on the REVELSBERG SPUR (CRUCIFIX CORNER)	
		10 pm	Things quietened down. Garrison were left in posts Remainder returned to Camp. Took up No 10 Pro in form S.M. 13.9. Fairly quiet night.	1/20.000
	15th		Very misty raw morning. 2nd A. G. Bottoms and 80 O.R. 2nd Corps & 3 O.R. 2nd H.	
			killed 4 O.R. Defeat 26 Stragglers joined Bn. during day. Carried on improving the posts. System in touch with H.N.Lancs.	
			Who were holding line on our left. And to stand to about 4 pm.	
Hill 70			enemy were shelling the camp behind very heavily, harassed the posts.	
			Support came to our returning from the REVELSBERG SPUR made	
			heavy artillery fire. Received orders to furnish a Coy. of 4 officers & 150 O.R.	
			which together with a similar Coy. from 9th H.L.I. were to form a Composite	
			Bn. under Major Lumsden 9th H.L.I. reset 6 by take up a position	
			at the CRUCIFIX CORNER.	

WAR DIARY
or
INTELLIGENCE SUMMARY.
(Erase heading not required.)

Army Form C. 2118.

Place	Date	Hour	Summary of Events and Information	Remarks and references to Appendices
Hill 70	15		The Coy. marches to Bourgh, with 2nd/7th Cam, Jeffrey Libery had to form up at KEERSEBROM. Inspection New & Maj. Lamberton 9th H.L.I.	Ry/Map
			2nd/7th Grey was wounded by M.G. fire on way down, enemy M.G. jealousy on	Belgium
			2nd/7th Hart/Hes of Bottoms took charge of boots and Br. H.Q's. 2nd/7th Coure	France
		8.15pm	duties of 10 O/R's Brig f/ 19/vs moved back to LOCRE CHAD M.28.C. (Patrols were pushed out & kept in with compy. 75th.)	Sheet 28
			12.33 am orders received that attack on CRUCIFIX (General Boxes) not to take place.	Sa
	16		and that Bn. was held Chateau dug-outs S.4.g.2 & S.6.c.3.8 (Kd.70) The enfilade fire was held by the E.N.R. operating in S.6.C.3.8, afterwards extended to Clayton Rly.	1/10000
			Maj. Lamberton took over as O.C. of front line from S.4.g.2 to S.6.C.3.8 at 5.30am. The mummy heavy enemy night ... this time was not compressed from the enemy. The disposition were 18th M.G.KS.	
			... were effectives from the ... Camp cycled ... S.4.g.1 held outpost firing ... W.N.Y...the two posts form Bm S.11.a S.4	
			2nd/7th Bottoms W.T.M.B's held support posts in rear. Bn. H.Q.'s. moved	
		9pm	back to HILLE FARM and passed H.Q. line of 19th X. of W. NOTE.	
			Patrols of three were sent out in early morning held down from RAVELSBERG I advancing in Hill 70 Artillery were called for. Advanced M.G. fires were from massage from Bill 6 any that reinforcements in great numbers opposite by Br.	
		8am	Artillery were coming up in support of the was to held in at all costs.	
			Railway bridge right front on Railway at KEERSEBROM. Enemy Gallery 75. very heavy artillery fire was on road at ... The men up to then Them gun.	
			Every rank's attack during afternoon several of our trench all over taken off	
			2nd/7th Crew badly wounded & Brig. was with also great numbers of men 1/2. enemy reported to be dropping in in R. M.G. any in front of KEERSEBROM artillery fire advised on that spot 2nd/7th Bottoms sent up to Coys from left sector	
			... Hallam + 12 then sent up to Coys from left sector it	

WAR DIARY or INTELLIGENCE SUMMARY

Army Form C. 2118.

Place	Date	Hour	Summary of Events and Information	Remarks and references to Appendices
Hill 70	16th		Things quieted down somewhat at night. Orders were sent up to be relieved at night. The front line especially the right & left had been badly knocked about and the garrison badly shaken & fatigued. Relief was got partly through by day but was not completed until day.	
	17th		Early in the morning heavy artillery fire became very heavy, the trench mortars opened out & an intense preparation on the Corps front was from about 7:45am to 8am. By 8am the enemy were seen to be caught under the barrage but were in strength. Being A.G. + Rifle fire all morning. Several attacks were driven off on our right & front, a Bn of the Northumberlands Fus? being especially good work on our right centre attacks. Hill 70 came in for a great deal of shelling during the day. Messages received from the front saying enemy had massed some front opposite us & a coy of R.S. Fusiliers between 6 Coy down was not very good. No. 16 Coy to long & 16 Coy Officers wounded. The HVs was ... the 3rd up right. Battn being a quick help to fill up the exciting enemy as they came to M.G. fire. Suspects of the left of the 15th made sure that we in the small sentries wet form line on left I Wood the enemy had penetrated a [150]yds & on bombing and without heavy artillery fire I was afraid that no trenches knowledge of him. Things became much quieter as it got dark.	
			Plan for relief: Halls by 16 & 148? by 15th crew in R.O.B. I'd opened and arranged relief. We went to S.F. take over by + of I'd & placed. Guides were sent down and the lines began to be held by up without incident. Relief completed between back to Bn. W.T. WESTOUT RE morning 3am 4am, the morning of Oct 18.
There follows...	

Army Form C. 2118.

WAR DIARY
or
INTELLIGENCE SUMMARY.
(Erase heading not required.)

April 1918

Instructions regarding War Diaries and Intelligence Summaries are contained in F. S. Regs., Part II. and the Staff Manual respectively. Title pages will be prepared in manuscript.

Place	Date	Hour	Summary of Events and Information	Remarks and references to Appendices
WESTOUTRE	18th	9 am	2/Lieut M Rowke (L Allen) with had prepared to form for men, the Platoon staff till gas Received orders to be prepared to move back probably by bus	HAZEBR OUCK #
		2 pm	refused to proceed to MONTU CATS by night worse arrangements about Shore hay Billets in Convent cellars we very comfortable.	5. a.m.
MONT TS CATS	19th		Had a good night. Congratulatory messages received on the good work done by the Bn. Rifle showing etc recommencing.	
			Cold morning. The men cleaned up & got to pieces Enemy shelled the vicinity of Convent during afternoon & also positions of which we were told to be in and the Cavalry having taken up S. of Convent causing S of P.E. enemy put a Barrage on the Chapel showing 10 of S.P.E. Warning orders received that Bn. would move to STAPLE BREW 20th	
		4th	Bn. moved off at 6. 15 a.m. The Bn. entered and moved at 4.30 a.m. 16/17 K.R.R.C. reaching Comaecked to MOORDPEENE arrived there about 12. 30 pm. what to go to top village OCHTEZEELE arriving there about 4. 15 pm. To 1 and final rest. Bn. rested about 12 midn.	
OCHTEZEELE	20th		Billets quite good but quite dead. Weather fine. Weather fine and sunny.	
	21st		Remained at TROIS ROIS Sent orders round for Bn. to prepare an immigae - branch ___	
		6.45 a.m	Bn. paraded inspected attended by nearly but 2 ZUYTPEENE Platoon were nearby officers there enthused as back to billets they waited there to move was ordered that B. would under d pet transport etc packed up other received Bn. "A" & "B" coy what notice Bn. to hand to reorganise Bn. 3/1 strong with 9 officers with B. to arrive C+D coys 2nd at 3 pm. Bn. heavy 3/1 strong with 9 officers 2 South (64 officers & 2 of R joined about 5. 30 pm. Have posted to Coys to make S.J. Lt. O.W. Clough "C" Coy, 2nd Lt. M.F. Savage "D" coy. 2nd Lt. E.M. Allen "E" coy the former very officers who belonged to Bn. before that appoint. New officers 2nd Lt B. Knight "B" coy. 2nd Lt S.H. Levitt D.coy. The men chiefly new men were sent to Coys. according to their strength up.	[illegible marginal notes]

(A7885) Wt. W807/M1672 D. D. & L., London, E. 350,000 4/17 Sch. 92a. Forms/C/2118/14
T E Pembleton

# WAR DIARY

Army Form C. 2118.

WAR DIARY
or
INTELLIGENCE SUMMARY.

(Erase heading not required.)

April 1918

Place	Date	Hour	Summary of Events and Information	Remarks and references to Appendices
OCHTEZEELE	22nd		2nd Lt. S.W. Clough took over command of "D" Coy. 2nd Lt. C.W.A.G. McLeod & 13 O.R. orders received for inspection of "B" Coy. by Divisional Commander next day.	Ref. Map Belgium & France
		10am	R.Q.M.S. paraded C.B. Qr paraded for inspection & arrangements of practice at 10am. Sgt & one mule cart on the other. Div¹ Commdr received guard, pleased with turnout of troops.	France Sheet 27 Edition 3
			Capt. Lloyd Lt. R.J. to "D" Coy and Sgt. Wes hurt & the 3rd Bn went to "D" Coy. Inspection of the Bn. after parade the Bn. carried on with its organising. Capt. Cook R.A.M.C. joined Bn. as M.O. (Temporarily) Still off to be noted.	1/40.000
	23rd		Capt at disposal of O.C. Coys. Training commenced. N.C.O.s of gas billetting, Lewis Gun, Stretcher Bearer classes commenced. Tel. Bn. had only 2 S.B. 12 L. Gunners. "9 Sigs. alllrs. w/t, every few transit men apparently in the draft.	
	24th		Coys on short range work in village, and on all Bayonet fighting practices from 12.30. Bn Bds at NOORDPEENE billeted to 13. 2pm to 8pm. Capt King Corbin Highlanders (on attached to Bn) from Sch. school to instruct. 14 men in Lewis Gun. 2nd Lt. H.R. Kindly reported 12.15pm from Base with our draft of 199 ORs. 2nd Lt. Crowe with took up the duties of the Asst. Adj. Officer Coy Sheridan carrying carried on. First range allotted C. Coy.	
	25			
ST MARIE CAPPEL	26	11.5am	Orders received at 5am for Bn to move to aerodrome near STMARIE CAPPEL. No air petrol. Bn. moved off 7.45am arrived destination about 12 noon. Men billeted in hangers & tents.	

Army Form C. 2118.

WAR DIARY
or
INTELLIGENCE SUMMARY.
(Erase heading not required.)

April 1918

Place	Date	Hour	Summary of Events and Information	Remarks and references to Appendices
ST MARIE CAPPEL	26th		2nd Lt Penney & 36 O.R. proceeded to LUMBRES on 2 days course of Lewis Gun firing.	Ref Map Belgium
	27th		Coy. & Specialist Training Carried on. Bn. moved into the village of ST MARIE CAPPEL.	France Sheet 27
CAPPEL	28th		Bn. accommodated in Tents. B.H.Q. in Private Billets. Voluntary Church service. 4 Coy Commanders & 16 Spl Officers reconnoitered 2nd Sys. forward area. Warning orders received for Bn. to move to WARDRECQUES area about 10 am 29th.	E.3 Various
	29th		2nd Lt. Elvin & 9 Middle O.R. proceed to 102nd T.M.B. 2nd Lt. Jeffery & 10 O.R. commenced N.C.O's Cos (Temp). Move orders received 1.15 am. Bn. paraded & moved off at 9 am. Train cancelled without the knowledge of higher command had to come back to billets about 10-10.45 pm.	
	30th		Coy & Specialist Training carried on. 50th Range allotted to Z Enn. Teams	

WAR DIARY or INTELLIGENCE SUMMARY

Army Form C. 2118.

(Erase heading not required.)

Place	Date	Hour	Summary of Events and Information	Remarks and references to Appendices
NEUVE			April 1915	
EGLISE			List of Casualties for Action 12/13 April 1915	
&			Lt. Col. A.C. Johnston D.S.O. Bombing Officer - Wounded 13/4/15 2/Lt. M.W. Bensaline - Missing 16/4/15	
			Capt. N.K. Balfour Signalling - Wounded & Missing B. Hodges -do- 13/4/15	
Avril 10.			A/Major E.A. Hilliers Wounded K.A.W. Lea Killed 13/4/15	
(S 5 c 7 2)			2/Lt. W. Sullivan M.C. South Africa Missing L.O. Jellett Wounded 16/4/15	
			A/Capt L.B. Scott O.C. "H" Coy Wounded R.W. Edwards -do-	
			Capt E.A. Park M.C. O.C. "G" Coy Missing 15/4/15 J.E. Nichols (missing) -do- 15/4/15	
			L.B. Francis M.C. O.C. "C" Coy -do- 13/4/15 W.H. McLean -do- 15/4/15	
			E.T. Sargent M.C. -do- 15/4/15 T.B. McCrone -do-	
			Local/Capt H. Heaney M.C. Bomb "D" Coy -do- 15/4/15 J. Grey (Wounded) Wounded 15/4/15	
			L.C. Hezlet O.C. "D" Coy (Commanding Coy) -do- 15/4/15 J. Brown N° 2 (Commanding) Died of Wounds 17/4/15	
			2/Lieut/Lt. R. Aldcroft (Ammunition Reserve) -do- 15/4/15 H.C. Brown N° 2 (Commanding Reserve) Wounded 16/4/15	
			W. Chatham Wounded 13/4/15 2/Lt. B.F. Lowe Witty 17/4/15	
			Lieut W. Hoggar (M.S.O. M.O.) Wounded & Missing 13/4/15	
			Killed 27 2nd & 3rd Mid. Dev. admitted 15/4/15 L.T.A. 15/18	
			Wounded 125	
			Other Ranks { Missing 337	
			Wounded & Missing 25	
			514	

16 KRRC

WAR DIARY
or
INTELLIGENCE SUMMARY.
(Erase heading not required.)

Army Form C. 2118.
Vol 31

Place	Date	Hour	Summary of Events and Information	Remarks and references to Appendices
ST MARIE CAPPEL	Sept 1st 1918		Battalion moved from ST MARIE CAPPEL to LA SABLON. Col J.R. LAMBERTON assumed command of the Battalion, vice Major E. WENHAM to Reserve Battalion on 30th Aug 1918.	Ref Sheet 36A
LA SABLON	2nd		Lt Col B.J. CURLING D.S.O. assumed command vice Col J.R. LAMBERTON. Appt St Stephen? Special orders issued to Company at OC's disposal. New Commander Warned and Orders for move to STEENVOORDE area received.	
	3rd		Battalion marched at 6.20 a.m. and arrived for STEENVOORDE area	
			2/Lt. Transport move. Ship at 7.30 a.m.	
			2/Lt H.E. KING evacuated sick	Ref Sheet 27
STEENVOORDE	4th		Coys remained quiet. Company Commanders	
			Battalion sent of Move noted by Names.	
			2/Lt B.J. CROWE assumed duties of Adjutant.	
	5th		Bn's were at stages of in bridges from 8.30 - 10.30am. Lecture	
			In attendance and hostility of arms	
WATOU AREA	6th		Battalion moved to LM.L.G. 91. Army HQ Command Training	
			Coys. Trench Regulations and Explosives Amy.	
			Letter of Support to join of Officers	
	7th		Company assisted of HQ in new commander. Geographical changes amongst of officers.	
			2/Lt. R.G.H. MURRAY 7th Bde to A Coy	2/Lt H.W. WALDEN
			Captain O. COUGHTRIE 7th Midland 2/Lt W.C. WHITMAN	2/Lt W.A.S. EVERTON
			2/Lt F.J. TROTTER	2/Lt R.C. NAYLOR
			2/Lt L.J. STONEY 2/Lt N.F. CARVER	2/Lt A.R. SUGDEN
			2/Lt J.H. CRUIT 2/Lt D.R. WILSON	
			2/Lt G.C. MORRONGER 2/Lt F.G. RUDD	
			2/Lt A. CAMERON 2/Lt G.S. HOGAN	
			2/Lt N.L. HANNAFORD	
	8th		Lectures were to G.W. L.O.! Areas of Tables T.P. + troops etc of officers	Sheet 2B
			wounded parts of machines	
			A company took up positions 9.30 a.m to 9.30 - 9.3	
			B company took up positions 9.30 a.m to HIGH ? 3 (Strong positions) O.4.21.2.18	
			2/Lt L.J. STONE described expects of Reg'l in Effect 2/Lt W.H. HUNT lost over?	
			2/Lt A.C. MURRAY (7 W?) use of his lost army on own patrol	

Army Form C. 2118.

WAR DIARY
or
INTELLIGENCE SUMMARY.
(Erase heading not required.)

Instructions regarding War Diaries and Intelligence Summaries are contained in F. S. Regs., Part II. and the Staff Manual respectively. Title pages will be prepared in manuscript.

Place	Date 1917	Hour	Summary of Events and Information	Remarks and references to Appendices
BRANDHOEK AREA	May 9		A Company moved to H.30.c.4.1 to G.30.c.9.2. B Company at G.30.a.2.3	Ref Sheet 28.
	10		Remainder of Officers & Warrant Officers reconnoitred YPRES-YSER line and approaches.	
	11		A & B Companies withdrew from their positions to 6.17.B.1.2 in the evening.	
	12		Conference of Officers of Company Commanders. CAPT. G. RITSONS assumed duties of Adjutant vice CAPT. B. COLQUHOUN assumed command of A Company.	
	13		Conference of disposal of Company Commanders.	
	14		Training carried out all the day as before. 2/Lt R.O. CROWE reconnoitred Ypres.	
			14/15 Dems Gas drill were practised as before and remainder of Coy	
			Company parties carried out as per programme.	
	15		Company carried out as per programme. Officers Ranges, Musketry carried out as fine. 9 Officers Ranges, Musketry carried out as ranges. All Company found for work	
POPERINGHE EAST AREA	16		Company moved out and 98 carried to fire on new fire	
	17		Ranges carried out to fire programme. Westhoek ranges used	
	18		C of E Church Parade in attendance of 100 Other Ranks.	
	19		Parade as per programme. C Company proceeded to RUBROUCK for 3 days Range.	
	20		Parade.	
			Evening Lecture by Commander issued by Battalion. 2/Lt R.T. CROWE rejoined from Brigade.	
	21		Company carried out a full Programme.	
			Inspects W.Comp & practised inspection by Army Commander. (2 Platoons A Company, 1 Platoon B Coy + 1 Platoon D Company)	
			4 Other Ranks wounded by shell. 2/Lt N.F. CRYER. 2/Lt DH.A. WELSEN. Proceeded to School of Instruction at 2nd Corps Infantry School.	
			Reinforcement Draft over to 19th Brigade Rifles on 24th received.	

WAR DIARY
or
INTELLIGENCE SUMMARY
(Erase heading not required.)

Army Form C. 2118.

Place	Date 1/18	Hour	Summary of Events and Information	Remarks and references to Appendices
POPPERINGHE EAST AREA	May 22nd		Enemy shelled out bns field programme. Camp Cr & company inspected by Army commander Br Gen SWINN ++ attached Lt Col OFG CRM of 2nd WORCESTERS. HQRS. MR - THE president of the court HAYES - Not guilty GWINN - 10-30am. R.S.	Ref Sheet 28
	23rd		Enemy carried out no field programme CSM GOSLING - AGS and B & D companies with CT morning D company proceeded to RUBROUCK for range practice. C company returned from RIBROUCK	
WATOU AREA	24th		Battalion moved to K.12.A.64 in early morning. JAN TEG BIEZEN	Ref Sheet 29
	25th		Enemy carried out no field programme Lance Cpl Sergeant Magnus Corporal. One Company D company returned from RUBROUCK Capt MATHER rejoined from 1 base Depot in LE TOUQUET	
	26th		Cpl E C.QMS WOOD pd at 11.35am Pte. Cpl E 10.30am	
	27th		Enemy carried out no field programme 2/Lt O ROBINET 5/Lt HC SMITH 2/Lt JH BLOOMER from RIFLE BRIGADE Joined Mill Lt R C HANN & JONES Major of No. 5 from 8th Leinsters assumed command of 15 company Brigadier Generals Scheme carried out	
	28th			
	29th		Brigade Tactical Scheme was carried out. Major of Major To M Reed as around 4pm Complete company presented to engaged as attached Rpl HUDSON Captain V KNOWLTRIDGE was a member of F.C.C.M reported at 2nd WORCESTERS HQRS	Ref Sheet 23
DIVL. RESERVE CORNER	30th		Battalion moved to A.30.N.1.9 - + took over trenches from 1st MIDDLESEX Parade 3.45 am Arrived about 7.45 am	

Army Form C. 2118.

WAR DIARY
or
INTELLIGENCE SUMMARY.
(Erase heading not required.)

Place	Date	Hour	Summary of Events and Information	Remarks and references to Appendices
DIRTY BUCKET CORNER	May 3/18		All Coys. companies on working parties on POPERINGHE EAST LINE. A + B Coys under CAPT. O COUGHTRIE to 222 FIELD COY. RE. C + D Coys under CAPT. HEMMATHER to 18th MIDDLESEX. Work for good hours commencing 5 am.	

B. Hutchins Lt Col
Comdg 16th K.R. Rifle
Corps

WAR DIARY
or
INTELLIGENCE SUMMARY
(Erase heading not required.)

Army Form C. 2118.

YPRES VII 32

Place	Date	Hour	Summary of Events and Information	Remarks and references to Appendices
DIRTY BUCKET CORNER	June 1st 1918		Training was carried out according to programme. The sentence in the case of Rfn. GRONIN Rfn. GWINN was commuted to 2 years I.H.L and was put into execution. Rfn. GWINN was handed over to the A.P.M. Cpl. MATHER was admitted into hospital sick. 2nd Lt. R.O. BINET was sent to Gas Course at 22nd Corps School. 12 O.R.'s jt. casuals joined for duty.	Ref. Sheet 28.
	2nd		Church Parades were held in C. of E., R.C's and Nonconformists.	
	3rd		All Companies were employed on Working Parties. The C.O. and Adjutant attended a Conference at Brigade H.Q. at 6.30 p.m. The enemy shelled the vicinity of the Camp. Honours and Awards. Bar to Military Medal.— R. 3196 Rfn. A. Hallam M.M.	
			C.174 Sgt. G. Oakley M.M.	
			Military Medal.	
			C. 22 Rfn. F. WOOD	
			R.19338 Sgt. A.A. WINGROVE.	
			C. 1197 L/Cpl. C. DEAN	
			C.744 Rfn. G. HIRST	
			C.522 Rfn. E. WRAGG	
			R.3379 Rfn. H. DAWSON.	
			A.20316 Rfn. A. ROUSE.	
			R.19753 Rfn. J. WILSON	
			A.26338 Rfn. P DONOVAN.	
			C. 953 A/Cpl F. PUTMAN.	
	4th		Companies went out at the disposal of Company Commanders in tactical schemes. 2nd Lt. T.E. PEMBERTON was transferred to T.M.B. 9 O.R's jt. casuals joined in duty.	
	5th		Companies were out at the disposal of Company Commanders. The Range was allotted to the Battalion.	
	6th		Companies were at disposal of Company Commanders. Range at A.30.d.3.9. allotted to Battalion.	
YPRES CANAL			The Battalion moved up to the line at night and relieved 1st LEICESTERS in Left Sub-sector of Right Brigade Sector. 1 Casualty while going up. Relief was completed at 12 M/N. Disposition of Companies on YPRES CANAL:— Out-post Line, Left "D" Coy (2nd Lt. BROWNE) Right "C" Coy (Lt. REID) Front Line, " "B" " " "A" " (Capt. OUGHTRED) Support Line.	Ref. Sheet 28.

WAR DIARY
or
INTELLIGENCE SUMMARY.

Army Form C. 2118.

Place	Date	Hour	Summary of Events and Information	Remarks and references to Appendices
YPRES CANAL	June 7th 1918		Training was carried out by minimum Reserve at ROSENDAEL Sector. Early in the morning a patrol went out under 2nd LT LEVITT from our left company. They obtained some information about an enemy M.G. post. Enemy defences to our front are chiefly composed of M.G. and Sniper posts. "A" and "B" Companies suffered in depth and improved defences of front and support lines. There was no infantry action. The Artillery was engaged only slightly. LT PG DE PARAVICINI joined the Battalion for duty. 2nd LT R.O. BIXBY returned from course. 3 OR's were wounded.	Ref. Sheet 28
	8th		In the morning the Reserve at ROSENDAEL Sector carried on training under R.S.M. In the early morning our right outpost Company sent out a patrol under 2nd LT A ARMAREY to beat a suspected enemy post and to obtain an identification. The patrol failed in its object attributing its non success to the darkness of the night. "A" and "B" Companies carried on working on the defences. In the early morning the French immediately north of us were SCOTTISH and RIDGE WOODS. They were unable to maintain their positions in RIDGE WOOD. The Battalion did not come into action but caught the edge of the hostile bombardment we passage. There was intermittent shelling throughout the day particularly on back areas and roads probably the result of the French attack. The following Officers proceeded on courses — 2nd LT F.G. MARANT L.G. Course 2nd Army School	
			2nd LT E.W. JEFFERY General Course " "	
			2nd LT H.C. SMITH L.G. @ Musketry course " " "	
			2nd LT DR. WILSON Musketry Course " " "	
	8-9		In the evening the enemy attacked SCOTTISH WOOD and are counter attacked SCOTTISH CAMP. The French counter attacked at this front and regained except at PRESTON CAMP. The trenches "C" Company were subjected to a somewhat severe gas bombardment probably as a consequence of this operations	

Army Form C. 2118.

WAR DIARY
or
INTELLIGENCE SUMMARY.
(Erase heading not required.)

Instructions regarding War Diaries and Intelligence Summaries are contained in F.S. Regs., Part II. and the Staff Manual respectively. Title pages will be prepared in manuscript.

Place	Date	Hour	Summary of Events and Information	Remarks and references to Appendices
YPRES CANAL	June 9th 1918		Church Parade was held Jn. C/o/E and then companies at "B" Schelden, ROSENDAEL Sector. "A" and "B" Companies worked as before. A Raid was sent out from the left Outpost by "D" under 2nd Lt. SUGDEN. They returned without casualties bringing regal we but useful information. A patrol from right out post Coy "C" went out under 2nd Lt PINNINGTON to reconnoitre an enemy Revet and if possible obtain a prisoner. The Trench was reached and found to be unoccupied. A very quiet day was passed by the Battalion. 2 O.Rs were wounded of whom 1 died of wounds. Capt. D.W. CLEUGH 6/J.O.R. sent to an Anti-Gas Course at 2nd Corps School. 7/O.R.s / lst Casualty joined for duty.	Re/ Sheet 28
	10th		Training was carried out by Companies. Relieve at ROSENDAEL sector. On the YPRES CANAL Sector there was a Company on duty each Coln. day. The Battalion was relieved by the 1st Hull Lads on the night 10/11th. The Relief was very good, being completed 11.59 p.m.	
BRANDHOEK	11th		"A" and "B" Coys had some shelling on the way up but no casualties. Training on Divisional Reserve. The Trench was occupied in line "A" on the Right "B" on the left BRANDHOEK to Divisional Reserve. The purpose of work rather than train the period was out of and R.S.M. KENT (9th R.B.) joined the Battalion. H.Q. of ERIE FARM. Training was carried on by Company Regmnt. Instruction in Q.M.S. duties th O.R. (1st casual) John Rollis, two months attachment for instruction and a general clean up took place. were allotted under Coy arrangements.	
	12th		Training was carried out by Company in Reserve. R/n LONGLEY was tried by F.G.R.M. at H.L 1 Hd QR and was sentenced to 90 day F.P No 1. A working party of 150 O.R. was employed burying a cable Jn 33rd Divl Signal Coy. Equipment was cleaned and posts were improved. C/ and 1.O. Pr its Counter-Battery Officer. Capt COUGHTRIE and Lt INIGO-JONES visited found — enquiry and flash-spotting officer. The Divl Genl visited the Battalion at 9.30 p.m. a Lat occupation of the line in depth was carried out — "A" "B" "D" Coys in front line + "C" in support.	
	13th		Training was carried on by Companies in Reserve. 2nd Lt. H.R. KINSLEY joined the Battalion from Base Camp. The working party of 150 O.R was employed burying cable as before. 12th.	
	14th		Training was carried on by Companies in Reserve. 2nd Lt A.R. KINSLEY went to 2nd H.Q. A working party was employed as a 12th & 13th Inst. 2nd LTs JERRY STONE reconnoitred the lines of the line to be relieved. Capt. BOTTOMS, 2nd Lts WHITMORE and BINET Came up from "B" Schelden	

WAR DIARY or INTELLIGENCE SUMMARY

Army Form C. 2118.

Place	Date	Hour	Summary of Events and Information	Remarks and references to Appendices
BRANDHOEK	June 15th 1918		Training was carried out by minimum Reserve at ROSENDAEL Rest. Capt. CLEUGH returned from his course. 2nd Lt. R.C. NAYLOR was evacuated sick. In consequence of information received the Batta lion prepared for an enemy offensive on a large scale and was ready to stand to at 2.45 a.m. the Rifleman are issued with extra ammunition and Rifle bombs but acted to no 36 Grenades	Ref. Sheet 28.
YPRES CANAL			The day passed quietly. At night the Battalion relieved the 1st CAMS: in the right subsector of the left sector of p.w.t. area. The relief was completed at 2 a.m. The dispositions were :- "A" Coy Right front "B" Coy left front "D" & "C" Coys in general Reserve. The 2nd WORCESTERS occupied the left Sub Sector. The night was quiet except for occasional bursts of Shelling	
	16th		Church Parades were held at Bn. HQ, "D" Coy HQ, "C" Coy HQ, Roven Farm, and E.D. Junio the Letter in the day was quiet. Work was done on Posts and Q H Q, 1 and 2 Junio the High but the Quiet but our patrols assembl ed with no Rivetions of O.C. no 11 Field Coy. The night was quiet but our patrols were out and no news of enemy	
	17th		Training was carried out by minimum Reserve. 2nd Lt. BUDD returned from leave. The day was quiet & Coys carried out work on Posts and Q.H.Q 1 and 2. Junio the night was quiet. Our Quiet patrols were out in information in anticipation of a raid by us. 1 O.R. died of wounds and 1 was wounded	
	18th		Training was carried out by minimum Reserve. Capt. J.W. LIPSCOMB proceeded on leave. The day was quiet by quiet. Outpost Coys were ordered to night, agains BEDFORD HOUSE and STABLES definitely in order there please might serve of best penetration. The and localities the reconnaissance of our line in case of need. Bn. Recontance with Coy programme, night was quiet and work was carried out and an acc ordance with Coy programme. A patrol brought information regarding enemy wire another patrol from the enemy Posts and brought information about enemy dispositions. 2 O.R. wounded. 1 S.I. wounded.	
	19th		Training was Carried out by minimum Reserves and a kit inspection was held in the afternoon. The day was very quiet Work in line of defence were carried out and arrangements were made to have efficient Q H Q line. At night Parties of the YPRES CANAL were issued the C 4 party line of aight 2nd Middlesex on to Batt. Right and by 2nd WORCESTERS on Batt. left. Gun am munition of Rifle and G.C. front was been covered by this but only a few Cas. alles were caused. 2nd Lt G.C. ASHBURNER wounded and evacuated. 1 O.R. wounded. Honours and Awards Capt. BOTTOMS awarded M.C. C.S.M. HALLAM M.M. "DCM"	

A6945 Wt. W14422/M1160 350,000 12/16 D.D. & L. Forms/C./2118/14.

Army Form C. 2118.

WAR DIARY
or
INTELLIGENCE SUMMARY.
(Erase heading not required.)

Place	Date	Hour	Summary of Events and Information	Remarks and references to Appendices
YPRES CANAL	June 20th 1918		Training was carried out by minimum Reserve. The day was very quiet with some Farm which caused a little delay to work. Drainage and the rebuilding of parapets blown in on the previous night was carried out. At "Stand to" Stand to be. A single man was observed wandering near our posts. He was secured and proved to be a man of the 439th Inf. Regt. He was sent to Bat. H.Q. Without delay. At night with-ey relief was carried out. "A" Coy relieving "B" Coy. The hour of darkness were not long enough to allow a full relief to be effected. The "B" Coy. 1 O.R. killed 3 O.R. wounded.	Ref Sheet 28.
	21st		Training was carried out by minimum Reserve. The day was quiet and work was carried out according to programme. At night the relief was completed by 12.40 a.m. and this unit was quite some time after the relief. Hours and awards:- R.S.M. awarded M.S.M.	
	22nd		Training was carried out by minimum Reserve. At 4 A.M. 2nd Lt. D.W. Grungeuden PARKER and Lt. WALDEN returned from Course. The day was quiet and work was carried on according to programme. At night our posts were withdrawn to admit of the discharge of gas and also in order that heavy Artillery might bombard LANKHOFF FARM. 3 O.R. wounded.	
	23rd		Church Parade was held by minimum Reserve. Our posts remained vacated throughout the day. LANKHOFF FARM was bombarded by 9.2" Hows: and swept damage done. 30 of the garrison retired from the Farm and were Shrapnel. The Receupation of the forward posts was carried out uneventfully at night. There is no evidence to suggest that Honours and awards:- Military Medal to R.21183 Pte. H. NEAVE R.135-79 L/Cpl. E. DEARDEN C.55707 Sgt. T. CLEMENT.	
	24th		Major LAYE left the minimum Reserve and Training was quiet. Work was carried out according to programme. England in M.G.C. The day was quiet. Lt. REID went in consequence of news received from his parents the Batt. 2 prepared to meet an attack preceded by 2 Kryts. bombardment in working of 25th. The night however passed quietly. Training and a Route march was carried out by minimum Reserve. The day was	
	25th		Very quiet. Colonel of parties were sent to take over Craeberies. The Batt. took up positions relieved by the 2nd A and J.A. the relief being off without event. YELLOW LINE. H Q at G. 11. d. 10. 15.	
BRANDHOEK				

A6945 Wt. W1422/M1160 350,000 12/16 D.D. & L. Forms/C/2118/14.

Army Form C. 2118.

WAR DIARY
or
INTELLIGENCE SUMMARY.
(Erase heading not required.)

Instructions regarding War Diaries and Intelligence Summaries are contained in F. S. Regs., Part II. and the Staff Manual respectively. Title pages will be prepared in manuscript.

Place	Date	Hour	Summary of Events and Information	Remarks and references to Appendices
BRANDHOEK	June 26th 1918		Training was Carried out by the minimum Reserve. The Battalion bathed at TORONTO BATHS.	Ref Sheet 28.
	27th		Minimum Reserve joined the Battalion and new training was laid down. Battalion found Working Parties on the defences in the YELLOW LINE and at QUERY FARM. Major Allpol RAWLAYE took command of the Battalion vice Lt Col T.S. CURLING D.S.O. who accompanied the Brigade.	
	28th		Battalion found working Parties on the defences in the YELLOW LINE and at QUERY FARM. Some shelling of the YELLOW LINE throughout the night. A & B Coys moved to positions in rear of the line. Seventeenth Chinese carry on at minimum Reserve.	
	29th		Battalion found Working Parties in YELLOW LINE and at QUERY FARM. Battn. Hd.Qrs. and A&B Coys marched camp on drying sheet. The remainder carried on at Minimum Reserve.	
	30th		Battalion found Working Parties at YELLOW LINE and in QUERY FARM. Battalion was warned that at 9.30 p.m. to take over the position of the 1st QUEENS in support of Right Brigade of the Division. Relief went off without incident and at	

[signatures]

To:- 100th Inf Bde.

Herewith War
Diary for
July.

H Trotter.
2nd Lt & adjt
for Lt Col.,
Comdg 16th K.R.R.C.

WAR DIARY or INTELLIGENCE SUMMARY

Army Form C. 2118.

Place	Date	Hour	Summary of Events and Information	Remarks and references to Appendices
YPRES CANAL	Monday 1st/18		Training carried out by Pioneers. Regiment on Rosindael area. 12 O.Rs. proceeded to 2nd Army Regtl. out. conf. by R.C. Large. Nom. return from Courts. The Bath returned to 197 Bde. on the night 30th Jan/1st Feb. The attack went with and quietly, there was no casualties.	
	2nd		Training carried out by Pioneers. Regiment 250 points on range. Major H.J. Willis joined for duty. Capt Waters and 2/Lt C.J. Willis return to duty. Batn. supplied working parties as follows 5 officers and 186 O.R. for work on Bde fortl. under supervision of 222 Field Coy R.E. B Coy. of Bn detailed for work except on salvage situation, C Coy.	
	3rd		Training carried out by Pioneers. Regtl. supplied working parties as above, also D Coy.	
	4th		Supplied a guard for a wounded aeroplane (Breitis) which fell in our area. Situation quiet. Regtl. carried out by Pioneers. Recons. Batn. supplied working party returning to B. Echelon. Baths supplied.	
	5th		Working parties as previous. 185 O.R. for work on Bde fort. Training carried out by Pioneers. Baths supplied. Working parties for work in the Rodes area. 1 O.R. killed 1st Bn. RR order No 351	
	6th		The 2/4 Y. & L. sounded. Firearms for 1 Coy B. 2nd Leicesters were provided in the Rodes area. The Bn Commander asides slipping movement of the 87th on the night 5th/6th July. B Echelon C.O Sidhaus Pioneer Major K. 2/Lt H. Willis 24 OR less Major H.J. Willis 1 Officer, W/Nov R.Q + 2 Servants. B Coy Rest. The C.Q.M.S. (2/4 Y.&L.) camied out a Recce not with 1 Company. Also W.O. R.Q.M. 2 Servants. B Coy Rest. 18 B Coy. men also crossed to Advanced position to Cocquart unit. B Coy.	
	7th		Church parades as follow. 2 officers and 9/4th AR Bath 25 D Coy as only available. At Rebreux was sent to hospital. Ve Reatt. Supplies working parties as follows.	
	8th		We took G.A. Coy on our books. 8/4 Y.R. Engineer officer from Trivera 2/Lt L.J. Froun proceeded to hospital via field ambulance. Baths supplied working parties as before for 212 Field Coy. by Pioneer Reserve. 8 officers and 220 men for each Coy.	

WAR DIARY
or
INTELLIGENCE SUMMARY.
(Erase heading not required.)

Army Form C. 2118.

Place	Date	Hour	Summary of Events and Information	Remarks and references to Appendices
	9th		10R and 8B Pioneers. Training carried out by Maximum Platoon. 4/Lt W.P. Felber awarded the M.C. The Batt. supplied the same working parties as for July 8th. & complete the wiring of the	
	10th		New C.H.L. Education was great. Training carried out by Maximum Platoon. R/9846 A/C J. Brant and V/131 A/C A.E. Lewton awarded M.M. 10R KWS and 10R awarded. The Batts was relieved by the 4th Kings. The relief was carried out quietly and situation was quiet after which the Batts took up position at Brandhoek & the Rd for the Middlesex.	
BRANDHOEK	11th		Training carried out by Maximum Platoons. Roop allotted. Batts were given baths & clean clothes. No casualties have been left.	
	12th		Training carried out by Maximum Platoon. Coys. Companies at the disposal of the following Commanders for entering and the improvement of Company areas. 150 men found for A + B Coys for work on the Yellow Line. 110 men from D Coy for strengthening ERIE FARM (Bdls HQ) + Lt B.J. Curling R.S.O. took command of the Pike (Pak) during temporary absence to Brig. Hd. of Y. Brind OMG. BEO Major J.A.C. Coy command by the Batts. in the absence of A/Lt B.J. Curling R.S.O.	
	13th		Training carried out by the Bn. Pa. 4/Lt P.W. Yaffey returns from course. Companies at the disposal of the Commanders for entering and improvement of their own areas. 150 men found for detail to the Yellow Line, & man for improvement of ERIE FARM (Bn. HQ) Major R.A.W. Lays a/d by A/Lt Willis attended. B.C.M. at HQ 33rd Bn MGC at 27/L.13.a.	
	14th		Church Parade for Brig. Bn. 2/Lt H.H. Chitty wounded and IOR. 2/Lt C.S. Wilson attacks T.M.B. A/Lt Cheer & Curtis [joined] with 60R & Many Branch Post. Comp. Capt. Clayton to Hospital. Working parties as for 13th ans. For small support parties own particular erected in the Yellow Line and work entering on strengthening ERIE FARM.	
	15th		Training by Coys; Pas; 2/Lt Pound to hospital evacuated workout parties as for 14th + one sent out for small support shelter to follow line entered and work on ERIE FARM R.O.P. proper with that of the division 134 Canadians. Relief completed by 12.50 am entirely quiet.	

WAR DIARY or INTELLIGENCE SUMMARY

Army Form C. 2118.

(Erase heading not required.)

Instructions regarding War Diaries and Intelligence Summaries are contained in F. S. Regs., Part II. and the Staff Manual respectively. Title pages will be prepared in manuscript.

Place	Date	Hour	Summary of Events and Information	Remarks and references to Appendices
YPRES CANAL	16th		Training carried out by Min. Res. Range allotted. 2/Lt. R.O. Blunt proceeded to Hospital. Quiet day. For record two Corp. B 2/125th Regt A.E.F. for experience. One Battn. had 1 killed and 4 wounded by shell fire during the activity. Shelling continued towards Bn. rgt. as in the early morning, probably Bois Kn. Artillery situation carried out by us on VORMEZEELE. At midnight and subsequently American troops were intermingled with our own into the vicinity of FM. Station pits for this Coy and Bn. accommodated at BEDFORD HOUSE for the night to HQ. Casualties caused by Min. Res.: 1 OR killed and 1 OR wounded. 2/Lt A.A. Whitney to hospital.	
	17th		Quiet day. Work carried out in front lines & Reserve Gun posts. 2 coys. American troops reduced instruction. Rate were now two Companies in Support of BELGIAN BATTERY CORNER (A Right Platoons and 1 American Platoon) & R. BELGIAN CHATEAU. Training was carried out that	
			An enemy attack would probably take place later in the morning 8th to 18th. Coy. positioned two fired on the enemy front. During the night a big suspect. Strained for Companies in outpost positions in Support - in Reserve. Retaliation was carried out over heavy & no infantry action developed.	
	18th		Training carried out by Min. Res. 2/Lt J.Y. Cann wounded by bomb while asleep 4/Lt W.E. Shaw returns from hospital. Quiet day. Work was carried out for the improvement of B. Defences and Battn. outpost support & Reserve Coys. Americans were formed into platoons for the purpose of holding platoon posts, & working as platoons.	
	19th		Quiet day. Training carried out by Coys Res. Raising of Americans continued by platoons. Work carried out on Defence of Canal Bank line - laid for a Chateau Communications between Bn. plan.	
			160x for BELGIAN CHATEAU in order to safeguard communication between Bn. plan	
			and B.H.Q.	
	20th		Training carried out by Min. Res.: 1 OR wounded. At 9.h. Bloom returns from hospital. Quiet day. 1 Coys of the 9th UL moved into the 60 Bn. at disposition as follows:—	

WAR DIARY or INTELLIGENCE SUMMARY

Army Form C. 2118.

Place	Date	Hour	Summary of Events and Information	Remarks and references to Appendices
YPRES CANAL	July 20th		1 Coy outpost at IRON BRIDGE. 1 Coy support vicinity of SWAN CHATEAU. 1 Coy Reserve at BELGIAN CHATEAU. H.Q. Armouries. Reliefs not all actually completed mostly owing to enemy shelling. Bn was Bde Res. Bn Coys. Reliefs not all actually completed by 12.30 am without incident.	
	21st		Afternoon and Evening: Quiet day. Morning and evening received info as enemy attack evidently started. Counter barrage on our line. Res. Positions taken. Two unimportant forward patrols during the morning by the 9/22. Precautions taken and enemy seemed to report abnormal movement. Initial artillery counter preparation was fired on the Corps front for bombs a certain amount of retaliation. No infantry action took place.	
	22nd	at H 18 d 6.2	Wiring carried out by 5th Pion. Res. 1 O.R. wounded. Enemy artillery more active in forward areas. O.C. 9th H.L.I. took over command of his Battalion on his return with H. Qrs.	Sheet 28.
	23rd		2 Lieut Reid wounded by Bullet. Reserve in Battle Res. alert. 2/Lt. W.A.J. Scott to carry out reconnaissance. Unit was working according to programme carried out. A certain amount of counter preparation fired by our artillery which proved very little response from the enemy.	
	24th		Normal ordered at by him. Res. 2/Lt. M.C. Smith returned from hospital. Capt. J.W. Chisholm from leave. Capt. W.S. Cobb joined for duty. Quiet day. Enemy shelled area of SWAN CHATEAU slightly during the afternoon.	
	25th		Quiet amount of aerial activity. 2nd Lt... 95. Hogan returned from course. 2/Lt. R.C. Wayte returned from hospital. Quiet day. Work carried out according to programme. The Bn was relieved by 1st Middlesex Regt. Relief being complete by 12.65 pm.	

WAR DIARY
or
INTELLIGENCE SUMMARY.
(Erase heading not required.)

Army Form C. 2118.

Place	Date	Hour	Summary of Events and Information	Remarks and references to Appendices
BRANDHOEK	July 25th /17		adv. moved into positions on the YELLOW LINE. HQrs at ERIE FARM.	Sheet 28.
	26th		Rain; Bn training + rest. attd. Capt EHD KING M.C. joins for duty. 2/Lt F.G. Rudd from Hospital. Fine day that is batting 2/W kit + Clothing, inspection. Certain alterations were put into operation in the Defence Scheme of the YELLOW line.	
	27th		Rain; Bn. training. Capt Cahir assumed command of B Coy. & Capt Kerr of D Coy. Working parties found for the Yellow line. B.Bn to Bde. to Et Col R.J. Curling DSO took command of Bn. C Coy Seal AWF. Band CMG DSO. Major P.F.W. Kaye assumed command of Bn. Relin.	
	28th		Church parade for Pres; Res: Working parties found for Yellow line. Voluntary Church Service held in hut near BHQ.	
	29th		Fine; Res: training. Rain. all day. 4/H B.T. Cross & ORS front Rept. Camp. A + B. found Working parties on Yellows line. C + D Corps S.O. Tactical Scheme. on one W.B. QUERY FARM.	
	30th		Fine; Res: Raining. Maj Kaye returns to B Bn. So OR and 2 officers proceed to photos lorry for a day to the Seaside. C+D Cops found working parties on GREEN LINE. 2/Lt R.J. Curling assumes Command of K Bn. W.B QUERY FARM. 2/Lt A.W.F. ISAIRD CMG DSO. to command 100th Brigade. on the return of Brig. Gen. A.W.F. ISAIRD C.M.G. D.S.O. to Relief of 1st Division Battalion moves into support on eight Support post immediately on arrival. Pres; Res: or Ltd C Coy found working party 88 SR. men	
	31st		Rain; Res: Raining 2/H W.J. Jenner, joined on Ross Emit Ss. Bath Pres; Res: Lombard parties reln. 212 {U.W. Co5 RE. St. Kirby 5/4/17. 10 10 Coln command 16 K.R.R.C.

SECRET.

To:- 100th Inf. Bde

Herewith War
Diary for Month
of August

H Trotter
Lt/N a/adjt
for Major,
2/9/18   Comndg 16th K.R.Rif.C.

16/KRRC

Army Form C. 2118.

WAR DIARY
or
INTELLIGENCE SUMMARY.
(Erase heading not required.)

Place	Date	Hour	Summary of Events and Information	Remarks and references to Appendices
	August 1st		Training carried out by Bombers and Lewis MG. L.O.R. proceeded to Scottish Rest Camp. Quiet day. Baths. Some working parties under 222nd Field Coy RE and 18th Middlesex Bn. 2/Lt. H.C. Smith to Hospital.	
	2nd		Some artillery active during the night. First OR on our right. Bn. found working parties under the 222 Field Coy RE & 18th Middx Regt. "C" Coy moved the position the BROWN LINE to H 11 C.	
	3rd		First Officer + HQ O.R's joined from the 9th Bn. Quiet day. Night Shelling near Ravine on the Boesinge-Ypres road (sand) near the R.E's. Alterations were made to the dispositions as follows:- in order that troops on the forward area might not be crowded B Coy moved from Coy HQ to H.22.d.95.65. The platoon in Ravine and posts astride Rd. VYVERBEEK D Coy moved 2 platoons to OPIUM FARM. A Coy HQ moved to BOLTON FARM. - Bn H.Q. at H22.a 35.15	
	4th		Church Parade for Gnrs. R.C's Quiet day. Work carried out by Bn & Coys during the day. Ringing and improving positions.	
	5th		Bn found working parties as above. Quiet day. Work carried at occurred to programme.	
	6th		Quiet day. Bn. supplied working parties as before under supervision of 222nd Field Coy RE. Relieving by Grin R.Regt. Quiet day. Work as usual. Night shelling near Bn.HQ. No casualties. Capt Chapman (9th Bn) joined for duty.	
	7th		Quiet day. Work as usual. Night shelling near Bn HQ. No casualties.	
	8th		Quiet day. Work on platoon posts in Ravine progressing. Parties supplied for RE's as usual. 2/Lt H.H.A. Whitney returned from Hospital. Capt Bottoms MC proceeded on leave to U.K. R/N P. Bacon to Hospital.	
	9th		Very Quiet. Bn was relieved, on the night 9/10th by the 1st Wiltshire Regt. Quiet relief completed 12.40 a.m. Bn took up position in the YELLOW LINE with HQ at ERIE FARM. Lt Col B.G. Curling A.S.C. took Command of 100th Inf. Bde. during the temporary absence of Brig. Gen A.W.F. BAIRD C.M.G. D.S.O. Brig. Gen R.W. LAYE took command from Baths. 2/Lt 29 Buscher returned from Course.	

WAR DIARY or INTELLIGENCE SUMMARY

Army Form C. 2118.

Place	Date	Hour	Summary of Events and Information	Remarks and references to Appendices
BRANDHOEK	10		Training by Coys. R.O.: Bay. Spot in Bakes refitted &c. Coys at the disposal B.O.C. Coys C + D Coys supplied working parties under 2ir.O/field Coy R.E.	
	11		Hd Qr B.P. Parties R.E.O. act as relief umpires for training field operations 8/11. R.O. Bart. & M. Clergh for Hospt.	
			Church Parade for Divis. Pres. Special Service at TERDIGHEM (4 O.R. attached) Coys at the disposal of Coy commander for scheme drill etc. A + B Coys working under N.C.R.E.s	
			Lt. R.C. Snugo Jones or Conner. 2/Lt. R.H. Blomer from Conner	
	12		Training by Coy R.O. Coys at disposal of Coy commanders for training 9th Bn. training Staff came up + joined H. Bn. C+D Coys in training parties	
	13		Training carried out by Coys A + B Coys had a small Tactical scheme. Lt C/S B.P. Curley took command of the Bn. or return of Bty. Lt. A.W.F. BAIRD. CMG D.S.O. assumed command of the Bn. Lt. C.I.B. Curles D.S.O. proceeded to 1/5 Echelon	
	14		3 P.M. 4/B Wilts Major P.A.W. Lege proceeded on leave Major H.Y. Willis. H. Bn. relieved the 1st Camerons on the right sub of the left B.F. Post. Dispositions as follows A SWAN CHATEAU. Left Support	
			B H22 d 4.4. R do	
			C BEDFORD STABLES Left Support	
			D IRON BRIDGE R do	
			Relief passed off well + quickly. Relief complete 11.30 p.m. 1 O.R. wounded (remains at duty. 8/LN C.G. Wilks to hospital from TMB.	

Army Form C. 2118.

WAR DIARY
or
INTELLIGENCE SUMMARY.
(Erase heading not required.)

Place	Date	Hour	Summary of Events and Information	Remarks and references to Appendices
CANAL SECTOR	15th		Training by Coys. Res: Lewis Bay Pl. Casualties. Warning order received from Bde that the Bn. was to be relieved and that the Bde would be relieved by 1st Bn.I.R.	
	16th		American Regt. ok April 17/18th. Defence Schemes were submitted by companies with sketch maps to Bn. HQrs. They ought to be passed before being handed over. Advanced party of Americans arrived in the evening - 3rd party to the troops Rest Camp LOOS 2/Lt J. E. Bryant, 6 Pass to U.K. 2/Lt E.W. Cheek to Hospital.	
	17th		Training by Bn. Res. Very quiet. Bn was relieved by A & C Coys 1st Bn 125th F.I.R. Relief was conducted quickly & was complete by 7:35 pm except for 1 Coy B Coy. Relief whose outfit was all entrained till 2 am. After relief Coys moved at independently and entrained at the Light Railway at ATHERLEY JUNCTION advanced to PUGWASH SIDING in PROVEN & then they marched to TUNNELLING CAMP	
PROVEN	18th		PROVEN. R/M. N.E. Lorry returned from leave. Boy given to Coys. for Baths & refitting. A,B+C Coys only were able to get baths	
	19th		43 OR. reported for Pulford Camp. B Coy to HQrs. Baths. Remainder hit & clothing inspection and a little drill. 2/Lt A H Pennington posted as censor Lt R.C Bugg passed from L.E convoy	
	20th		Coys and platoon drill carried out. Transport proceed to WORMHOUDT by road on its way R.R	
	21st		WATTEN AREA Billeting Party under 2/Lt E Baxter proceeded to WATTEN. Bath entrained at PROVEN at 12 noon & arrived at WATTEN at 5:30 pm. Went by road to ZUDROVE & SERQUES	Sh.27A N.E.

WAR DIARY
INTELLIGENCE SUMMARY
Army Form C. 2118.

Place	Date	Hour	Summary of Events and Information	Remarks and references to Appendices
ZUDROVE	21st		Coy HQ as follows: A. G.31.C.8.5. B. R.13.6.8.4. C. R.7.6.9.6. D. R.13.c.5.8. Bn HQ. R.7.2.1.4	
	22nd		9th Bn EW Jeffery proceeds on leave to UK. Day devoted to Company work. Coys bathing in the Canal & refilling. The 1st Brigade complete with all attached units now passed near MOULLE & did a practice.	
	23rd		General fast. Preparatory to an inspection by the Bn.l Commander. 4th Bn R L Davidson attached for duty.	
	24th		2/Lt 9AP Thomas joined for duty. Bn paraded at 6:15 am the proceed to ground for the Bn.l Commanders inspection. This however was put off owing to rain. Bn paraded at 12 noon and was inspected by General Perry who criticised and allowed to the Bn who later too over tasks. After which the Bn. marched past. Capt Bettono MC returned from leave. Lt. SWEENY joined for duty as MO. vice Capt V.P. Mullison to M.G.C.	
	25th		Church parade in the Bn. HQ. recreation field at 8 am. Service by Rev Blackam the Bn. chaplain. Lt. J.J. Hark (9th Bn.) joined for duty.	
	26th		Training carried out as per programme. Warning order received for Bn. to move out another Army. Lt. Sweeny to M.G.C. for duty. Lt. Emerson (USA) joined as M.O.	

Army Form C. 2118.

WAR DIARY
or
INTELLIGENCE SUMMARY.
(Erase heading not required.)

Instructions regarding War Diaries and Intelligence Summaries are contained in F.S. Regs., Part II. and the Staff Manual respectively. Title pages will be prepared in manuscript.

Place	Date	Hour	Summary of Events and Information	Remarks and references to Appendices
2ND ROVE.	27th		Coys at disposal of Coy Commdrs. Baths paraded at 9.45 pm and proceeded to Arzew and entrained for BOUQUE MAISON	
	28th		Train arr 2.27 am Bn detrained BOUQUEMAISON about 9 am and marched to S.O.S. ST. LEGER.	
SOS. ST. LEGER	29th		Coys at disposal of Coy Commdrs.	
	30th		Normal parades out. Capt. Grimmond proceeded on course (to Army Cadet School)	
	31st		Training carried on. Maj. J.R.W. Kaye & Lt. J. Broadbent returned from leave. 2/Lt. A.H. Vickers joined for duty. 2/Lt. A.H. Pennington from course.	

H.S.Kaye
2/Lt Adjt.
for Lt Col commdg.
16th KRRC.

WAR DIARY
or
INTELLIGENCE SUMMARY.
(Erase heading not required.)

Army Form C. 2118.

Place	Date	Hour	Summary of Events and Information	Remarks and references to Appendices
SUS ST LEGER	Sept 1st		Lt. J.P. Hook proceed on leave to U.K. Companies under Coy arrangements. 2/Lt. S.N. Wait from course	
	2d		Coys under Coy Commanders. Lt. Col. B.O. Curling DSO Mans Battalion to command 189th Infantry Brigade. Lt. Col. R.L. Poulton VD (attached) assume Command of Bn. 2/Lt J.L. Morrell returns from leave.	
	3d		Tactical Schemes under Records. C.O. had all Coy Commanders	
	4th		Tactical Scheme & Cloze order drill under Coy arrangements. 8.30 am - 12.30 pm. 2/Lt. P.A.P. Homan to Lieut. 2/Lt. T.J. de Pancorini relinquish acting rank. A/Capts J.W. Lipscomb & P.J. de Pancorini relinquish acting rank. 2/Lt. J.S. Budd proceeds on leave to U.K.	
	5th		Training under Coys arrangements. 8.30 - 12.30 pm. Lt. R.C. Phipps of 2/no proceeded on leave	
	6th		Signalling under the Signalling Officer. Companies training under Coy arrangements. Lt. Col. C.H.N. Seymour DSO joined for duty and assumes Command. Lt. A.R. Kirkby appointed Bn. Intelligence Officer. Struck off Strength as from 4/8/17	
	7th		Raining as per programme	
	8th		Church service for all denominations	
	9th		2/Lt. E.A. Lloyd going from hospital	
	10th		Training under coys arrangements. Capt. J.R.E. Mason to 19th Inf. Bn for Potatotory Staff Course	
	11th		Training under coys arrangements from 8.30 am to 11.30 am	
	12th		Battn Sports commenced at 1.30 pm. Sergio proceeds to	

WAR DIARY
or
INTELLIGENCE SUMMARY.
(Erase heading not required.)

Army Form C. 2118.

Place	Date	Hour	Summary of Events and Information	Remarks and references to Appendices
SUS-ST-LEGER	12th	2pm	Successful Competitions by Brigadier General A.W.F. BAIRD CMG. DSO.	
			All ranks now had complete outfit to include wristlets and the work of the programme.	
	13th		Training as usual. — Sports continued at 5 pm.	
	14		Orders received to be prepared to move by lorry on the night 14/15th. Men were carefully inspected and allowed to sleep 15/16th.	
	15th		Revised orders received. — 52 ORs reported from attentional unit RE. Short letter by Divisional Commander to all officers & sergeants at Bde HQrs at 9 am. Church parade at 11 am. Bath. Men B. Coy entrained as SUS-ST-LEGER – SOMBRIN Road. about 10 pm. and arrived at BAZENTIN – LE – PETIT about 5 am. 16-9-15. Transport (Brigade) moved to LOUVENCOURT Area.	
BAZENTIN-LE- PETIT	16th		Bivouacked at about 3 am. Battalion (less B. Coy) in Bivouacs and huts Area HIGH WOOD B. HQrs at Offr of HIGH WOOD. Lieut F.G. BUDD agreed from France. B. Coy. arrived from SUS-ST-LEGER about 8 am. and Transport about 5 am.	
	17th		Bath. Baths, tactical scheme carried out. Billeting Party proceeded to take over LETHELLE Area. 5 ORs. proceeded to 3rd Army Rest Camp. F.G.C.M. at HQrs & O to disguised – Major at 7. L.Y. Antler presided. Prize-prayer Bureau of 11 officers and 93 ORs proceeded to Camp at LES BOEUFS at 5 pm water Bearer 9 A.M. Loge. Commanding Officer Conference at Bde HQ at 6 pm	

Army Form C. 2118.

WAR DIARY
or
INTELLIGENCE SUMMARY.
(Erase heading not required.)

Instructions regarding War Diaries and Intelligence Summaries are contained in F. S. Regs., Part II. and the Staff Manual respectively. Title pages will be prepared in manuscript.

Place	Date	Hour	Summary of Events and Information	Remarks and references to Appendices
LECHELLE	Sept 18		Battalion marched to LECHELLE starting at 2 a.m. Route DELVILLE WOOD - LES BOEUFS - LE TRANSLOY - ROCQUIGNY - BUS - LECHELLE. The Batln. was camped in huts.	
			The Bn. was sent half an hour earlier to move warning order to EQUANCOURT Area	
EQUANCOURT	19th		Batn. marched at 2 and took up posns. to bivouac at V17 b 7. Bn. H.Q. at V19 a 9.5 near PERONNE - CAMBRAI Road. Bn. undro 2 hrs. notice to move.	
	20th		Training under Coy. arrangements.	
	21st		Training under Coy. arrangements. 1 platoon per Coy. digging and improving trenches S.E. EQUANCOURT.	
	22nd		Voluntary Church Service at 10 a.m. Batln. moved into the line to relieve units of the 19th Inf. Bde. S. of VILLERS - GUISLAIN and attend. elements of the 1st Cameronians and 5th Seaforth Rifles. Situation very obscure. 2nd Cameronians ordered to do a minor operation to clear the situation on the right flank around Limerick Post. This spoiled all attempts to get information. Repts. received from Brigade that the 2nd Argyll & Sutherland Highlanders had made good MEUNIER TRENCH as far South as LEITH WALK. Coys spent disposition as under: A Coy. in MEATH POST. B Coy. 2 platoons in TARGELLE TRENCH. 2 platoons in MEATH LANE.	X22 603

WAR DIARY
or
INTELLIGENCE SUMMARY.
(Erase heading not required.)

Army Form C. 2118.

Place	Date	Hour	Summary of Events and Information	Remarks and references to Appendices
	Sept 22nd		C. Coy. 2 Platoons in MEUNIER TRENCH from X15.d.4.5 to MEATH POST. 1 Platoon in MEATH LANE as a defensive flank.	
			1 Platoon in PARRS TRENCH. X21.c.5.2. looking S. to gain touch with unit on the right.	
			D Coy in reserve in SUNKEN ROAD at X20.b.	
			Attempts made by C. Coy to work along MEUNIER TRENCH to gain touch with the 2nd A. & S.H. were repulsed by bomb fire. One wounded prisoner captured during these attempts.	
	23rd		Orders issued to A & C Coys to establish posts E. of GLOSTER ROAD. On attempting to carry this out the companies found GLOSTER ROAD occupied in strength by the enemy with shalon swa.	
			The 2nd Worcesters passed through A. Coys lines at 5.10 am to carry out an operation on LIMERICK POST and neighbourhood. Report received from A. Coy that the 2nd WORCESTERS had established communication with Division on right at X22.c.3.2. at 7.10 am.	
			Report from C. Coy that enemy bombing parties had been seen working up MEUNIER TRENCH. These parties were being reinforced by dribbling along LEITH WALK	
			C. Coy find on their parties into houses obtained cover for lookes along the right side of the road.	
			B Coy to support were moved up also down the M.G.C. into full strength in advance on loss of ground. Enemy snipers. D. Coy were ordered to train 1 platoon in readiness for immediate counter attack.	

WAR DIARY or INTELLIGENCE SUMMARY

Army Form C. 2118.

(Erase heading not required.)

Place	Date	Hour	Summary of Events and Information	Remarks and references to Appendices
	Sept 23rd		Lt. Col. C.H.N. SEYMOUR, D.S.O. proceeded to Bde. H.Qrs. for the purpose of arranging details of a combined Bombing attack on MEUNIER TRENCH in conjunction with the 2nd A+S.H. At 3.40 pm Brigade reported that M.G. at X15 c enfilading & harassing the 2nd A+S.H. Stokes Mortar taken to Australian H.Qrs. A.Coy report that Stokes Mortars were fired on a M.G. posn. & caused casualties. Our guns of the 7th in the post were disabled. Lt Col C.H.N. SEYMOUR D.S.O. returned from Brigade and arrangements were made for an operation to clear up the situation in MEUNIER TRENCH. C. Coy under Capt. Milner Riding and A. Coy under Capt. Mann in support to take part. B.Coy H.Qrs. Men in by a Shell. and Capt Cooke + 2/Lt Linton Leslie shaken and 1 Officer and 2 Machine Gunners killed. Two platoons of B. Coy (5+6) detailed and sent to relieve platoon. 1 sect of A+C Coy to take part in the operation. The Bomb got getting stock & part of Field Ambulance. Application made to Brigade H.Qrs. for CSM DEWHURST & 1 p B. Coy also 1 n.c.o. & 2 Sergeants. Lt Col SEYMOUR proceeded to A Coy H.Qrs. to be in to superintend the final arrangements. During the post that No 9 Platoon C. Coy was lost their Officer (2/Lt BINNEY) No 1 platoon was placed under the command C. Coy & No 9 Platoon under A Coy. 2/Lt WARDEN proceeded to MOUQUET FARM to H.Q. 1st Middlesex Regt. to act as Liaison Officer to that Bn.	

WAR DIARY
or
INTELLIGENCE SUMMARY.
(Erase heading not required.)

Army Form C. 2118.

Place	Date	Hour	Summary of Events and Information	Remarks and references to Appendices
	Sept 26th		Heavy Barrage was placed on BHQ and area at 5pm lasting for 20 min. After which Artill. was not quiet. Moon fish & Minnie bombing went behind our line. At 2.30 am report was received from the 2nd Worcesters that GLOSTER ROAD was LIT. in five flarelight flares. At 3.0 am an addition of MG barrage came down. Capt Ruland reported that owing to B Coy using his platoon late he was late at the assembly position. He had orders to propose and he formally was lit later it was ascertained that the attack on GLOSTER ROAD had been held up by a strong point at X.15.d.9.3. At 4.0 am it was ascertained that MEUNIER TRENCH was held by no of enemy & 300 of KEITH WALK. BOMBS been used & sent up SOS lights. Rudock stated that Capt. Ruland & Wanner lit. 2/Lt. Pennington missing (later found wounds only). 2/Lt. HOGAN killed. 2/Lt. RUDD wounded. Capt Ruland returned at dusk after he was hit and made a personal reconnaissance of the total trench front of the final attack reports of the situation. 2nd Lt BUDD was also wounded at dusk, after he was hit & onwards excellent service. Lt Leyman directed the remainder of the party attacking GLOSTER ROAD & Lookshaw. Frank Arthing was thought to have on suspects complaints in GLOSTER ROAD. Enemy counter attack succeeded in driving in on four other portions however to the attack Lewis guns spark in playing the post system were employed as & HQ Lewis gun team took 2 spare	

WAR DIARY
or
INTELLIGENCE SUMMARY.

Army Form C. 2118.

Place	Date	Hour	Summary of Events and Information	Remarks and references to Appendices
	Sept 24th		Lt. Jones assumed command of C Coy in the line and 2/Lt NAYLOR of A Coy.	
			At about midday an attack developed on our right which appeared to have been repulsed.	
			Division on right reported concentration of troops in SHUL MLR position at X.2.b. and requested confirmation by us.	
			A Coy. report no movement in X.2.a.b. but that a post could be seen at X.21. C.8.4. in a small ruin. Of trench with communication leading to MEATH POST.	
			A Coy. ordered to deal with this post. Stokes Mortars and Lewis guns.	
			Stokes Mortars bombarded the often accurately	
			Warners was owned all fire that projects for would be fired.	
			Bn H.Qrs removed into VILLERS - GUISLAIN on night 24/25th.	
			Casualties sustained on patrols — the day. Shells of all calibres.	
			Killed. 2/Lt. G.S. HOGAN & 7. O.R.	
			Wounded Capt & 2nd D. WARNER. M.C.	
			" 2/Lt de Casey - Molland. M.V.O. M.C.	
			2/Lt. H. PINNINGTON	
			2/Lt F.G. BUDD (remains at duty.)	
			and 68 other Ranks.	
			Missing 9 O.Rs	

WAR DIARY or INTELLIGENCE SUMMARY

Army Form C. 2118.

Place	Date	Hour	Summary of Events and Information	Remarks and references to Appendices
	Sept 25th (cont'd)		Night passed quietly. Our front was unusually pakolled in order to find out the positions the enemy had taken up.	
	26th		Day passed quietly. Corps in front line improved their trenches. Occasional bursts of heavy shelling mixed with gas were fired on THRUSH VALLEY - W. B's H.Q. Batn. were relieved by GLASGOW HIGHLANDERS. An excellent exchange of duty, owing to comrades being in CAVALRY TRENCH moved to support for position in CAVALRY SUPPORT. Relief completed by 1.0 pm.	
	27th		In the early morning a heavy barrage was put down by Bosch. Our casualties 2 killed and six wounded. & missing. Bn. HQ moved to Gros Sergent on Cavalry Support in order to make room for 19th Bde H.Q. 7 Broadbent and 31 O.R. joined. It Broadbent to C. Coy and to command their respective Coys.	
			Night passed quietly. Heavy barrage put down on our flanks to early morning. No retaliation of any magnitude on our immediate front. Propaganda received that large supplies of water tanks were doing well. Lt. Belton asked to find fresh water carts forward to obtain storage.	
	28th		3 more joined to strength improved. Bn. stood by to relieve Worcestors in the line. Counterattack order out. No orders received at noon. Commanding Officer of the line called around	

WAR DIARY or INTELLIGENCE SUMMARY

Army Form C. 2118.

Place	Date	Hour	Summary of Events and Information	Remarks and references to Appendices
	29th contd		to meet the Brigadier. Bn ordered to take up position in clor support to the 2/5 Dorsets. & Walton evacuated to hospital sick.	
			Bn moved into Supporting & assembly positions to trenches known as plans.	
			Withdrew FIR SUPPORT & BEECH AVENUE in X.26.B.	
			Zero at 5.30 am. 1/4 Bn ga attacked. At 6.0 am. B&D Coys started drifting up to the line evacuated. Assembly complete by 6.20 am.	
			Much information by Wounded re LIMERICK TRENCH in X.21. First reports received that attack was doing well. Bn HQrs moved to LIMERICK TRENCH Situation was obscure. Stonewalls set up at X.21.6.6. by a strong point. Two coys of the Regiment B & D. had moved forward in an effort to check the Enemy. The enemy put down a very heavy trench barrage at this time which caused the Coys A Coy to also moved forward to the direction.	
			Stonewalls attack was made to gain touch with the 2 coys. We were located about 10 am. At about noon it was found that the Enemy were too Brigade issued orders that LIMERICK TRENCH was to be held & organised for defence. This was forwarded with by two coys placed between LIMERICK POST & KILDARE POST. and a coy in support & TANKS TRENCH Bn HQ at LIMERICK POST. 2/4 K.P. KNIGHT & S.N. LEVITT afoot	
	30 F		Patrols that set out at about 7 am afterwards gained close touch with LIMERICK TRENCH would be missing. a considerable distance in front of LIMERICK TRENCH	

Army Form C. 2118.

WAR DIARY
or
INTELLIGENCE SUMMARY.
(Erase heading not required.)

Place	Date	Hour	Summary of Events and Information	Remarks and references to Appendices
	Sept 30th (cont)		B & D Coy ordered forward to make good PIGEON TRENCH (taken from pushed forward by two coys into eastward their advance and endeavour to take OSSUS. 13 working from the N & D Coy from the S. His advance was held up by M.G. fire from the W. bank of the Canal. A Coy was ordered to STONE TRENCH. C.Coy to Reserve in STONE LANE. At 4.30 p.m. 13R was ordered to take over STONE TRENCH so far S. as CATALET ROAD exclusive. At 8 p.m. the 13R was ordered to take over BOTTOM TRENCH. His own place by D Coy. By midnight the 13R had complete position which was as under. 13 Coy in reserve at X.24.a with a post (1 Rifle Section) at S.13.d.3.5. D. Coy. Posts in BOTTOM TRENCH. 1 platoon in front at X.23.d. 1 platoon in STONE TRENCH. A. Coy. STONE TRENCH from KILDARE AVENUE to CATALET RD. C. Coy. Reserve in dugouts in STONE LANE & vicinity. B.H.Q. Sunken Rd. at X.22.d.8.5. The night was very dark & heavy rain made movement & communication extremely difficult. Bodies of 2/15 Knight & Lunt were found (later sent at from left part Coy) made a thorough examination of the CANAL & environs. 2/M Wilson brought valuable information & found no the W. bank of the Canal.	

H. Statten
2/Lieut Adjt.
for Capt & Adjt.

M.1126.

Operations

An Account of the part taken by 16th K.R.R.C
in attack upon OSSUS on 29-9-18.

Ref. Sheet 57. c. S.E.

03.30 The Battalion left their Reserve position and moved up to Assembly points situated in FIR & PLANE TRENCHES. X.25.b. & X.19.d.

04.50 The Battalion was in position "C" Coy (Reserve Coy) found it necessary to move to SUNKEN ROAD X.26.c. as shelling was causing casualties.

05.50 Zero hour – at about 0615 the first wounded began to arrive.

06.30 The two leading Companies 'B' & 'D', were sent forward to fulfil the dual role of supporting the attack of the 2nd Worcesters Regt. if necessary, and afterwards of pushing on to OSSUS through the WORCESTER REGT. and secure the crossings over the CANAL. These two Companies advanced in lines of small columns distributed in depth and passed successfully through the enemy barrage, which fell mostly behind them.

07.30 The supporting Company, 'A' Coy, followed the leading Companies in the same formation.

The Reserve Coy & Bn. H.Q. followed after an interval & proceeded to LIMERICK TRENCH and established Bn. H.Q. there. At this time there was a dense fog of smoke & some gas and the situation was obscure. It was ascertained from the O.C. WORCESTER REGT. that his attack was held up by heavy M.G. fire from a Strong Point at X Roads in X.22.c.

The two leading Companies, realizing the situation, had on arrival pushed forward in support of the WORCESTER REGT.; the left Coy 'B' Coy, had actually attained a position between the S.P. and DADOS LANE and were practically behind the S.P.. They charged forward and carried the survivors of the WORCESTERS on their left with them for some 30 yards when the smoke fog came down and touch was lost.

'B' Coy and also 'D' Coy in the fog, drew away to the right and became involved with the 12th DIVn. on our RIGHT and fought with, & in some places, in front of them, in the neighbourhood of CROSSBILL ROAD. Later on, realizing that they had lost direction, they reformed and made their way to KILDARE LANE.

As soon as the whereabouts of Coys had been ascertained it was my intention to direct the Coys with the 12th DIVn. to make an encircling movement via CATELEY ROAD and DADOS LANE with a view to attacking the S.P. from E to W, the only feasible means of approach. I had at this time only one Coy 'C' Coy, about 50 Rifles, in hand and as the WORCESTERS

What had become of "A" Coy in his meantime & how had "C" Coy been reduced to 50 Rifles. What were the casualties of this Coy?

Sheet 2

appeared to have lost very heavily I did not feel justified in using my one Reserve Coy in an encircling attack, in view of the possibility of an enemy counter attack.

About 1230 acting on instructions from the Bde I issued orders to Coys to reorganise in the TRENCHES from LIMERICK POST to KILDARE LANE and hold the trench system in depth.

Orders were issued to patrol, but these were subsequently cancelled owing to a bombardment being contemplated.

The night passed quietly except for M.G. fire & some scattered shelling.

30th Sept. 1918.

0300	From this time onwards the enemy was abnormally quiet
0600	Patrols were pushed out and found the enemy had gone
0800	'B' & 'D' Coys. were ordered to push on towards the original objective of the WORCESTERS, i.e. STONE TRENCH, from KILDARE AVENUE to STONE LANE, and then push out patrols towards OSSUS and CANAL BANK. This was done, the Coys moving forward at a great pace, and meeting with no opposition.

Finding that the WORCESTERS and H.L.I. would not be under way for some time I sent orders to my Coys to wait until the WORCESTERS arrived in PIGEON TRENCH before advancing on OSSUS, as my left was in the air. On the right my Coys were in touch with the 12th Divn the whole time.

The two leading Coys, had, as a matter of fact pushed straight on before my order reached them and they established themselves in a good position overlooking & commanding the CANAL, the left Coy very rightly forming a defensive flank to their left which was then in the air. I had pushed up 'A' Coy after the leading Coys to occupy STONE TRENCH. Slight readjustments were made during the night in order to dispose the Coys more effectually in depth, and Bn. H.Q. was established at X22 d.8.5.

There was fairly heavy M.G. fire and sniping from the E side of CANAL where enemy appeared to be in some strength, and all crossings over CANAL had been destroyed.

I should like to place on record the invaluable assistance that I received throughout the operations from the BRIGADE MAJOR. Owing to his constant visits to the line I was enabled to keep in touch with the BRIGADE and ascertain

Sheet 3

the intentions of the BRIGADIER in a way which could never have been done by wire and runner only

2-10-18.

Seymour Lt Col
Commanding 16th K.R.R.C

WAR DIARY or INTELLIGENCE SUMMARY

Army Form C. 2118.

16 K.R.R.C.

Place	Date	Hour	Summary of Events and Information	Remarks and references to Appendices
	October 1st 1918		Uneventful time stated. Day quiet. Front Companies greatly troubled by Machine Guns and Snipers; difficulty being experienced in locating these. Patrols were sent out during the night who ascertained that the enemy held the E side of all CANAL crossings with M.G.'s and T.M.'s which were active. Some shelling of TARGELLE VALLEY and CATELET ROAD. Night was but dark. Lt. Colonel F.L. PARDOE D.S.O. joined for one month's tour of duty.	
	2nd.		Fine day, visibility good. Enemy Machine Guns active whenever movement in our lines was seen. Enemy Patrols reported in the enemy moving South of HONNECOURT, look-out kept and preparations made to open it. The Enemy seem considerable T.M. activity during the night.	
	3rd.		Our Artillery extremely active in the early hours of the morning and continued active throughout the day. Retaliation insignificant. a small amount of Gas Shelling on Battalion area only. Battalion was relieved, two Companies in the afternoon, two Companies in the evening, by 5th SCOTTISH RIFLES. Relief complete by 21.30 hours. Battalion moved into Support in area S. of VAUCELLETTE FARM.	

WAR DIARY
or
INTELLIGENCE SUMMARY.
(Erase heading not required.)

Army Form C. 2118.

Place	Date 1918	Hour	Summary of Events and Information	Remarks and references to Appendices
CAVALRY SUPPORT area S. of VAUCELETTE FARM	OCTOBER 4th		Day spent reorganising and in kit inspections. Companies at disposal of Company Commanders. Salvage work carried out.	
	5th		Report received that 96th Brigade had advanced and held the HINDENBURG LINE. Battalion warned to be ready to move in full Marching Order at 45 minutes notice. Lt Col PARDOE DSO accompanied the Battalion to the Line. Companies at disposal of Company Commanders. Company Training	
		6½	carried out. Church Service held.	
		7½	Voluntary Church Service held.	
		8½	Coys at disposal of Company Commanders. Tactical schemes carried out by Coys. Battalion moved at 1730 hours from CAVALRY SUPPORT to OSSUS. Transport and B Echelon moved at 1730 hours to TARGELLE RAVINE. A Echelon Transport and Cookers moved with Battalion to OSSUS. Colonel Seymour 250 pro- ceeded to Minimum Reserve at EQUANCOURT & 9th Bath. Colonel PARDOE DSO assumed command of the Battalion. Captain DINSMORE returned	
		9½	from leave. G. HINDENBURG line S. of LA TERRIERE and breakfasted there. Battalion moved to DEHÉRIES and onward in a wood E. of DEHÉRIES. B Echelon moved forward to DEHÉRIES and Rear Transport moved stating at 1030 hours. Route:— Our CANAL, DE L'ESCAUT near OSSUS, AUBECHEUL-AUX-BOIS, VILLERS-OUTREAUX, MALINCOURT, Edge of Bois du GARD, Battalion in Bivouacs, B Echelon and Transport	
		10½	at 0560 hours Battalion moved to TROISVILLE in Artillery Formation and lay in E. of that Village. Captain DINSMORE to Hospital. B Echelon & Rear Transport moved about 1130 hours to CLARY via ELINCOURT.	
		11th	Battalion stood to from 0500 hrs. to 0700 hrs. placing observation Posts at RAMBOURLIEUX FARM. Casualty to one other tank from Shell fire. Brigade received confirmation that Battalion Commanders to Brigade H.Q. orders received that Battalion would attack the following morning next objective the Line of the LE CATEAU—SOLESMES Railway and the high ground in K.10. and K.17.	

Army Form C. 2118.

WAR DIARY
or
INTELLIGENCE SUMMARY.
(Erase heading not required.)

Place	Date	Hour	Summary of Events and Information	Remarks and references to Appendices
E. of TROISVILLE	OCTOBER 12th 1918		Battalion moved at 0100 hrs and took up assembly positions on the Road E. of River SELLE. The River previously having been Bridged by the R.E. the units being marched from H.Q.S. on the Road being A.C.B. & D Companies Battalion Headquarters in the Ravine at K.14.d Central. At 0500 hrs the Battalion attacked without Barrage in two Columns consisting of A Company with C Company in support, Right Column and D. Company with B. Company on the LEFT Column on reports received by the Battalion Commander that actually at 0800 hours C. Company were to that the attack was proceeding satisfactorily. 2nd Lieutenant SURRY was killed and verily of that their O.C. had been found in position in the quarry. 2nd Lieutenant SURRY was killed and 2nd Lieutenant C. BUDD wounded at about this time. Leaving D Coy without Officers. This Company was therefore reported to be in the Quarry making C Company forwards the line of the Railway at 0900 hours. Colonel PARDOE D.S.O. Battalion Hd. Qrs. to the QUARRY in K.9.d. Reports divided to advance Battalion Hd. Qrs. to the QUARRY in K.9.d. Being very heavy Barrage was put up by the enemy on the Railway SELLE and the River H.Q. were Pushed on K.14.d.5. Bringing across the attack was resumed the Battalion in conjunction with the 2nd E. Surrey Regt. of A and C Companies. Battalion H.Q. arrived at the QUARRY to H.Q. in three by the evening Gun was brought up to the point of and the enemy Mounted very heavily wounded. Reserve at that Point Colonel PARDOE was so badly wounded. Reverse tried to Report to Sir Major WILLIS who was left at Report Centre in Ravine at K.14.d. Adjutant had Notified every Officer with him had been killed or wounded. for has been N. Battalion H.Q. by casualties very heavy Barrage on Machine Gun K.15.d.1.0 and endeavoured to get together with him at H.Q.s to effect touch with that of the Battalion H.Q. had been taken up the line of the Railway by now the first objective and unit shown disorganised began. The Brigade was ordered to attack the same objectives	
Lt. Col. THOMAS MIDDLESEX REGT.				

WAR DIARY or INTELLIGENCE SUMMARY

Army Form C. 2118.

Place	Date	Hour	Summary of Events and Information	Remarks and references to Appendices
	OCTOBER 12th 1918 (continued)		Zero hour altered to 17.50 hours later, subsequently this attack was cancelled, and the Brigade ordered to establish the line of the River SELLE with advanced posts beyond the River including the crossings over the road. 1st MIDDLESEX on the left, 2nd WORCESTERSHIRE Regt. Centre, 16th K.R.R.C. on the right, 16th K.R.R.C. ordered to take over portion of 8th H.L.I. but this was found impossible with the small available strength, so 70 men from 9th HUSSARS left in the line under command of 2nd Lieut. THOMAS. The night was fairly quiet except some slight shelling & machine gun fire. 1st Worcs making improvement and consolidation earlier difficulties. Gun fire. Battalion H.Q's moved to M.R. 26.C. At noon an attempt was made to establish Battalion H.Q's at M.R. 17.K. Offrs. Casualties were Capt. PARDOE wounded, 2nd Lieut. SURRY killed, 2nd Lieut. BUDD wounded (since died of wounds) 2nd Lt. A.H. VILLIERS wounded and missing. Lieut. P.G. Le Q. PARAVICINI and 2nd Lt. W.A.J. EVERTON to Coxyne at I Corps School. 2nd Lieut. R.S.A. HOLLAND joined for duty.	
	13th		Battalion held the line in the new position; 2 companies had been moved A & C under the command of 2 Lieut: THOMAS and BUDD under command of Capt. COATES. A & C Companies in front & B & D in support Lovely Artillery & Machine gun fire all day. Battalion were relieved by the 2nd R.W.F. (38th Division) Relief completed by 23.30 hours. On completion of relief Battalion to TROISVILLE for the night. 2nd Lieut. SUGDEN to Hospital sick. Lt. H.G. MATHER rejoined from leave.	
CLARY.	14th		Battalion marched out to CLARY. Brunwer rejoined.	
	15th		Reorganisation and refitting proceeded with. Companies at the disposal of Company Commanders for refitting. Lieut: J.H. BLOOMER proceeded on leave.	
	16th		Battalion was inspected by the Divisional General Representatives of the Brigade.	
	17th		Operations resumed part of the O.C. Companies Special Service of conforming at the disposal of the Church at CLARY.	
	18th		Thanksgiving held in the Church at CLARY. A "Staff Ride" was held in the afternoon by C.O's, Company Commanders, Adjutant and Company Commanders 2nd B.E.F. in Command of Alphaland Company.

Army Form. C. 2118.

WAR DIARY
or
INTELLIGENCE SUMMARY.
(Erase heading not required.)

Instructions regarding War Diaries and Intelligence Summaries are contained in F. S. Regs., Part II. and the Staff Manual respectively. Title pages will be prepared in manuscript.

Place	Date	Hour	Summary of Events and Information	Remarks and references to Appendices
CLARY	OCTOBER 19th 1918		Battalion route marched to DEHERIES and then retired moving as a Tactical Advanced guard. Lt J. ALLEN returned from leave.	
	20th		Church service held. 2nd Lt L.J. STONE and 2nd Lieut J.C. NAYLER proceed on leave.	
	21st		Battalion moved to BERTRY	
BERTRY			move forward from the force Brigade Sector. reinforcement of 60 O.R. and draftmate to Companies. Brigade called for information on disposition of Battalion officers. 2nd Lieut C.V.J. SNETT and 2nd Lieut M.G. GILL went for duty 2nd Lieut J.R. SUDDEN came to U.K. 2nd Lieut J.R. WILSON remained in line.	
	22nd		Battalion billeted at BERTRY. Orders received for Battalion to move forward to R 18 square Battalion moved at approx 20.30 from billeting area and arrived at Cambrai hauling order of March B.C. HQ. A & C Companies. Preliminary reconnaissances had taken off on the Railway Embankment near Solesmes where Battalion bivouacked for the night.	
K.16.9	23rd	0260 0530	At 0260 the attack by the 33rd Division commenced from this line into the 0530 news reaching us stating ... [illegible] ... that the Rifle Brigade was in sufficient strength ... FOREST that ...	
			Battalion moved forward about 0845 hours having again been in support on the right of the Leinsters. of VENDEGIES Wood but on the B Company in the right of the Battalion being short of men the Battalion being very short of men on the Direction ... of the ... 2nd Lieut C.V.J. ERRETT ... [illegible] ... Battalion casualties ... for the night ... and 38 O.R. casualties.	
	24th		Battalion ordered to take our outpost line from CAMERONIANS who were to go through that line later and take up the 4th and 5th Objectives. The Brigade would follow up and establish the general line LA COURE GORGE L.5.26.a.60 to S.16 Central	

WAR DIARY
or
INTELLIGENCE SUMMARY.
(Erase heading not required.)

Army Form C. 2118.

Place	Date	Hour	Summary of Events and Information	Remarks and references to Appendices
	OCTOBER 24th 1918 (cont'd)		CAMERONIANS resumed on the outpost line and advance of objective from this at 0400 hours. The 0408 hours an enemy patrol but was held up owing to the very obscure situation on the right. The retirement was continued. O.C. 1200 hours reported the line of the ENGELFONTAINE – LA COUPE GORGE Road. A Company left hold, C Company Right Support. 39 1600 hours the B Company left C Support. B Company Right Support. Reorganisation completed 1800. At 1600 hours the Battalion occupied the position with 600 yards. Strong fighting patrols were sent out to harass the enemy to occupy the right Battn. A and C Companies went forward about 500 yards, encountered Companies of enemy who owing to the line held by them, were accurately shot pretty by the Batteries. Slight but stubborn resistance was encountered.	ENGELFONTAINE
	25th		At 0730 hours enemy counter-attacked along the Battalion front, the Battn. front being successful in driving it off. Patrols from A and C Companies of HLI on the right. Shells stuck on road by 2 scouts MATHER strength of one of the Sections that of about 15 enemy and attacked, one horse and equipment and 3 machine guns. B Company was rushed up on the night of the LP/HLI who were supporting the B Company. At 1360 hours the line was again attacked. This affected the B Company commenced clearing of the ENGELFONTAINE – LA COUVRE GORGE Road and about 1800 hours these were clear. 1800 A Company established Outposts received orders to pass through the LP – the Queen's and the Batt. gave information for a large number of the objectives being the COLCHTRIE colony village of ENGELFONTAIN. Orders accordingly passed. About 2300 hours D Company at 0100 hours left to assemble by the Railway Line about 2 miles cut of LH GH COS and Cpt RJF NORTH wounded in LAYE was found.	
	26th		0107 A and C Companies moved along the Rue B Mahieu to reach Queen's road to Queen's posn and from there 34 OR cpm B line. A and C Companies advanced along the same line to the immediate north of the road of the objective of the Battalion had to relieve the 1st Queen's on the road running N and S through S 26 R.2.6. and a deployment finally being S.19. 2 through N.	

WAR DIARY
or
INTELLIGENCE SUMMARY.
(Erase heading not required.)

Army Form C. 2118.

Place	Date	Hour	Summary of Events and Information	Remarks and references to Appendices
	OCTOBER 26th 1918 (cont)		A and C Companies attained their objectives but D Company were held up by Machine Gun and Shell Fire. B Company was attacked by Germans from the South and by 08.29 hours all objectives were gained and touch established on the left. After reorganisation the position of companies was from North to South. A and C Companies D Company B Company Battalion was relieved during the afternoon and early morning by the 17 E.R.W.F. Relief being complete without incident by 2100 hours. On relief Battalion moved into Billets at FOREST. 1/2 O.R. casualties.	
	27th		Sunday. Battalion rested. 2nd Lieut E.F. WALKER and 2nd Lieut C. WOOD joined for duty.	
	28th		Companies practised gas mask on Tuesday, working on 53 Machine Gun Companies practised gas mask for use Tuesday and an Anti-tank Stretcher Bearer Parade under M.O. Lt Col. C.H.V. SEYMOUR D.S.O. and 2nd Lieut D.W. CLEUGHBOURNE came. 2nd Lieut F.L. TROTTER proceeded on Gas course.	
	29th		Companies employed on Salvage. Specialists under Instruction. 2nd Lieut P.B. di PARAVICINI attended Junior Course at II Corps School.	
	30th		Companies employed on Salvage. Companies practised in firing their own and the German Light Machine gun.	

WAR DIARY
INTELLIGENCE SUMMARY

(Erase heading not required.)

Army Form C. 2118.

10/R.R.C
Vol 37

Place	Date	Hour	Summary of Events and Information	Remarks and references to Appendices
FOREST	1/11/18		Battalion in rest at FOREST. Companies at the disposal of their Commanders for re-organisation	
	2/11/18		Reorganisation. Capt. O. C. DOUGHTIE to England for leave	
	3/11/18		Capt. the Hon. R. P. Stanley Commissar - Lt G.H. BLOOMER returned from leave. Coys at the disposal of their Commanders - Conference of all Company officers explaining role of Battalion in the forthcoming attack. the FIRST to be in MORMAL. Major RAWLINS to LONDON FRANCE Battalion moved to assembly position E.7. H.E.C.Q. Humm…. Rear rural GAS QUESTIONS etc …. attached to Division. Train Commanders Officers held conference explaining to the Scottish Rifles	
	5/11/18		Suddenness received to move forward owing to information of an enemy retirement across the SAMBRE. A Coy reported to B. Coy …, (….) J ……, of the village of LA PETITE NOIR with a few followers at 0300 hours. …… the brigade of BERLAMONT, …….. by 1000 hours A Coy with B Coy in the SAMBRE. C Coy …… was dispatched Coy in … Land was established on right and left flank by HQ ……. SART BARAS. Battalion …… about by 1st Division and moved into ……	
	5/11/18		Advance forward of SART BARAS. Road completed by 2500 hours. Battalion …… 1st Army …… crossed SAMBRE. Riv .…	
	6/11/18		MAUBERGE had been attacked. An advance guard from 6th Brigade …… with the right flank of the 2 WORCESTERS and forward patrols pushed forward to LEVAL. These were joined by the second LEVAL which …. held by our 1Pdrs and infantry occupied that town without casualty about 1600 in NE direction. Dawn arrival of 9th Brigade…… who advanced in keeping to 91st Division Comm… …………. BATTALION of the Naval …… to the Battalion who occupied MERVAL to night of B ... HQ …… at SASSEGNIES. An enemy …….. on the 7th. Lt Col C.H.N. SEYMOUR DSO …… took over command of ….. off at 0145 hours. Major A.N. WILLIS took Command.	
			Cont a …… ed at six. Major A.N. WILLIS took Command.	
			Company marched to Brigade assembly … Major John de Bussy from PETIT MAUBERGE en route. 2/14 P. BACON relieved L by rear ……. Battalion ……. Germans delayed us by 1000 hours LE PARIS to Brigade Battalion front line from …… at NOYE where it was …… through as the military sit ass ……	
	7/11/18		14.00	Coy to conform at …… by when early enemy had …… with the …… 1st Coy from B.P.M. 2nd …… marched without …… on right of Battalion …… across well defined enemy line a ……. Coy en ……	
			The PM 3 N w.… and …… orders were …… Battalion bivouac were …… on areas made …… across …… …… along ……. other road across the military line …… Battalion from Col …. by other tracks. Battalion members and to Bivouac on PETIT MARBERGE. 2/ Lt R.G. BINET, from had Capt D.SMITH & G. L. GARROBENT from Hospital	

WAR DIARY or INTELLIGENCE SUMMARY

Army Form C. 2118.

(Erase heading not required.)

Instructions regarding War Diaries and Intelligence Summaries are contained in F. S. Regs., Part II. and the Staff Manual respectively. Title pages will be prepared in manuscript.

Place	Date	Hour	Summary of Events and Information	Remarks and references to Appendices
PETIT MARBERGE	8/11/18		Summon Reserve regime Battalion at PETIT MARBERGE. MAJOR RAW. LANE assumed command of the Battalion on returning from leave in FRANCE. Coys at the disposal of their Company Commanders for rest and recreation.	
	9/11/18		Coys at the disposal of their Commanders. Observation that Germans had been communicating with every Cock he had been given till 1100 hours on the 11th instant. 2/Lt R G de PARDVINIEU Liason Officer reported to Bn from Brigade.	
	10/11/18		2/Lt R.C. NAYLOR from leave. 2/Lt F.E. NORTH from hospital. Sunday. Voluntary Service held in the Bungalow attended by R.I.E. BLOXAM & Officers 172 others ranks. 2nd Lieut (A.H. instant and was enclosed. Bn of q/136 other ranks joined the Battalion and were posted to Companies. 2/Lt SUGDEN from leave.	
	12/11/18		Battalion moved to BELLES at BERLAIMONT	
	13/11/18		Coys at the disposal of their Commanders. Attempt inspected by the Commanding Officer. Coys at the disposal of their Commander. Brigade did battle left by the Pioneers, a tea used with	
	14/11/18		Battalion moved by Route march to SINGLE FONTAIN. Pioneers came with by tea. Capt J.F. BLOXAM MC CF	
	15/11/18		(A Coy) was admitted Special Hospital. 2/Lt F.I. TROTTER from leave. Capt. HODSON M.C. 6th permits duties Medical Battalion moved by Route march to CLARY staying for details at TROISVILLE. 2/Lt MC OUGH joined for duty.	
	16/11/18		Lt. R.C. INIGO-JONES rejoined from Brigade Employment	
	17/11/18		Sunday. Voluntary Church Service held by all denominations	
	18/11/18		Coys at the disposal of their Commanders. New shafts from leave 11th R.S.M. FuRP/S Sn.L.C. Cr-Col C.M.N SEYMOUR D.S.O. from Brigade. Coffee R.H. WILLIS H.Lane.	
	19/11/18		Coys at the disposal of their Commanders. Promotion of the Battalion attended Lecture in Bungalow, disposal of the Command Division (6th) Colonel CHIDKING, M.C. supported D.S.O. 2/Lt WAS. EVERTON from Course. 2/Lt J.B. HERION & 2/Lt W.F. JACKSON 2/Lt J.A. BARTLETT. joined for duty. Capt O. COUGHTRIE from leave.	
	20/11/18		Battalion reported for Commander but rained the Commanding Officer	
	22/11/18		Battalion paraded for Command Review and the Commanding Officer 2/Lt W.A.I. EVERTON to leave. 2/Lt R.S.A. Holland from Musical Bunker.	
	23/11/18		Battalion devoted Handgrenade Service with Brigade arrangements. H.Col M.L.S CLEMENTS joined for duty. Lt F.L. TROTTER proceed to see to attend Battalion will shortly move and Shelling Bois. Battalion visited the Aerodrome of 2nd Squadron R.A.F & heard a Lecture in the entertainment of Aeroplanes	
	29/11/18		Battalion enlarged Church Service Memorial of Glory of W.N. missed. Lt F.W. LISCOMB(?) detained Brigade Town feast Official with effect from 9th September 1918. Captain Acottims M.C. Lt & F BLOXAM M.C. awarded Bar to M.C. Lt G H BIRTHER & 2/Lt ROBINET awarded M.C.	

(A9725) W. W4358/P.580 650,000. 10/17. D.D.& L. Sch. 52a. Forms/C2118/13

WAR DIARY
or
INTELLIGENCE SUMMARY

Army Form C. 2118.

Place	Date	Hour	Summary of Events and Information	Remarks and references to Appendices
CLARY	24/11/18		Sunday. Parade Service with Divisional Recreation Room CLARY.	
	25/11/18		Battalion paraded for usual day work. The Commanding Officer, Lt. Col. C.H.N. SEYMOUR D.S.O. left Battalion. 2/Col. M.E.S. CLEMENTS assumed command.	
	28/11/18		Battalion paraded for recommencing usual training (Company & Specialist). 2/Lt. P.G. de PARAVICINI from 2/4 M.G. Gns. to Educational Corps.	
	29/11/18		Battalion proceeded on Education Parade by Companies. 2/Lt. HARDINER M.C. & 2/Lt N.G. GILL to Educational Corps.	
	28/11/18		Battalion proceeded on Education Parade by Companies. Battalion transport inspected by the Brigade Commander. 9/Lt. A. CAMERON and 22 [...] recruits joined for duty.	
	30/11/18		Battalion parade for Commanding Officer with the Commanding Officer. 19 other ranks to Base for Home Employment.	

2-12-18

Arthur Crant
Col Comdg
11th KRRC

19
100/33
16 K.R.R.
C/N 38

WAR DIARY
or
INTELLIGENCE SUMMARY
(Erase heading not required)

Army Form C. 2118.

Place	Date	Hour	Summary of Events and Information	Remarks and references to Appendices
CLARY	Sept 1st		C.O.E. Lectures held in Bn. Recreation Room. – Educational classes started. – Sports issued at 2000 hrs. daily. Command'd. 6. day.	
	2nd		Batts. for the whole Bn. Salvage work (carried on). – Education classes. – 2/Lt. F.G. BUDD awarded the Military Cross. (2nd ARO. 1877).	
	3rd		Route march via Troisvilles, Bertry, Maurois, Bertry & Clary.	
	4th		His Majesty King George V. passed through the Divisional Area, stopping a few moments at CLARY. Troops lined the Route & cheered lustily.	
	5th		Batn. Route march ELINCOURT. – MARETZ – CLARY	
	6th		Batn. Route march. CAULLERY. – SELVIGNY. – WALINCOURT. – DEHERIES. – SERAIN. – ELINCOURT.-CLARY. Bn. Gas Casualty examined took Rev. H.V. HODSON. C.F. 4/Lt. S.A.P. THOMAS appointed acting Captain whilst Commanding a Company. Lt. J.W. Lipscomb to be acting Captain (additional) C/86 Sgt. being awarded M.M. and C/1132 L/C. R. SMURTHWAITE	
	7th F.		C.O.E. lectures in the Divisional Cinema at 11:00 hrs. Lectures also for R.C's. & Non-conformist. Batn. work march.	
	8th F.		Batn. started to march to Horney Area taking 8 days. reached MASNIERES first day.	
	9th F.		Batn. marched to HERMIES via MARCOING. – RIBECOURT. – HAVRINCOURT. –	
	10th F.		Batn. marched to FAVREUIL via DOIGNES. – BEAUMETZ. – VELU. – FREMICOURT. – BEUGNATRE. a very hot day.	
	11th F.		Batn. marched to a fort W. of ALBERT via BAPAUME. + was accom'd.d in tents.	
	12th F.		Batn. marched to BUSSY LES DAOURS. Div' Commdr. saw the Batn. march past.	
	13th F.			

Army Form C. 2118.

WAR DIARY
or
INTELLIGENCE SUMMARY.
(Erase heading not required.)

Instructions regarding War Diaries and Intelligence Summaries are contained in F. S. Regs., Part II. and the Staff Manual respectively. Title pages will be prepared in manuscript.

Place	Date	Hour	Summary of Events and Information	Remarks and references to Appendices
BREILLY.	14th.		Batn. marched to BREILLY.	
CAMPS EN AMIENOIS.	15th.		Batn. marched to CAVILLON AREA H.Q. & 2 Coys billeted in CAMPS EN AMIENOIS. and 2 Coys in HALLIVIERS.	
ANDAINVILLE.	16th.		Batn. reached its destination at ANDAINVILLE. Troops marched in exceedingly well, after 8 days marching in very bad weather & trying conditions.	
ANDAINVILLE.	17th.		Coys at the disposal of their Commanders for rest & improvement of billets.	
	18th.		Coys at the disposal of their Commanders. Cross country runs training under Rev. H.V. HODSON J.P. for the 31st Cross country race.	
	19th.		Coys at the disposal of their Commanders. The Batn. played the 9th H.L.I. at football & won unfortunately, both.	
	20th.		Coys at the disposal of their Commanders. NCOs passed under the R.S.M. Lewis gun & rifle. Inspected by the Padmore Sgt.	
	21st.		Coys at the disposal of their Commanders. Major PAN LAYE assumed Command of the Batn. vice A.B. W.S. CLEMENTS. C. Company Command of 100th Inf Bde.	
	22nd		V/usher CB & Lurico.	
	23rd.		Batn. go to the wtld. Batn. at FRESNOY.	
	24th.		Coys at the disposal of their Commanders. Preparations for Xmas dinner in full swing.	
	25th.		Voluntary service in the morning. The Batn. Band gave a choral service in the Parish Church which was attended by many inhabitants. and was greatly appreciated. Rations L. Corp. W. (warned) all Bakers & the Batn. Cpl. go. the Batn. was told informed for a short afternoon. In fact Xmas day & Xmas given by the Cpl. L. Said & hoped we should all remember the first Xmas day & peace after 4.	

WAR DIARY or INTELLIGENCE SUMMARY

Army Form C. 2118.

(Erase heading not required.)

Place	Date	Hour	Summary of Events and Information	Remarks and references to Appendices
	25th		Xmas & Coln. Spent with Bn allies and Bn. It was deer. Bat: all his parishioners would remember today a great day. It had been too a great success. Col. Clement spoke a few appropriate & well chosen words at the commencement. Coys at the disposal of their commanders. Xmas dinner for B Coy. CO attended again 20h coms from Brigade. to personally wish his men a happy Xmas, which was much appreciated by all ranks.	
	26th			
	27th		Coys at the disposal of their Commanders. C. Coys Xmas dinner.	
	28th		A Baton paraded to him asked on which the Brigadier Commander was going to give medal ribbons to then. Men who had not yet received them. Owing to the weather the ceremony was cancelled and the Brigadier Commander gave the ribbons in the Baton Orderly room. Voluntary service for all denominations.	
	29th			
	30th		Coys at the disposal of their Commanders. Morning used for the Brigade with Battn. Move to the Brigade area shortly. Bn played football against the 101st Field Ambulance which resulted in a draw.	
	31st		Coys at the disposal of their Commanders. Major ALY toothes assumed command of the Baton vice Major F.A.W. Lays to hospital. A Battalion Officers dinner was held, at which many excellent speeches were made. The Battalion afterwards assembled and a hope begin to see the New Year in.	

R.W.W...
Major
Commanding 16th K.R.R.C.

Army Form C. 2118.

WAR DIARY
or
INTELLIGENCE SUMMARY.
(Erase heading not required.)

Instructions regarding War Diaries and Intelligence Summaries are contained in F. S. Regs., Part II. and the Staff Manual respectively. Title pages will be prepared in manuscript.

Place	Date	Hour	Summary of Events and Information	Remarks and references to Appendices
ANDAINVILLE	1/1/19		Coys at the disposal of their Commanders. The Battalion goes on to the defence of the Village. Major A.M. WILLIS and one Coy of Engineers at the H.Q. of the 9th H.L.I.	
	2/1/19		Coys at the disposal of their Commanders. Advance party proceeds to MARTIN EGLISE near DIEPPE	
	3/1/19		Battalion moved to FOUCARMONT AREA and Billeted in VILLERS en route for MARTIN EGLISE	
	4/1/19		" " " " LONDINIERES " " " WANCHY	
	5/1/19		" " " " MARTIN EGLISE where the DIEPPE EMBARKATION CAMP was taken over by the 100th Brigade for administration.	
MARTIN EGLISE	6/1/19		Companies at the disposal of their Commanders for refitting. Lecture to all Officers by the Brigadier Major on the Scheme of working the Demobilization Camps.	
	7/1/19		Battalion Parade. 2/Lt Col M.L.S. CLEMENTS resumes command of the Battalion on return from 100th Infantry Brigade. Major A.N. WILLIS assumes the duties of 2nd in Command	
	8/1/19		Confidential orders on the Demobilisation scheme. Confirmed appointment of their absence duties. Major PANLAYA assumed the duties of 2nd in Command in return from England. Appointment of Companies carried on. Major A.N. WILLIS takes on Command of A BLOCK Coys at the disposal of the Block Commander	
	9/1/19		" " " "	
	10/1/19		" " " "	
	11/1/19		" " " "	
	12/1/19		Sunday. Voluntary Service held	
	13/1/19		The first drafts arrived for demobilization carried	
	14/1/19		on the evening and are expected every day from now onwards	
	15/1/19		Work of demobilization carried on. Capt & Q BOTTOMS M.C. and 2/Lt W.A.S. EVERTON return from leave	
	16/1/19		" " " "	
	17/1/19		" " " "	
	18/1/19		Fourteen other ranks left the Battalion for demobilization.	
	19/1/19		" " " " " village	
	20/1/19		P.A.W. LANE to leave in England. The whole Battalion paraded the new Camp Arrangement received a lecture about change. Practicals &	
	21/1/19		Reveilts were also discussed.	
	22/1/19		Work of Demobilisation carried on. " Seven men left Battalion for Demobilisation.	
	23/1/19		Unity ma " Capt H.V. HODSON M.C. C.F. to leave in France	
	24/1/19		to Proceed as Asst Staff Captain, above men left Battalion for Demobilization. Lt Col F.L. TROTTER	

Wt. W14422/M1160 350,000 12/16 D. D. & L. Forms/C./2118/14.

Army Form C. 2118.

WAR DIARY
or
INTELLIGENCE SUMMARY.
(Erase heading not required.)

Instructions regarding War Diaries and Intelligence Summaries are contained in F. S. Regs., Part II. and the Staff Manual respectively. Title pages will be prepared in manuscript.

Place	Date	Hour	Summary of Events and Information	Remarks and references to Appendices
MARTIN EGLISE	25/1/19		Work of demobilisation carried on. Six men left Battalion for demobilisation. Capt. W. C. COATES. Lt. F. S. HORTH and 30 men left Battalion for demobilisation.	
	26/1/19			
	27/1/19		Work of demobilisation carried on. B. Coy reduced to cadre strength by the transfer of surplus personnel to other Companies in equal proportions. Two men left Battalion for demobilisation.	
	28/1/19		Work of demobilisation carried on. 2/Lt W. B. JACKSON from leave.	
	29/1/19		" " Lt. H. C. GILL and 2 men left Battalion for demobilisation.	
	30/1/19		Major P. A. W. KAYE returned to Battalion during from leave.	
	31/1/19		Work of demobilisation carried on. Capt. M. G. MATHER. Lt. J. B. HEATON. Lt. P. G. de PARAVICINI. 2/Lt W. B. S. EVERTON. 2/Lt H. C. OUGH and 17 other ranks left Battalion for demobilisation.	

Bottom(?)
Capt + Adjt
16th KRRC

A6945 Wt. W1142/M1160 350,000 12/16 D. D. & L. Forms/C./2118/14.

Army Form C. 2118.

WAR DIARY
INTELLIGENCE SUMMARY.
(Erase heading not required.)

16 R.R.R. 1/5/40

Place	Date	Hour	Summary of Events and Information	Remarks and references to Appendices
Martin Eglise	1/2/19.		Work of Demobilisation carried on.	
	2/2/19.		do 33 men demobilised. Voluntary Church Services held.	
	3/2/19.		do	
	4/2/19.		do 9 men demobilised.	
	5/2/19.		do	
	6/2/19.		do	
	7/2/19.		do	
	8/2/19.		do Voluntary Church Services held.	
	9/2/19.		do Draft of 5 Officers and 126 other ranks arrive from 11th Bn The Kings Royal Rifle Corps.	
	10/2/19.		do	
	11/2/19.		Work of Demobilisation carried on.	
	12/2/19.		do Battalion Christmas cards arrived from the Printers. Lt and Q.M. J. Allan to leave in England.	
	13/2/19.		do Lt C.M.C. Turner to leave in England. Battalion Bathed.	
	14/2/19.		do	
	15/2/19.		do Lt B. Paterson to leave in England. 10 men demobilised.	
	16/2/19.		do	
	17/2/19.		do	
	18/2/19.		do 2/Lt R.S.A. Holland from leave in England.	
	19/2/19.		do	
	20/2/19.		do 2/Lt L.J. Stone from leave in France. 10 men demobilised.	
	21/2/19.		do	
	22/2/19.		do	
	23/2/19.		do Voluntary Church Services held. 2/Lt R.C. Naylor to leave in England. 5 Officers and 182 other ranks from 8th and 2/10th London Regt joined for duty. Major P.A.W. Laye to leave in England.	
	24/2/19.		do	
	25/2/19.		do 2/Lt J.A. Bartlett to leave in England. Capt. C.H.D. King D.S.O. M.C. from leave in France.	
	26/2/19.		do 20 other ranks demobilised. 10 Officers and 300 men from 11th and 12th Battns Rifle Brigade joined for duty.	
	27/2/19.		do	
	28/2/19.		do	

Mottram
Captain
16th KRR

Army Form C. 2118.

WAR DIARY
or
INTELLIGENCE SUMMARY.
(Erase heading not required.)

Instructions regarding War Diaries and Intelligence Summaries are contained in F.S. Regs., Part II. and the Staff Manual respectively. Title pages will be prepared in manuscript.

Place	Date	Hour	Summary of Events and Information	Remarks and references to Appendices
~~DUNKIRK~~ ~~LE×HAVRE×~~ DIEPPE.	Mar 1st		Work of demobilisation carried on. Lt and Q.M. J Allen from leave in England.	
	2nd.		do Voluntary Services held.	
	3rd.		do Advanced party consisting of Capt Hick.M.C. Lt. Dennett and 14 other ranks proceeded to HAVRE to take over No 1 Reception Camp to which the Battalion will shortly move.	
	4th.		Work of demobilisation carried on. Lt. D.W.Cleugh from leave in England.	
	5th.		Work of demobilisation carried on. Battalion moved to Martin Eglise Station to entrain to HAVRE. Owing to a Railway accident the train did not arrive. Battalion moved back to D Block, Martin Eglise Embarkation Camp to await instructions. Raining Camp very muddy. Men accomodated in tents.	
	6th.		Battalion stood by to wait for train. Moved into C. Block of the Camp to better accomodation. 2/Lt C.M.C.Turner and Lt. E.B.Wastall from leave in England.	
	7th.		Battalion moved by train to HAVRE preparatory to taking over No. 1 Reception Camp from 1st. Middlesex. Travelled all night.	
SANVIC. LE.HAVRE.	8th.		Arrived at HAVRE at 0230 hours - raining - moved to No. 1. Reception Camp and rested for the day. Selected parties attached to 1st. Middlesex for the purpose of learning new duties.	
	9th.		Battalion carried on the process of taking over.	
	10th.		do	
	11th.		do	
	12th.		A Coy. took over X Wing of No. 1. Reception Camp from 1st. Battalion Middlesex Regt. B and C Coys. took over DeLouser.	
	13th.		Capt. Hick.M.C. and 1 Platoon B Coy and 1 Platoon C Coy took over Y Wing. D Coy. took over Y Wing from 1st. Middlesex Regt, thus completing relief. Lt B. Paterson from leave in England. 2/Lt L.J.Stone to be Lt.	
	14th.		Work of demobilisation carried on. 2/Lt. A.A.Whitney from leave in England.	
	15th.		do	
	16th.		do 2/Lt.J.R.Sugden and 2/Lt R.C.Naylor from leave in England.	
	17th.		Lt O Hunting 2/Lt G.D.Chamberlain and 100 ranks joined for duty from 1st. Bn. Rifle Brigade.	
	18th.		Work of demobilisation carried on.	
	19th.		do Lt. L.J.Stone to leave in England.	
	20th.		do	
	21st.		do 2/Lt O.C.Venus, 2/Lt. C.Chisnell, 2/Lt.G.A.Wallace and 2/Lt. A.McLeod from Draft Conducting Leave.	
	22nd.		Work of demobilisation carried on.	
	23rd.		do Voluntary Services held. 2/Lt. H.G.Smith from Hospital.	

Army Form C. 2118.

WAR DIARY
or
INTELLIGENCE SUMMARY.
(*Erase heading not required.*)

Instructions regarding War Diaries and Intelligence Summaries are contained in F. S. Regs., Part II. and the Staff Manual respectively. Title pages will be prepared in manuscript.

Place	Date	Hour	Summary of Events and Information	Remarks and references to Appendices
SANVIC. LE HAVRE.	Mar. 24th.		Work of demobilisation carried on. 2/Lt. H.W.Walden from leave in England.	
	25th.		do	
	26th.		do	
	27th.		do	
	28th.		do	
	29th.		32, other ranks proceeded for training to 100th Brigade School.	
	30th.		do Voluntary Services held.	
	31st.		do	

Lieutenant
Cmdg K.R.R.C.
16/4/19

Army Form C. 2118.

WAR DIARY
or
INTELLIGENCE SUMMARY.
(*Erase heading not required.*)

Instructions regarding War Diaries and Intelligence Summaries are contained in F. S. Regs. Part II. and the Staff Manual respectively. Title pages will be prepared in manuscript.

16 KRRC

Place	Date	Hour	Summary of Events and Information	Remarks and references to Appendices
SANVIC.	April 1st.		Work of demobilisation carried on.	
	2nd.		do.	
	3rd.		do.	
	4th.		2/Lieut. E.W.Jeffery to be Lieutenant. Lieut. L.J.Stone from leave. Capt. H.B.Emerson.U.S.A. M.C. to A.E.F. for demobilisation.	
	5th.		Lieut. F.L.Trotter from leave.	
	6th.		Voluntary Church Services held. Lt. A.O.Hunting to leave in England.	
	7th.		do.	
	8th.		2/Lt. R.O.Binet, and Lt. L.J.Stone demobilised.	
	9th.		2/Lieut.W.A.G.MacLeod returned from duty with 100th. I.B. Battalion collection of 1560 francs sent to St Dunstan's Institute.	
	10th.		Lieut. G.A.Wallace from Hospital.	
	11th.		Major. P.A.W.Laye from leave in England.	
	12th.		do.	
	13th.		Capt. S.A.Smith.M.C. from leave in England. Voluntary Church Services held.	
	14th.		do.	
	15th.		Lieut. R.A.Burton, to leave in England.	
	16th.		2/Lieuts. G.A.Wallace and G.C.Chisnell to be Lieutenants.	
	17th.		do.	
	18th.		do.	
	19th.		Voluntary Church Services held.	
	20th.		Capt. R.C.Hollond from 100th. Brigade School. Parade Services held.	
	21st.		do.	
	22nd.		Major. A.L.Y.Willis assumed command of the Battalion vice Lt. Col. M.L.S.Clements to General Base Depot.	
	23rd.		Training carried out in accordance with programme. Capt. R.C.Hollond and 2/Lieut. W.A.C.Mc Leod to 53rd. R.B. for duty.	
	24th.		Training carried on in accordance with programme. Subaltern officers paraded under Adjutant and R.S.M.	
	25th.		do.	

Army Form C. 2118.

WAR DIARY
or
INTELLIGENCE SUMMARY.
(Erase heading not required.)

Instructions regarding War Diaries and Intelligence Summaries are contained in F. S. Regs., Part II. and the Staff Manual respectively. Title pages will be prepared in manuscript.

Place	Date	Hour	Summary of Events and Information	Remarks and references to Appendices
SANVIC.	April 26th.		Work of demobilisation carried on. Training carried on in accordance with programme. Capt. F. Noble. M.C. to Hospital.	
	27th.		do. Parade Services held.	
	28th.		do. Lt. A.O.Hunting from leave in England. Capt. C.H.D.King. D.S.O. M.C. to leave in England. Training carried on in accordance with programme.	
	29th.		do. Training carried on xxxx in accordance with programme. Major Willis and 16 Officers attended 33rd. Divisional School for purposes of liaison. 2/Lieut. G.T.Taylor to leave in England.	
	30th.		do. Training carried on in accordance with programme. 16. Officers attended 33rd. Divisoanl School in continuation of the visit made the preceding day.	

[signature]
[signature] Col. KRRC

WAR DIARY
or
INTELLIGENCE SUMMARY.

(Erase heading not required.)

Army Form C. 2118.

16 KRR
1/6/43

Place	Date	Hour	Summary of Events and Information	Remarks and references to Appendices
SAMAC 16 HOUSE	1-8-39		Capt G Bortoma MC proceeded to Inwilisation at the Depot experience courses of England	
			Capt R.A.O. Moore to leave in England	
	2		Routine work R.H.Q. + Companies (Ingonish)	
	3		Routine Work	
	4		Church parade for Coy 3 service	
	5		Routine Work. Lt De Maroin + em De Neana to 33 Art School for Potential Signalling Course	
	6		Routine Work	
	7		Routine Work	
	8		Major E.L. Hopkins MC 2nd Worcestershire Regt attached, ceased from leave appendices to leave in England	
	9		Routine Work	
	10		Routine Work	
	11		Wednesday Church Service	
	12		Routine Work	
	13		Routine Work. Major Willis assumed command on his return from leave	
	14		Routine Work	
	15		Routine Work	

WAR DIARY
or
INTELLIGENCE SUMMARY.
(Erase heading not required.)

Army Form C. 2118.

Instructions regarding War Diaries and Intelligence Summaries are contained in F. S. Regs., Part II. and the Staff Manual respectively. Title pages will be prepared in manuscript.

Place	Date	Hour	Summary of Events and Information	Remarks and references to Appendices
JANUARY	16		Rouen. Brigadier General F.E.G. GINSBERG CMG DSO inspected the transport.	
	17		Rouen. Capt Bell-Irving to DES Havre & 2/Lt J. Elliott posted for duty from 1 Bn. 2/Lt J.F. Taylor from leave	
	18		Veterinary Board duties	
	19		Rouen. Capt Austin Brown posted to Bn. at work	
	20		Rouen.	
	21		Rouen. Signallers taken a variety of Bn. HQrs for Kinemas	
	22		Rouen. Capt G.C. Huck M.C. R.S. acts H.Q.O. assumes duties of Adjutant vice W.J. Taylor & asst Adjt. Lt. E. Wood & 2nd Holland posted for organization	
	23		Rouen. 2/Lt J.F. Taylor appointed Bn. Gassing Officer	
	24		Rouen	
	25		Veterinary Church Service. 2/Lt W.R. Powell to leave	
	26		Rouen. W.R. Powell assumes duties of Adjutant vice Capt G.C. Huck M.C. to leave	
	27		Rouen. 2/Lt Violet to leave	
	28		Rouen. Major Lowe to Genl Base Depot	
	29		Rouen.	
	30		Rouen.	
	31		Rouen. 2/Lt W.J. Taylor 6 Ret? DSO MC to England for appointment to Regular Bn.	

16 KRR (Army Form C. 2118.)

9/11 44

WAR DIARY
or
INTELLIGENCE SUMMARY.
(Erase heading not required.)

Place	Date	Hour	Summary of Events and Information	Remarks and references to Appendices
SANVIC (Le Havre)	1/6/19		Routine Work. Capt.C.H.D.King D.S.O., M.C., to England to join Regular Unit. Lieut.A.R.Pope 3rd Ox & Bucks L.I., joined for Duty and is posted to "C" Company.	
	2/6/19		Routine Work, 2/Lt.H.W.Walden assumes command of "D" Company vice Capt.C.H.D.King D.S.O., MC.; to England.	
	3/6/19.		Routine Work.	
	4/6/19.		General Holiday in honour of King's Birthday.	
	5/6/19.		Routine Work. Lieut.& Q.M.A.Allen to leave.	
	6/6/19.		Routine Work. 2/Lieut F.E.Mitchell joins from 4th/Bn.K.R.R. C. and is posted to "D" Coy. Lieut.O.W.Davis to leave.	
	7/6/19.		Routine Work. Battn.Weekly Conference held.	
	8/6/19.		Voluntary Church Services.	
	9/6/19.		General Holiday.	
	10/6/19.		Routine Work. Lieut.D.Cleugh to leave.	
	11/6/19.		Battn.Sports Meeting. "A" Company won Sports Cup. Capt.G.C.Hick M.C. assumes duties of adjutant vice Lieut. F.L.Trotter on return from leave. 2/Lieut.R.C.Naylor is appointed Assistant Adjutant from this date.	
	12/6/19.		Routine Work.	
	13/6/19.		Routine Work. Lieut.D.R.Martin and 2/Lieut.J.Collett return from leave. 2/Lieut.C.J.Thornton to leave.	

Army Form C. 2118.

WAR DIARY
or
INTELLIGENCE SUMMARY.

(Erase heading not required.)

Place	Date	Hour	Summary of Events and Information	Remarks and references to Appendices
SANVIC. (Le Havre)	14/6/19.		Routine Work. 2/Lieut.B.Paterson to leave.	
	15/6/19.		Voluntary Church Service. Lieut.F.L.Trotter to England to join Regular Unit.	
	16/6/19.		Routine Work.	
	17/6/19.		Routine Work. Lecture to "B" & "C" Companies by Capt.Scott R.A.M.C. 2/Lieut.R.G.Naylor to leave.	
	18/6/19.		Routine Work. Lecture to "A" & "D" Companies by Capt.Scott R.A.M.C.	
	19/6/19.		Routine Work. 2/Lieut.W.H.Fletcher to leave.	
	20/6/19.		Routine Work.	
	21/6/19.		Routine Work. Battalion Weekly Conference. Lieut & Q.M. J.Allen from leave.	
	22/6/19.		Voluntary Services.	
	23/6/19.		Routine Work. 2/Lieut.O.C.Venus to leave. Lieut.O.W.Davis from leave.	
	24/6/19.		Routine Work. Advance Party of Lieut.G.A.Wallace - 2/Lieut G.T.Taylor and 60 O.R. to Harfleur.	
HARFLEUR. (Le Havre)	25/6/19.		Battalion moved to Harfleur by March-Route and were accomodated in Camp 15. Camp taken over from 2/5th Gloucester Regt.	
	26/6/19.		Routine Work. Lieut.D.W.Clough from leave.	
	27/6/19.		Routine Work.	
	28/6/19.		Routine Work. Battalion Weekly Conference. Rear party of 11 O.R. under Lieut & Q.M. J.Allen rejoin.	

Army Form C. 2118.

WAR DIARY
or
INTELLIGENCE SUMMARY.
(Erase heading not required.)

Place	Date	Hour	Summary of Events and Information	Remarks and references to Appendices
HARFLEUR.	29/6/19.		Lieut.G.A.Wallace to leave.	
	30/6/19.		Routine Work. 2/Lieut.C.J.Thornton from leave. Lieut.G.C.Chisnell. to Hospital.	
1.7.1919.				

[signature]
Lieut Colonel.Commanding
16th Battn.King's Royal Rifle Corps.

16 KRR Army Form C. 2118.
Vol 45

WAR DIARY
or
INTELLIGENCE SUMMARY.
(Erase heading not required.)

Instructions regarding War Diaries and Intelligence Summaries are contained in F.S. Regs., Part II. and the Staff Manual respectively. Title pages will be prepared in manuscript.

Place	Date	Hour	Summary of Events and Information	Remarks and references to Appendices
HARFLEUR	1/7/19		Routine Work.	
	2/7/19		Battalion Holiday to Celebrate Peace, Football Match in afternoon and Concert, Supper and Sing Song round fire large bonfire after. 2/Lt.J.A.Bartlett to leave, 2/Lt.R.C.Naylor from leave.	
	3/7/19		Routine Work. 17th Worcestershire Regt's guards taken over. 2/Lt.H.W.Fletcher from leave.	
	4/7/19		2/5th Gloucester Regt took over all guards for a period of 24 hours from 1600 hours.	
	5/7/19		100th Brigade Ceremonial and Thanksgiving Service. 16th K.R.R.C. won universal praise from all quarters for excellent turnout and remarkable steadiness.	
	6/7/19		Resume normal Guard Duties and routine work.	
	7/7/19		Routine Work.	
	8/7/19		2/Lt.O.C.Venus from leave.	
	10/7/19		Take over guards of 17th Worcestershire Regt for 3 days. Capt.H.Dinsmore MC., and 2/Lt.J.R.Semple to leave.	
	13/7/19		Lt.Col.A.L.V.Willis,Lt.Clough R.S.M. and 12 other ranks N.C.Os leave for Paris. 2/Lt.H.W.Walden to leave.	
	14/7/19		Capt.G.A.P.Thomas T/Commanding Battalion. Composite Company under Capt.S.A.Smith MC., took part in grand March Past of troops in Havre Special Physical Training Class gave a display at Base Sports in afternoon and won universal approval. Battalion Relay Team won Base Relay Race. General Holiday.	

Army Form C. 2118.

WAR DIARY
or
INTELLIGENCE SUMMARY.
(Erase heading not required.)

Instructions regarding War Diaries and Intelligence Summaries are contained in F. S. Regs., Part II. and the Staff Manual respectively. Title pages will be prepared in manuscript.

Place	Date	Hour	Summary of Events and Information	Remarks and references to Appendices
HARFLEUR.	15/7/19		Day Off. Cleaning up. Paris Leave Party return. 2/Lt.G.M.Fenwick to leave.	
	16/7/19		Battalion take over all Brigade Guards for period of 12 days. Lt.Col.A.L.Y.Willis assumes Command. Lt.G.A.Wallace from leave.	
	17/7/19		Guards.	
	19/7/19		Peace Holiday for all not on Duty. Firework display in evening.	
	20/7/19		Guards. Lieut.G.C.Chisnell to leave.	
	21/7/19		Guards.	
	22/7/19		Guards. Battalion Concert Party give their opening Concert to the Battalion and are named "Purple Patches"	
	23/7/19		Guards. 2/Lt.J.A.Bartlett from leave.	
	25/7/19		Battalion Dance in evening. 2/Lt.J.R. Semple and Capt.H.Dinsmore MC., from leave.	
	27/7/19		2/Lt.H.Walden from leave.	
	28/7/19		17th Worcestershire Regt take over all guards. Capt.B.D.Melville MC.,joins for duty and is posted to "D" Company.	
	29/7/19		Training and Education. Lt.A.O.Hunting to leave.	
	30/7/19		T/Lieut.(A/Capt.) G.A.P.Thomas is granted authority to wear badges of rank of Major,and assumes duties of 2nd in Command from 28.6.1919	
	31/7/19		Divisional Commanders Inspection. Ceremonial Parade in morning. Inspection of Transport and Camp. Books and Interior economy. Excellent report on all branches. Capt.B.D.Melville MC., to leave.	

ALYWillis Lieut.Col. Commandg.
16th Bn K.R.R.

Army Form C. 2118.

WAR DIARY
or
INTELLIGENCE SUMMARY.
(Erase heading not required.)

Place	Date	Hour	Summary of Events and Information	Remarks and references to Appendices
Harfleur.	1.8.19.		Training and Education. Appreciation from Divisional Commander, Maj.Gen.F.Duncan, C.B,C.M.G., D.S.O., on excellent performance at Inspection.	
	2.8.19.		Weekly Conference. Lieut.Col.Willis, Major G.A.P.Thomas, C.Q.M.S.Johnson, Sgt.Rose, L/C.Sillett, R, L/C.Wood J.W.C. mentioned in March despatches for "gallant conduct".	
	3.8.19.		Voluntary Service. Battalion selected out of all units in France & Flanders for special mission in Denmark.	
	4.8.19.		General Holiday,(Bank Holiday). Battalion addressed by C.O. on new mission in morning. Sports in afternoon. Lieut. G.C. Chisnell from leave.	
	5.8.19.		Training and Education. 1 O.R. for demobilisation.	
	6.8.19.		2 O.Rs. for demobilisation.	
	7.8.19.		100th Bde. Ceremonial farewell parade by Brigadier General Guggisberg, C.M.G, D.S.O., on relinquishing command.	
	8.8.19.		Training and Education. Lt.Col.Willis to leave. Major G.A.P.Thomas assumes temporary command. 1 O.R. for demobilisation.	
	9.8.19.		Cleaning up.	
	10.8.19.		Voluntary Services.	
	11.8.19.		Capt.H.Webb, R.A.M.C, joins for duty. 1 O.R. to demobilisation.	
	12.8.19.		17 Officers and Five hundred and fifty men or Denmark draft to leave.	
	13.8.19.		Routine. Lieut. A.O. Hunting from leave.	
	14.8.19.		Routine.	
	15.8.19.		Routine. Captain B.D.Melville, M.C., from leave.	

Army Form C. 2118.

WAR DIARY
or
INTELLIGENCE SUMMARY.
(Erase heading not required.)

Instructions regarding War Diaries and Intelligence Summaries are contained in F. S. Regs., Part II. and the Staff Manual respectively. Title pages will be prepared in manuscript.

Place	Date	Hour	Summary of Events and Information	Remarks and references to Appendices
Harfleur.	16.8.19.		Routine.	
	17.8.19.		Routine.	
	18.8.19.		Routine.	
	19.8.19.		Routine. Captain W. Prier, R.A.M.C, joins for duty.	
	20.8.19.		Routine. 1 O.R. for demobilisation.	
	21.8.19.		Routine. Lieut. A.O. Hunting for demobilisation.	
	22.8.19.		Routine. Capt. & Q.M. H. Armishaw, Royal Warwickshire Regt. joins for duty.	
	23.8.19.		Routine.	
	24.8.19.		Routine.	
	25.8.19.		Routine. Capt. B.D.Melville, M.C, returns from leave and assumes temporary command of Battalion, vice Major.G.A.P.Thomas to leave. 7 O.R. for demobilisation.	
	26.8.19.		Routine. Capt. H. Webb, R.A.M.C, off strength. 9 O.R. for demobilisation.	
	27.8.19.		18 O.R. for demobilisation.	
	28.8.19.		Routine. Battalion returns from leave, and draft of 275 O.R. from 25th K.R.R.C. joins for duty. 1 O.R. for demobilisation.	
	29.8.19.		Routine. 22 O.R. for demobilisation. Inspection of new draft by G.O. Lieut. G.S.Young, Lieut.W.A.Lawrence, Lt.G.Jones, North Staffs Regt, join for duty.	
	30.8.19.		Routine. Warning order to move on 1st September received.	
	31.8.19.		Routine.	

D.A.G.
G.H.Q.
British Troops in France and Flanders.

Herewith   A.F. C. 2118   (War Diary) for the month of September 1919.

3.10.19.

N. Chaplor

Lieut. & Asst. Adjt.
for Lieut. Col. Cmdg.
16th. K.R.R.C.

Army Form C. 2118.

16th KRRC

WAR DIARY
or
INTELLIGENCE SUMMARY.
(Erase heading not required.)

Instructions regarding War Diaries and Intelligence Summaries are contained in F. S. Regs., Part II. and the Staff Manual respectively. Title pages will be prepared in manuscript.

Place	Date	Hour	Summary of Events and Information	Remarks and references to Appendices
HARFLEUR	1/9/19		Routine work. C.O. Inspects new draft from 25th K.R.R.C. 2 Other ranks for demobilization.	
	2/9/19		Training continued. 36 other ranks proceeded for demobilization.	
	3/9/19		Training. 9 other ranks proceeded for demobilization.	
	4/9/19		Training. Major G.A.P.Thomas assumes command of Battalion vice Lt.Colonel A.L.Y.Willis to G.H.Q. on duty. 4 Other ranks for demobilization. Major.E.Hopper Royal Engineers.Joined for duty.	
	5/9/19		Lieut.Colonel A.L.Y.Willis resumes command of Battalion on return from G.H.Q.	
	6/9/19		Training. 5 Other ranks proceeded for demobilization.	
	7/9/19		Parade Service. 3 Other ranks proceeded for demobilization.	
	8/9/19		Training. 4 Other ranks proceeded for demobilization.	
	9/9/19		Training. 1 Other rank proceeded for demobilization. Lt.A.R.Pope and 2/Lt.J.A.Bartlett to U.K. on leave.	
	10/9/19		Training.1 Other rank proceeded for demobilization.	
	11/9/19		Training.	
	12/9/19		Guards. "D" Company to Rouxin P.O.W. Depot on Pimple. 1 Other rank proceeded for demobilization.	
	13/9/19		Commanding Officers Inspection of Camp.	
	14/9/19		Parade Service. 3 other ranks proceeded for demobilization.	

Army Form C. 2118.

WAR DIARY
or
INTELLIGENCE SUMMARY.

(*Erase heading not required.*)

Instructions regarding War Diaries and Intelligence Summaries are contained in F. S. Regs., Part II. and the Staff Manual respectively. Title pages will be prepared in manuscript.

Place	Date	Hour	Summary of Events and Information	Remarks and references to Appendices
HARFLEUR	15/9/19		Guards and training. 1 other rank proceeded for demobilization.	
	16/9/19		Guards and training. Major G.A.P.Thomas assumes T/Command of Battn. vice Lt.Col.A.L.Y.Willis to U.K Leave. Revd.F.W.Welbon C.F.,M.C., joined for duty.	
	17/9/19		Guards and Training. 2nd Draft from 25th K.R.R.C. arrives.	
	18/9/19		Guards and training. Lt.Colonel.A.L.Y.Willis resumes command on return from U.K. leave.	
	19/9/19		48 Other Ranks for demobilization.	
	20/9/19		53 Other ranks proceeded for demobilization.	
	21/9/19		Voluntary Church Service. 53 Other ranks proceeded for demobilization.	
	22/9/19		Guards and training. 40th Northumberland Fusiliers take over some guards. 64 Other Ranks proceeded for demobilisation.	
	23/9/19		"D" Company return from P.O.W.Depot Pimple. 40th Northumberland Fusiliers take over remainder of Guards. 64 Other Ranks for demobilisation.	
	24/9/19		Training. 60 Other Ranks proceeded for demobilisation. Lt. A.R.Pope and 2/Lt. J.A. Bartlett from leave.	
	25/9/19.		Training. 24 Other Ranks proceeded for demobilisation.	
	26/9/19		Training.	
	27/9/19		Cleaning up etc.	
	28/9/19		Parade Service.	
	29/9/19		Training. All demobilisation and leave cancelled owing to Railway Strike.	
	30/9/19		Training.	

30.9.1919.

[signature]
Lieut. Colonel Commanding.
16th Bn.King's Royal Rifle Corps.

Army Form C. 2118.

WAR DIARY
or
INTELLIGENCE SUMMARY.
(Erase heading not required.)

Instructions regarding War Diaries and Intelligence Summaries are contained in F. S. Regs., Part II. and the Staff Manual respectively. Title pages will be prepared in manuscript.

Place	Date	Hour	Summary of Events and Information	Remarks and references to Appendices
Harfleur.	1/10/19		Training. Capt. C.L. Balkwill R.A.M.C. joined for duty. Capt. W.R. Low D.S.O.,M.C. 17th Bn., K.R.R.C. joined for duty, 21 other ranks for demobilization.	
	2/10/19		Guards resumed from 40th Bn. Northumberland Fusiliers.	
	3/10/19		Guards. Promotions:- 2/Lt. Taylor & 2/Lt. J.R. Semple to be T/Lieuts: 3 O.Rs. for demobilization.	
	4/10/19		Cleaning up. Capt.W.R. Low D.S.O.,M.C. assumes command of "C" Company.	
	5/10/19		Voluntary Services. Winter Time resumed.	
	6/10/19		Guards. 1 O.R. for demobilization.	
	7/10/19		Guards. 2/Lt. C.J. Thornton for demobilization. 2 O.Rs. for demobilization.	
	8/10/19		Guards. Capt.C.L. Balkwill R.A.M.C., Capt. H. Armishaw, and Lt. A.U. Vinall to leave.	
	9/10/19		Guards.	
	10/10/19		Guards. 2 O.Rs. for demobilization.	
	11/10/19		Guards. Guards handed over to 40th Bn. Northumberland Fusiliers.	
	12/10/19		Voluntary Services.	
	13/10/19		Training. Chinese Picquet duties commenced. 2 Officers and 50 O.Rs. daily. 6 O.Rs. for demobilization.	
	14/10/19		Training. Chinese Picquet. 2 O.Rs. for demobilization.	
	15/10/19		Training. Chinese Picquet.	
	16/10/19		Training. Chinese Picquet. 3 O.Rs. for demobilization.	
	17/10/19		Training. Chinese Picquet. Base Hd.Qrs. move to No.2 Rest Camp. 1 O.R. for demobilization.	

Army Form C. 2118.

WAR DIARY
or
INTELLIGENCE SUMMARY.

(Erase heading not required.)

Instructions regarding War Diaries and Intelligence Summaries are contained in F. S. Regs., Part II. and the Staff Manual respectively. Title pages will be prepared in manuscript.

16th (S) BATTALION

Place	Date	Hour	Summary of Events and Information	Remarks and references to Appendices
Harfleur.	18/10/19		Training. Chinese Picquet. Cleaning up.	
	19/10/19		Training. Chinese Picquet. Voluntary Services. 4 O.Rs. for demobilization.	
	20/10/19		Training. Chinese Picquet. Lt. G.E. Taylor to demobilization. Lt. A.C. Vinal 17th Bn. K.R.R.C. joined for duty and posted to "B" Company. 2/Lt. J.I. Daly 17th Bn. Worcertershire Regt. joined for duty and posted to "A" Company.	
	21/10/19		Training. Chinese Picquet. 1 O.R. for demobilization.	
	22/10/19		Training. Chinese Picquet.	
	23/10/19		Training. Chinese Picquet. 1 O.R. for demobilization.	
	24/10/19		Training. Chinese Picquet. Capt. C.L. Ballkwill R.A.M.C. Capt. H. Armishaw, and Lt. A.C. Vinall from leave. 2 O.Rs. for demobilization.	
	25/10/19		Training. Chinese Picquet. Denmark Orders finally cancelled. Orders received for reduction of Battalion to Equipment Guard. All M.S.A. men to be demobilized.	
	26/10/19		Chinese Picquet. Voluntary services.	
	27/10/19		Chinese Picquet. 2 O.Rs. for Demobilization.	
	28/10/19		Lt. O.C. Venus (Rifle Bde.attached) appointed Equipment Guard Officer. Battalion Farewell Dinner and Farewell Concert by the "Purple Patches." 1 O.R. for demobilization.	
	29/10/19		Demobilization commenced. 200 O.R. Dispatched for dispersal.	
	30/10/19		200 O.R. for demobilization, and 5 Officers for demobilization. 2nd Farewell Concert by "Purple Patches." Sergeants Mess Farewell Dinner and Sing-Song.	
	31/10/19		203 Other Ranks for demobilization.	

LT-COL.
COMMANDING 16th K. R. R. C.

Army Form C. 2118.

WAR DIARY
or
INTELLIGENCE SUMMARY.
(Erase heading not required.)

Instructions regarding War Diaries and Intelligence Summaries are contained in F. S. Regs., Part II. and the Staff Manual respectively. Title pages will be prepared in manuscript.

Place	Date	Hour	Summary of Events and Information	Remarks and references to Appendices
Harfleur.	1/10/19		Training. Capt. C.L. Balkwill R.A.M.C. joined for duty. Capt. W.R. Low D.S.O.,M.G. 17th Bn., K.R.R.C. joined for duty. 21 other ranks for demobilization.	
	2/10/19		Guards resumed from 40th Bn., Northumberland Fusiliers.	
	3/10/19		Guards. Promotions:- 2/Lt. Taylor & 2/Lt. J.R. Semple to be T/Lieuts. 3 O.Rs. for demobilization.	
	4/10/19		Cleaning up. Capt.W.R. Low D.S.O.,M.G. assumes command of "C" Company.	
	5/10/19		Voluntary Services. Winter Time resumed.	
	6/10/19		Guards. 1 O.R. for demobilization.	
	7/10/19		Guards. 2/Lt. G.J. Thornton for demobilization. 2 O.Rs. for demobilization.	
	8/10/19		Guards. Capt.C.L. Balkwill R.A.M.C., Capt. H. Armishaw, and Lt. A.C. Vinell to leave.	
	9/10/19		Guards.	
	10/10/19		Guards. 2 O.Rs. for demobilization.	
	11/10/19		Guards. Guards handed over to 40th Bn. Northumberland Fusiliers.	
	12/10/19		Voluntary Services.	
	13/10/19		Training. Chinese Picquet duties commenced. 2 Officers and 50 O.Rs. daily. 6 O.Rs. for demobilization.	
	14/10/19		Training. Chinese Picquet. 2 O.Rs. for demobilization.	
	15/10/19		Training. Chinese Picquet.	
	16/10/19		Training. Chinese Picquet. 3 O.Rs. for demobilization.	
	17/10/19		Training. Chinese Picquet. Pte. H. Oats A.C. moved to No.2 Rest Camp. 1 O.R. for demobilization.	

Army Form C. 2118.

WAR DIARY
or
INTELLIGENCE SUMMARY.
(Erase heading not required.)

Instructions regarding War Diaries and Intelligence Summaries are contained in F.S. Regs., Part II. and the Staff Manual respectively. Title pages will be prepared in manuscript.

Place	Date	Hour	Summary of Events and Information	Remarks and references to Appendices
Harfleur.	18/10/19		Training. Chinese Picquet. Cleaning up.	
	19/10/19		Training. Chinese Picquet. Voluntary Services. 4 O.Rs. for demobilization.	
	20/10/19		Training. Chinese Picquet. Lt. G.T. Taylor to demobilization. Lt. A.C. Vinal 17th Bn. K.R.R.C. joined for duty and posted to "B" Company. 2/Lt. J.I. Daly 17th Bn. Worcestershire Regt. joined for duty and posted to "A" Company.	
	21/10/19		Training. Chinese Picquet. 1 O.R. for demobilization.	
	22/10/19		Training. Chinese Picquet.	
	23/10/19		Training. Chinese Picquet. 1 O.R. for demobilization.	
	24/10/19		Training. Chinese Picquet. Capt. C.L. Bailkwill R.A.M.C. Capt. H. Armishaw, and Lt. A.C. Vinall from leave. 2 O.Rs. for demobilization.	
	25/10/19		Training. Chinese Picquet. Denmark Orders finally cancelled. Orders received for reduction of Battalion to Equipment Guard. All M.S.A. men to be demobilized.	
	26/10/19		Chinese Picquet. Voluntary services.	
	27/10/19		Chinese Picquet. 2 O.Rs. for Demobilization.	
	28/10/19		Lt. O.C. Venus (Rifle Bde. attached) appointed Equipment Guard Officer. Battalion Farewell Dinner and Farewell Concert by the "Purple Patches". 1 O.R. for demobilization.	
	29/10/19		Demobilization commenced. 200 O.R. Dispatched for dispersal.	
	30/10/19		200 O.R. for demobilization, and 5 officers for demobilization. 2nd Farewell Concert by "Purple Patches". Sergeants Mess Farewell Dinner and Sing-Song.	
	31/10/19		205 Other Ranks for demobilization.	

LT-COL.
COMMANDING 16th K. R. R. C.

Army Form C. 2118.

WAR DIARY
or
INTELLIGENCE SUMMARY.
(Erase heading not required.)

Instructions regarding War Diaries and Intelligence Summaries are contained in F. S. Regs., Part II. and the Staff Manual respectively. Title pages will be prepared in manuscript.

Place	Date	Hour	Summary of Events and Information	Remarks and references to Appendices
Havre.	1/11/19		Work of handing over "Denmark Stores" commenced till 5th. Lieut. W.A. Lawrence proceeded for demobilization. 151 other ranks for demobilization.	
	2/11/19		Work of closing down continued.	
	3/11/19		Work of closing down continued. 15 Officers to No.2 Rest Camp to await disposal. 15 other ranks for demobilization.	
	4/11/19		Work of closing down continued. 10 other ranks for demobilization.	
	5/11/19		Rev: D.J. McHugh O.B.E., to P.C. Boulogne. 32 other ranks for demobilization.	
	6/11/19		Work of closing down continued.	
	7/11/19		Work of closing down continued. 15 other ranks for demobilization.	
	8/11/19		Work of closing down continued. 4 other ranks for demobilization, including R.S.M. Mitchell C. and C.S.M. Peach A.E. M.M. & Bar. Croix de Guerre (Original member of Battalion).	
	9/11/19		Work of closing down continued. 1 other rank for demobilization.	
	10/11/19		Work of closing down continued. 2 other ranks for demobilization. The following officers off Strength:- Capt. S.A. Smith M.C.; Lt. O.C. Venus; Lt. G.S. Young M.C.; Lt. J.R. Semple; Lt. C.W. Jeffery; Lt. H.W. Walden; Lt. G.C. Chisnell; Lt. A.R. Pope; 2/Lt. J.I. Daly; 2/Lt. G.D. Chamberlain; 2/Lt. B. Paterson; and Capt. C.L. Belkwill R.A.M.C. attached.	
	11/11/19		Work of closing down continued. Armistice Anniversary. 39 other ranks for demobilization.	
	12/11/19		Work of closing down continued. 1 other rank for demobilization.	
	13/11/19		Work of closing down continued.	
	14/11/19		The following officers left the Battalion:- Lt.Col. A.L.Y. Willis; Major G.A.P. Thomas; Capt. H. Dinsmore M.C.; Capt. W.R. Low D.S.O., M.C.; Capt. E.D. Melville M.C.; Lt. A.C. Vinall; Capt. The Rev: G.C. Hamilton.	

16th KRRC 35 to 2

Instructions regarding War Diaries and Intelligence Summaries are contained in F. S. Regs., Part II. and the Staff Manual respectively. Title pages will be prepared in manuscript.

Army Form C. 2118.

WAR DIARY
or
INTELLIGENCE SUMMARY.
(Erase heading not required.)

Place	Date	Hour	Summary of Events and Information	Remarks and references to Appendices
Havre.	1/11/19		Work of handing over "Denmark Stores" commenced till 5th. Lieut. W.A. Lawrence proceeded for demobilization. 131 other ranks for demobilization.	
	2/11/19		Work of closing down continued.	
	3/11/19		Work of closing down continued. 15 Officers to No.2 Rest Camp to await disposal. 13 other ranks for demobilization.	
	4/11/19		Work of closing down continued. 10 other ranks for demobilization.	
	5/11/19		Rev: D.J. McHugh O.B.E., to F.O. Boulogne. 32 other ranks for demobilization.	
	6/11/19		Work of closing down continued.	
	7/11/19		Work of closing down continued. 15 other ranks for demobilization.	
	8/11/19		Work of closing down continued. 4 other ranks for demobilization, including R.S.M. Mitchell G. and C.S.M. Peach A.E. M.M. & Bar., Croix de Guerre (Original member of Battalion).	
	9/11/19		Work of closing down continued. 1 other rank for demobilization.	
	10/11/19		Work of closing down continued. 2 other ranks for demobilization. The following Officers off Strength:- Capt. S.A. Smith M.C.; Lt. C.C. Venus; Lt. G.S. Young M.C.; Lt. J.R. Semple; Lt. C.W. Jeffery; Lt. H.W. Waldem; Lt. G.C. Chisnell; Lt. A.R. Pope; 2/Lt. J.I. Daly; 2/Lt. G.D. Chamberlain; 2/Lt. B. Paterson; and Capt. C.L. Balkwill R.A.M.C. attached.	
	11/11/19		Work of closing down continued. Armistice Anniversary. 39 other ranks for demobilization.	
	12/11/19		Work of closing down continued. 1 other rank for demobilization.	
	13/11/19		Work of closing down continued.	
	14/11/19		The following Officers left the Battalion:- Lt.Col. A.L.Y. Willis; Major G.A.P. Thomas; Capt. H. Dinsmore M.C.; Capt. V.R. Low D.S.O., M.C.; Capt. B.D. Melville M.C.; Lt. A.C. Vinall; Capt. The Rev: C.C. Hamilton.	

Army Form C. 2118.

WAR DIARY
or
INTELLIGENCE SUMMARY.
(Erase heading not required.)

Instructions regarding War Diaries and Intelligence Summaries are contained in F. S. Regs., Part II. and the Staff Manual respectively. Title pages will be prepared in manuscript.

Place	Date	Hour	Summary of Events and Information	Remarks and references to Appendices
Havre.	14/11/19 continued		Final Disbandment of 16th Battalion King's Royal Rifle Corps. Details under Command of Capt. G.C. Hick M.C. moved to No. 2 Rest Camp. 22 N.C.Os., N.C.Os., and men (Volunteers for Army of Occupation) To "C" Pool, Column Camp, Boulogne, including CQMS. Baker F., and Sgt. Snelling E. original members of Battalion. 30 other ranks for demobilization including C.S.M. W. Oalley D.C.M., M.M., and CQMS. Johnson A. original members of Battalion.	
	17/11/19		Work of closing down continued. Following Officers off Strength:- Lt. C.S. Dennett; Lt. D.W. Clough; 2/Lt. J.A. Bartlett; 14/11/19 and 2/Lt. G.M. Fenwick 17/11/19.	
	18/11/19		Work of closing down continued. 5 other ranks for demobilization. Final handing in of all Stores drawn for Denmark commenced.	
	19/11/19		Handing in of "Denmark Stores" Continued. 1 other rank for demobilization.	
	20/11/19		Handing in of "Denmark Stores" continued. 21 other ranks for demobilization. 4 other ranks Volunteers for Army of Occupation to D.G.R. & E. St. Pol.	
	21/11/19		Work of handing in "Denmark Stores" continued. 1 Ford Touring Car; 3 Ford Box Cars; and one Sunbeam Ambulance returned to 21 V.R.P. Rouen.	
	22/11/19		Handing in of "Denmark Stores" continued.	
	23/11/19		" " " " "	
	24/11/19		" " " " "	
	25/11/19		" " " " " 1 other rank for demobilization.	
	26/11/19		" " " " "	
	27/11/19		" " " " "	
	28/11/19		" " " " " 1 other rank for demobilization. Lt. D.K. Martin to reposting.	
	29/11/19		" " " " " Remainder of Transport returned to Rouen.	
	30/11/19		Work of transporting and handing in "Denmark Stores" completed.	

Commdg., 16th Bn. King's Royal Rifle Corps.
Captain,
Details.

Army Form C. 2118.

WAR DIARY
or
INTELLIGENCE SUMMARY.
(Erase heading not required.)

Instructions regarding War Diaries and Intelligence Summaries are contained in F. S. Regs., Part II. and the Staff Manual respectively. Title pages will be prepared in manuscript.

Place	Date	Hour	Summary of Events and Information	Remarks and references to Appendices
Havre.	14/11/19. continued.		Final Disbandment of 16th Battalion King's Royal Rifle Corps. Details under Command of Capt. G.C. Hick M.C. moved to No. 2 Rest Camp. 22 W.Os., N.C.Os., and men (Volunteers for Army of Occupation) To "C" Pool, Column Camp, Boulogne, including CQMS. Baker F., and Sgt. Snelling E., original members of Battalion. 80 other ranks for demobilization including C.S.M. W. Oakley D.C.M., M.M., and CQMS. Johnson A. original members of Battalion.	
	17/11/19		Work of closing down continued. Following Officers off strength:- Lt. C.S. Dennett; Lt. D.W. Clough; 2/Lt. J.A. Bartlett; 14/11/19 and 2/Lt. G.M. Fenwick 17/11/19.	
	18/11/19		Work of closing down continued. 5 other ranks for demobilization. Final handing in of all Stores drawn for Denmark commenced.	
	19/11/19		Handing in of "Denmark Stores" continued. 1 other rank for demobilization.	
	20/11/19		Handing in of "Denmark Stores" continued. 2 other ranks for demobilization. 4 other ranks Volunteers for Army of Occupation to D.G.R. & E. St. Pol.	
	21/11/19		Work of handing in "Denmark Stores" continued. 1 Ford Touring Car; 3 Ford Box Cars; and one Sunbeam Ambulance returned to 21 V.R.P. Rouen.	
	22/11/19		Handing in of "Denmark Stores" continued.	
	23/11/19		" " " " "	
	24/11/19		" " " " " 1 other rank for demobilization.	
	25/11/19		" " " " "	
	26/11/19		" " " " "	
	27/11/19		" " " " "	
	28/11/19		" " " " " 1 other rank for demobilization. Lt. D.R. Martin to reposting.	
	29/11/19		" " " " " Remainder of Transport returned to Rouen.	
	30/11/19		Work of transporting and handing in "Denmark Stores" completed.	

Commdg., 16th Bn.King's Royal Rifle Corps Captain, Details.

www.ingramcontent.com/pod-product-compliance
Lightning Source LLC
Chambersburg PA
CBHW080845010526
44114CB00017B/2374